THE LIFE I'VE PICKED

A BANJO PLAYER'S

NITTY GRITTY

JOURNEY

CHICAGO
REVIEW
PRESS

An A Cappella Book

Published by Chicago Review Press Incorporated
814 North Franklin Street
Chicago, Illinois 60610
ISBN 978-1-61373-895-5

Library of Congress Cataloging-in-Publication Data

Names: McEuen, John, 1945- author.
Title: The life I've picked / John McEuen.
Description: First edition. | Chicago, Illinois : Chicago Review Press, [2018] |
    Includes bibliographical references.
Identifiers: LCCN 2017053523 (print) | LCCN 2017055330 (ebook) | ISBN
    9781613738962 (adobe pdf) | ISBN 9781613738979 (kindle) | ISBN
    9781613738986 (epub) | ISBN 9781613738955 (trade paper)
Subjects: LCSH: McEuen, John, 1945- | Banjoists—United States—
    Biography. | Country musicians—United States—Biography. | Bluegrass
    musicians—United States—Biography. | Nitty Gritty Dirt Band. | LCGFT:
    Autobiographies.
Classification: LCC ML419.M357 (ebook) | LCC ML419.M357 A3 2018
    (print) | DDC 787.8/8092 [B] —dc23
LC record available at https://lccn.loc.gov/2017053523

Cover design: Marc Whitaker / MTWdesign.net
Cover photo: Henry Diltz
Typesetting: Nord Compo

Printed in the United States of America
5 4 3 2 1

Contents

Preface

What seemed to happen so quickly took a long time. I didn't think I would get here from there. I love what I do and have a passion for travel and for meeting people. As I looked back on my life in the process of this writing, it became apparent that from my earliest days in school, I was searching for something.

I started looking for acceptance in those early school years as a dork who worked his way up to nerd level by high school. I practiced my autograph in high school for no apparent reason. I wasn't doing anything notable, but I had a vague dream that it was possible to become known somehow, by doing something. As a teenager, I filled my time with magic tricks and dreams of being on stage. I learned magic from old books and at the Disneyland Magic Shop, and continued dreaming. Then I was on stage! For three years, I worked at Anaheim's Disneyland doing magic tricks all day. It was there that I met and became friends with Steve Martin, who at sixteen, like me, was a natural performer always reaching out for an audience. As seniors in high school we became Magic Shop coworkers.

Then music lit up the seventeenth year of my life, thanks to my older brother showing me guitar licks. After seeing the bluegrass group the Dillards six months later, I knew what I wanted to do: play the banjo (and through that, get on the radio and see the world). Steve and I discovered banjo at the same time; he became my first student.

After playing in four music groups as a teenager, the Nitty Gritty Dirt Band (NGDB) was born, all of which led to a music career that has taken me through fifty-plus years of radio, film, and television, and to stages all over the world. This teenager's dream came true, despite multiple warnings to not go the music route. Steve soared beyond all expectations. I guess we both did. His dedication to his work, which led to his successes, has been a lifelong inspiration to me.

For many years, interviewers have said to me, "You should write a book," as many interview stories seemed to be more than just funny reminiscences to them. They sensed a deeper resonance, as if in describing my experiences, I was describing their own lives.

And what a broad range of experiences I'm able to share. We were the first American band to go to Russia, and our recordings are in the Grammy Hall of Fame *and* the Library of Congress. I've done more than ten thousand shows in fabled venues like Carnegie Hall and the Grand Ole Opry, as well as on remote flatbed trucks and in obscure halls located everywhere from Armenia to the Alaskan bush. Others certainly had more blockbuster success than NGDB, but none of our contemporaries covered as much varied ground. We opened for Jack Benny, the Doors, and Bobby Sherman all in one year, and have played with Maybelle Carter, Earl Scruggs, Doc Watson, Sammy Hagar, and ZZ Top. Our years together have generated stories both light and dark, and as I go on my own the stages get better and people keep coming.

I was seldom content with the band's successes and struggled with others' lifestyle excesses, as I felt more could be done about both. The drug years were very difficult for me. I never joined that club and became the outcast I had been during my early school days. Raising kids a lot earlier than others I knew made it necessary to again push the solo front, because I had to bring in enough money for a large family. But something else simultaneously drove me to search out other creative things: writing film scores, making other albums, producing concerts, writing for a magazine, selling a script, producing a play, recording someone as a producer, making film documentaries. "Make it and they will come" was my philosophy, so I make things—and hope they will come.

It's been a lifetime of comings and goings. For more than fifty years I've been hitting the road, literally, as a traveling musician with banjo, guitar, mandolin, and fiddle—an "acoustic traveller," as I like to say. But life is also full of great journeys and new beginnings. More than once, the band fell apart and then came back together as resentments grew and faded between the oldest friends and partners. My marriage came undone, partially under the weight of a lifetime on the road and its influences, but again, new love rose up in its place. Grounding and sustaining me through it all was the desire to create—to make art and music, but also to create unbreakable bonds of love with my family and children. When I had the chance to create projects with my grown kids, I truly felt the strength of the circle unbroken.

That's the life I want to share with this story. It's a story with chapters yet to be written. I feel like my career is just now getting under way, and I hope to have more great music and experiences to share with fans and listeners.

Time to get ready for a show. Thanks for tuning in. Enjoy the ride. I have.

1

You Can't Get Here from There

Born in Oakland, California, in 1945, a month ahead of the boom, I think the first thing I learned to say was "Get me out of here," because even then I thought that things could get better. What I remember hearing most often in early school was "Who gets *McEuen?*" I couldn't figure out how, before even seeing me play, they knew I sucked at sports. During fifth grade, I faithfully paid a dollar a week to the Space Rangers Club, until the club president used three months' worth of my dues to buy *himself* a green transistor radio. He was the only other member—and my only brother, too—but he did let me listen to it a few times.

Though mostly ignored in school, I was a happy kid. Serving as crossing guard and operating my school's movie projector gave me a feeling of status and worth in those elementary school years. I lasted about three weeks in the Cub Scouts, as that did the opposite. From an early age, I hated uniforms, until they became costumes. That kind of group's activities always made me feel like I wasn't good enough, that I didn't fit in. This inferiority complex stuck with me, I guess, but I never saw any solution other than to drive on.

My first business was selling Christmas cards door-to-door in fifth grade. The more cards you sold, the more prizes you could earn, but I don't remember the prizes. I just wanted to make the sales, and I always sold out. That was exciting for me. Next, I begged my dad to bring mistletoe from the mountains; I would put it in little plastic bags that I sold for fifty cents apiece. That was killer, and the next year I cleaned up again at Christmas. Then I figured out how to put on a backyard carnival. I charged ten cents to play the balloon popping dart game, the BB gun target shoot, or the ping-pong ball toss. It felt like a big event, and I picked up $8.25 of my own. That was an exciting year. I also won third prize, and then second, at the school yo-yo contest. These were the first things that I could do that were really my own. They did win me recognition, but no real friends.

When we moved to Fremont, I started junior high school with renewed hopes for social acceptance, but by day two I was already hearing "Dog pile on McEuen!" My dad started a new business in Long Beach, south of Los Angeles, and most of the week my mom and I were home alone. My brother, Bill, who was five years older than me, and my sister, Maureen, who was three years older, were also down in Long Beach. Bill was working for my dad's diesel equipment business; Maureen was starting business college. My mom and I had a ritual of having a frozen pot pie while watching *The Tonight Show Starring Johnny Carson* together. It made her so cool to me, and I felt fortunate to have a mom everyone liked.

Beginning somewhere around eighth grade, during the monthly air-raid drills, I'd deduced some cracks in governmental logic. To get ready for the big flash, we'd get under our desks as we were told, and when the siren went off, we'd put our hands over our necks. When the fireball didn't come, we would get a cookie. I quit paying attention when it dawned on me how stupid it was to wait for the fireball under a big piece of kindling.

Down south, my dad's surplus business grew. My family moved to Southern California's Orange County, where I started high school in Garden Grove. This provided my first exciting destination away from the house: Disneyland. And, amazingly, my sports ability improved! I excelled in badminton and ping-pong, but just try to win friends in a baseball/

football/surf world with that claim. I still spent a lot of time alone. By the end of freshman year, I had become very proficient at climbing Disneyland's fence to get in free. I found it as advertised: "the Magic Kingdom, the happiest place on earth." In the backstage lots of the park, I made the exciting discovery that if you just acted calm and confident, and looked like you belonged there, you could walk into the park and no one would stop you. I mastered this "I belong here" attitude—that people would later call "let the force be with you"—to such a degree that I managed to never need a stage pass around most concert venues.

I'd climb over the fence that was topped with barbed wire, sneak through the back lot to Main Street, and then get the back of my hand stamped to come back "later that day." It also helped me to raise cash. At the front gate, I'd approach ticket buyers with an offer to get them in for two dollars each. Then, I'd enter the park on the right side by using my ultraviolet hand stamp, go to the exit on the left side to get stamped again, and tell the stamper, "Please put on a lot. I'm going swimming later." After pressing the stamp from my left hand onto my right, and holding it there to keep it wet, I'd meet my geeks at the restroom area and transfer the stamp from my right hand to their left, which made the pattern appear correctly. I got caught climbing the thirteenth time and quit.

I was drawn to magic tricks by my fourteenth year and spent all of my free time at Disneyland, mostly at the Main Street and Fantasyland Magic Shops. I saw how people liked being fooled, how they *admired* the person fooling them. I bought as many tricks as I could, took them home, practiced dutifully in front of a mirror, and became the family jester for any occasion. My mom would parade me in front of visiting aunts and uncles or friends, subjecting them to my tricks. It is a kid's thrill to do something adults cannot figure out, and I loved that I could finally do something my brother couldn't. But he never wanted to see my tricks. Magic shows for kids and parties earned me between twenty and thirty-five dollars for thirty minutes of work. I'd feel like the king of show business for that half hour. I was totally ready for the big time and even had a "have magic wand—will travel" business card.

I guess I was a pretty industrious kid, or maybe I just liked having some pocket money. My fifteenth year, I started my own pool-cleaning business with seven clients who each paid fifteen dollars a month. I steam cleaned diesel equipment at my dad's depressing place for fifty cents an hour and learned to drive a forklift well. I borrowed $200 from him to import two gross of toy airplanes from Hong Kong, and I sold them in a month at a small profit. I cleaned more diesel equipment, did yard work, followed various family dogs with a shovel, made magic tricks for my future boss Aldini the Magician, cleaned diesel equipment one last time, and made it to my junior year.

One of my biggest high school accomplishments was winning a bet with a teacher just by cashing a check. But it was no ordinary check. According to what the teacher said, a person could, in theory, cash a check written on anything, as long as the account information was right. So I challenged him with a crazy idea, and he bet me it wouldn't work. That was the first time I made it into a newspaper: "Student Cashes Check Written on Watermelon!" I liked that.

Another time I felt special in high school actually typified my youthful existence, but because of it, I still have a debt to pay to the guy who showed great kindness and concern for someone he didn't know. During one lunch time, I was circled by a bunch of big, big-shot football jocks who were pushing me around; I remember thinking I should try out to be the poster boy for the guy who gets sand kicked in his face. They were closing in, jabbing harder for no apparent reason, getting ready to go in for the kill, and I felt certain my life was going to be short and miserable. At the last moment, just as I was about to strike out in self-defense by blacking out, I heard loud yelling from the back of this mob of dumb assholes. I thought it was my death knell.

"Hey! Come on, you guys! Hey!" A huge football player pushed his way into the tightening circle of bullies and said, "Just back off. There's no reason to pick on this guy. Leave him alone—or deal with me first!" They dispersed, and I nerded along to class. I have yet to find this guy and thank him for a great save—one I've often thought about throughout my life. I hope to find him, and wonder if he might want to meet Willie Nelson, Steve Martin, or Dolly Parton, or maybe have some backstage food. He could use my backstage pass that I still never bother to get.

Things got a little better during my last year of high school. Until then, I hadn't even been an outcast in school; I just wasn't "cast." I accepted school life as an unaccepted dork, with three good friends and no noticeable achievements other than good grades. I challenged the PE teacher to a badminton game for my grade, since I couldn't get graded for fence climbing. He knew he would lose and turned me down, so my only C grade was in gym. I did list myself in the senior yearbook as president of the chess club, but in truth, there was no club, only one other player: my new friend Steve.

The most auspicious event of that year had taken place in early summer, before school started: I met Steve Martin. The two of us met hanging around the Disneyland Magic Shop, both trying to get jobs there, one May day, and then ate lunch in Tomorrowland by the House of Tomorrow. Here was a friendly guy I wanted to know. Later that week, after going over the fence to get back into D-land, I saw Steve at his work; he was a stock boy for the Tiki Hut, an Adventureland souvenir store.

Steve and I played chess every lunch hour during our senior year. By year's end, the score was eighty-five to eighty-seven, but neither of us remembers who was ahead. Eight-five to eighty-seven is also about the total number of words we said to each other during the lunchtime matches, other than "check/checkmate" and "adjusting" (something I could only seem to do on a chessboard).

In the middle of my senior year, I landed that dream job: working at the Main Street Magic Shop. Feeling this was good as it could get, I first ran the hand-set printing press in their print shop. I put people's names in newspaper headlines or on "Wanted: Horse Thief" posters or on fake marriage licenses. I even made an unknowingly prophetic one with "John & Marilyn" to display on the wall, because I thought it sounded nice. I was proud to hold the record for the most posters printed in an hour. During one rush I did forty-two posters—get the name, set the type, ink it, put in the poster, print it, clear the poster, roll it with a rubber band around it, clean and reset the type in the rack. That put twenty-four bucks in the till! Finally, I was good at something, and I was getting noticed for it, and getting paid, and they let me fill in behind the magic counter.

Even in high school Steve was a standout guy. As a cheerleader, he wore a pink tutu to lead cheers. I was glad he invited me to be in the Drama Club yearbook photo, as I wanted *something* more than just faux Chess Club president. I wanted to feel like I belonged. I found that feeling from working at Disneyland, where being on stage, even if only to hawk merchandise, made me feel at home.

I made two other close friends in those four years. Jim Arnold, whose mother worked for my dad, is still a great pal to this day. I learned from watching Jim that throwing up a six-pack of beer on the hood of your car is not as funny as it sounds. The only alcoholic drinks I've ever had are about twenty-two strawberry daiquiris. Jim is now living a simpler life in Montana. I admire his honesty, his up attitude, and his constant smile.

Mike Van Horn is still a great friend, although we don't see each other that much. As it is with Jim, when we do get together it feels like hardly any time has gone by, and I'm not sure I've really done anything, as seeing them is like traveling back in time to the days before anything happened. Mike is one of the many unique people I have been fortunate to know, and he impresses me to this day with his drive and the many hats he wears: magician, hypnotist, window washer, photographer, funky blues musician.

There is a special value in old friends from our early lives. They can be a reality check, like a platinum record on the wall. It impresses visitors, but those who have them know the dark truth: those records have a date on them, often from *many* years ago. And, more often than not, the sight of those records only makes me think, *What did I do this year?*

With the post-graduation summer of 1963 right around the corner, Steve was working the Fantasyland Magic Shop while I was mainly at the Main Street Magic Shop. Sometimes we'd play chess by phone. (Phone rings. "King pawn to king pawn five," he'd say. Phone rings. "Queen bishop to king knight six.") That was to be the best summer of my life. I had a car, a great job, the beach, no girl problems (no girls!), and I was making my own money: $1.15 an hour! I'd moved up to pitching tricks and I was good at it.

It was a great training ground for showbiz, with a constant flow of people generating an audience of two to twenty that turned over every ten or fifteen minutes. You could fool them into parting with their money, and it was essentially risk free. If you blew it, a new crowd would be drifting through in a few minutes. I credit those years with giving me the confidence to go out in front of any audience and get their attention, and keep it. I felt respected, especially the day I sold a record 154 decks of Svengali trick cards.

My coworker, the ever-smiling Jim Barlow, was ten years older but had the air of a man-child, and could always make anyone laugh. He was my first live example of confused confidence. His smooth, seemingly fumbling but well-practiced magic put people at ease. His secret language was usually shouted, and helped us spot the cute girls. "Shadowbox time" meant a girl in a thin dress was standing in the doorway, and that the hot sun was hitting the sidewalk just right so you could see through her dress, like she didn't even have one on. "Family of four" alerted the boys that large breasts, capable of feeding a family of four kids, were coming in. "Punch the time clock" let us know that it was easy to see down the blouse housing said large breasts, especially if we got the woman to pick up something we would "accidentally" drop on the floor while showing a trick. This might not be considered polite today, but we were teenage guys having giggly fun, and nobody got hurt.

It was a wonderful, carefree existence. I'd go to work an hour or more before the park opened to get the store ready, and just to be there before the crowd. I remember foggy winter mornings spent reading Ray Bradbury's science fiction while sitting on an empty Main Street bench when I couldn't even see Fantasyland, even though I was right in the middle of it. Around eight thirty, the fog lifted and the opening rope across Main Street dropped, people rushed in, and the day's show began. It was like a giant circus, only cleaner. I had no worries about "the future," which never extended beyond the next few hours or so, except making sure that I'd have enough money for gas. I was happier than ever. One week, I put ninety-two hours on the time clock, earning the biggest paycheck of my life: $124. Getting it cashed with all $2 bills, I put them in a stack, painted the ends with glue, and put them in a checkbook wrapper, so when money was needed I would tear one out like a check. I liked that all I did was tricks, and realized then that "working for a living" was not for me. It never really dawned on me that any of this was work.

One unforgettable night, our boss, Aldini, was locking the door at about 1:30 AM after a great sixteen-hour day. The last tourist leaving the Magic Kingdom came up behind him and asked, "Pardon me, sir, can you tell me just how much of Disneyland Walt Disney actually owns?"

Without missing a beat or looking up from fumbling with the key, Aldini brusquely muttered, "Two cows and a horse." Then he locked the door and walked off, never even glancing at the shocked tourist. We laughed for an hour.

My three years there were the best, and they left me believing that one did not have to become old, and as the years went on I'd strive to become a retired kid. Rather than work for a living, I would live for some kind of work. Thanks, Walt, for teaching that lesson to this Walt. (My legal name is Walter.)

I didn't meet Walt, but I saw him three times in the park. Once, while working Merlin's (the other Magic Shop, in Fantsayland), I heard he was at the front of the castle and went to see him. He was explaining to landscapers how to deal with an interesting problem: the new statues of Snow White and the Seven Dwarfs were all the same size! Not wanting to wait for new smaller dwarfs from the Italian maker, nor wanting to make a Snow White that would have to be twelve feet tall, he took a sketch pad and drew out a V-shaped waterfall that pushed perspective to a point at the top and was wide at the bottom. "Put her at the top, and all the dwarves down in front by the river, right next to the fence.

She'll look bigger that way," he said. It worked. I learned even Walt Disney himself had to make lemonade from lemons.

———————

Then along came music, college, and discovering McCabe's Guitar Shop in Long Beach. There was music everywhere, and I fell in love with it. I discovered finger-picking on the guitar and could passably play songs like "Freight Train." I like the challenge of moving fingers on the strings. My hundred dollar Harmony guitar served me well for those first six months, but it seemed I couldn't learn anything my brother didn't already know.

These were the hootenanny years in Disneyland, with great folk musicians playing on Monday nights, after being booked by a guy named Tom Campbell. (And, twelve years later, I would hook Tom up with John Denver to do twenty antinuclear benefits, but I wasn't to know either of them personally for several more pages.) Tom would later cowrite "Darcy Farrow" with the great guitarist, and now folk legend, Steve Gillette.

Folk clubs were popping up all around Southern California, and budding guitar skills got me into my first fledgling group, a Christy Minstrels type of thing, all strumming guitars and singing harmony, with a tambourine, and songs about rowing boats to some shore or working on someone's farm that I never really understood nor cared about. But the chords were easy, and I was in a group for a few minutes. I liked the other people who were becoming musicians, and since we all sucked we had something in common. My brother had invited a new friend, Dave Simpson, over to the house one afternoon when Steve had also come by. Dave knew four songs on the banjo, and Steve and I were blown away by how cool that instrument sounded. I remember clearly Steve asking Dave (who owned the Long Beach music store McCabe's Guitar Shop) "Just how much is a good . . . used . . . cheap banjo?" (Steve soon bought that banjo and plays it to this day.)

A friend invited me to a show in Orange County at the Paradox, which was a club in Tustin, that would change my life. The Dillards, fresh immigrants to Southern California from Salem, Missouri, came on and Doug kicked off "Hickory Hollow." I think my heart stopped. They were the perfect combination of Flatt and Scruggs and the Smothers Brothers. They played hot music and knew how to excite an audience and get laughs. They had been featured as the Darlin' Boys on the *Andy Griffith Show*, and their first album, *Back Porch Bluegrass*, got so deep under my skin that I played and studied banjo music constantly for the next two years. I saw them perform so often—at least eight times a month—that my mom said I should change my last name to Dillard.

I lived in record grooves: from the Dillards and Bill Monroe's bluegrass, to Earl Scruggs and Bill Keith, Don Reno and Doc Watson. Slowing the LPs down to 16 2/3 rpm made the banjo an octave lower, and easy to follow. After watching Doug, I'd go back and listen to the record again. *Aha! That's how he did that lick!* Then I'd go see them again to pick up another one. I took one formal lesson each from three different people. One gave me a two-hour course on music theory that has stuck with me until today. Pete Seeger's book, *How to Play the Five String Banjo*, also gave great insight and a base to work from. Steve Martin and I would take our Magic Shop breaks and meet in Frontierland to catch the Mad Mountain Ramblers, with later-to-be-renowned musicians David Lindley, Richard Greene, and Chris Darrow playing bluegrass. We were obsessed with banjo.

But I needed the music to do something more, to be entertaining. My mom would say to the visiting aunts and uncles, "Why don't we have Johnny play the banjo?" But invariably, after "Dixie Breakdown" or "Foggy Mountain Breakdown," they'd ask: "Do you know any songs?" Even after playing "The Ballad of Jed Clampett" a few times, it was obvious that most solo banjo music couldn't hold a listener's interest for very long, and I was tired of doing magic tricks.

So, I learned Clementi's "Opus 36" because it could stand on its own on the banjo, and because I had never heard anybody else play it. I got my hands on the music at my friend Linda's house in exchange for giving her some banjo lessons. It took me two months to figure out "Opus 36," as I knew nothing about reading music, but this piece would show up in my life in strange places.

Linda was my first crush, but she was Steve's girlfriend and a fellow Magic Shop employee. The very thought of touching her as I looked over her shoulder to correct fingering on her banjo's neck made me feel like my life had begun. I confess that I fantasized that we *might* learn things other than music, but my hands stayed on the banjo.

This was California and I had wheels, so whenever Steve was working, Linda and I would drive around, anywhere and everywhere. Never did get in the back seat, and the front wasn't rewarding the way I fantasized. It was always worth that frustration just to hear her laugh. Steve missed this love boat, but he later paid homage to those years by naming a street in one of his films (*Dead Men Don't Wear Plaid*) with her last name: Rasmussen.

I enrolled at Long Beach State College as a math major, which enabled me to practice banjo eight hours a day, either in a campus music room, in my car, or eleven minutes away at McCabe's Guitar Shop in Long Beach. McCabe's turned out to be my gateway to show business. It was a place to hang out and sit around the coffee table, playing music with other itinerants, surrounded by acoustic guitars, banjos, and folk records and books. I am not sure exactly how I found it. I think my brother Bill told me about it. It became my second home in the daytime, where I would go between and after classes to hang out and play with whoever was doing the same.

While still working the Magic Shop during, and in the middle of my ersatz pursuit of college, I got my first band together. I played guitar with fifteen-year-old Les Thompson, who was hanging around McCabe's too, and who I would see at various Dillard shows. Les liked to sing and play guitar and mandolin, and was as much of a Dillards fanatic as I was. Truly a hard worker, a friendly puppy kind of guy, always-smiling Les wanted to please everyone. We formed the Willmore City Moonshiners and got a gig opening for Hoyt Axton at the historic Golden Bear in Huntington Beach. A big gruff guy, Axton scared me at first! A few months earlier, he had showed off one way to handle a bad crowd. The collegiate madras-shirt audience, too busy talking to each other about how cool it was to be in a folk club, hadn't been paying enough attention to his music. He suddenly stopped mid-song and glared out at the now quiet crowd.

"Well, you're not listening to my songs," Hoyt growled. "Maybe you'll listen to this." He raised his guitar over his head and smashed it to pieces against the chair. He wordlessly left the stage, walked out of the Bear to his car, got in, and drove away. Showbiz looked like it could be a huge amount of fun, if I could just figure out how to get in. (Twenty years later, Hoyt's mother, Mae, writer of "Heartbreak Hotel," would become my "biggest fan" in Nashville. Three Dog Night's take on Hoyt's song "Joy to the World," known by its opening lyrics, "Jeremiah was a bull frog," was still several years from croaking on the radio.)

Steve often came by my family's house after Magic Shop work, around one in the morning, and we would play our banjos. He was my first banjo student as music began to take the place of chess and magic. I'd show him something I learned from slowing my records down or we'd try to make up something. Often, Steve would try new jokes. Then, after about eight minutes and the predictable, "I'd better get going," he would leave. Later, Steve would become well-known in the entertainment industry for that eight-minute attention limit. When my mom said, "That friend of yours, Steve, always acts like he is *on*, performing, or thinks he's on stage, trying to be funny," I agreed. That's what I liked, and life felt like a natural extension of the Magic Shop. A few times during my transition from magic to music, I went to Steve's shows, backed up his banjo playing, and cued up a record for his magic act a few times. But I could tell he was more into his own thing and trying to find it—like I was. I wanted to be part of something, to work with others, and see where that would go. When not playing, I was drawn to the haunting records of Houston bluesman Lightnin' Hopkins, and I would go to sleep to his soulful music.

Music pretty quickly took the place of everything, except my first actual girlfriend, singer Penny Nichols. Penny helped me understand where the music of life came from. But, when she came back from a USO singing trip in Vietnam, we found we were in different keys, so we parted ways, though we're friends to this day.

———————

All hanging around McCabe's, Jimmie Fadden was a sardonic blues harmonica savant; quick-witted Jeff Hanna was into Ian and Sylvia and other folk music; and great finger-picker Ralph Barr and quirky singer/guitarist Bruce Kunkel hung around too. Sitting around that low, worn wood coffee table, we all were trying to learn from the records on the shelves around us. It was a very friendly atmosphere of teenage pickers learning and sharing. It was here that my fifth band would start, but that was still a year away.

One night while I was watching *Hootenanny* on TV, drooling over Doc Watson doing "Deep River Blues," my dad said, "Now, how a guy like that gets on TV, I'll never understand." (I knew then I wanted to be on TV, too.) Not knowing Doc's importance, my father would rather have sung along with Mitch Miller. But he did buy me my first banjo—from McCabe's of course. Up until then I had only been borrowing a cheap one.

Even though McCabe's had become the most important space in my life and had opened up doors to the future I dreamed of, I ended up transferring the next year to Santa Ana Junior College. It had better music practice rooms, and enrolling in the drama classes gave me access to the empty theater, which was a great place to sit on stage alone in the dark and practice.

———————

It was around then that I experienced my first standing ovation. Steve was performing in some unknown college theater, and I played the banjo while he recited a poem, "The Mountain Whippoorwill," to close the show. We finished—and were met with absolute silence. That five seconds seemed like five minutes, until the crowd burst into applause and rose to their feet. They just stayed there, standing and cheering. That same poem became the basis for my biggest artistic accomplishment at that time: a film project for my art history class term project. I recorded the two of us doing "Whippoorwill," which we both learned from our high school *Adventures in American Literature* textbook. My brother had shot the Topanga Banjo Contest the previous year, and I had a lot of 8mm footage of the mountains that I had shot on a family trip, and I was able to edit some of that together with our recording as a soundtrack. The teacher was amazed when his previously somnolent, failing student brought his film project/term paper to class one day. I was nervous as a cat but put on a good show of confidence as I set up the projector and recorder, cueing the tape to the film. That sixth-grade projectionist "training" was paying off! He made me show it to every class, and I ended up turning the F into an A+++.

I escaped the death throes in my music history class in much the same way. That teacher reluctantly allowed me do a class concert instead of a term paper. I called my new, blind Puerto Rican teenager friend, whom I had met at the Paradox. He had recently moved to Orange County from New York, and I'd drive us around to play together at the clubs. No one had heard of him, but Jose Feliciano liked my banjo playing, and thanks to our concert in that theater, I earned another A. I also got my first D that same term, in calculus, and realized math was no longer my major. Making things was more exciting; music, show bits, finding comedy routines, putting people together to play. That's what I wanted to do.

It was a great time for new music. Clubs and coffee houses of this growing music scene were everywhere. I'd walk in and ask the club manager if my blind friend (I had to explain his dog) and I could just play a few songs. At first reluctant, the managers would most often then let us play for an hour. On my own, with Jose, or with other musicians I met, we hung out at all of the coffee houses: the Rouge et Noir in Seal Beach, the Mecca in Buena Park, the Troubadour and the Ash Grove in Hollywood, the Ice House in Pasadena, and the Golden

Bear. Their walls had different artwork, the vibe was new, the people who worked them all seemed to be escaping something, too. It seemed like we were all the same age. Like the audiences who came, they were all brimming with and searching for what was coming in the music world. I wanted to be part of it, but wasn't sure what "it" was to be. I wanted to be on the radio.

On the way to college one morning, "Mr. Tambourine Man" came on the radio. I pulled over, stopped to listen, and then blew off classes and headed to the beach with my banjo. I waited for the Byrds to come on again. I knew that their bass player, Chris Hillman, was a mandolin player from a San Diego bluegrass group called the Scottsville Squirrel Barkers. I thought, *If he can get on the radio, well, so can I!* I still didn't have a clue how to do it, but that D in calculus pretty much settled things. I now knew my future would be in music. But I needed a band.

I wanted a future like the Byrds'. After the demise of the Moonshiners, my quest took me to Michael Murphey at the Glendale Ice House (one of those L.A. clubs). He wanted me in his group—my fourth one—with his partner from Texas, and we believed we could get on the radio. But after six months with their two guitars, my banjo, and a bass player, there were too many straws on that camel's back and it was time to head down a different road.

The first straw was the name of the group: the Texas Twosome. I wasn't from Texas, and there were four of us. Another straw: the publicity shot with just the two of *them*. The final straw: we got a booking on *The Linkletter Show*. (*This is it! On TV finally!*) Michael came up to me during camera blocking. "I really want you playing with us," he said, "but they don't have enough money in the budget to have four guys on camera." The final straw, and I was out. It felt like "Who gets McEuen?" all over again. I sat a couple feet off camera during the taping of *their* fifteen minutes, then went off to look for my own. My mom watched the show, imagining me sitting just out of the picture to the left. I didn't watch; it was too depressing. But I still loved his songs and voice, and thought he could be on the radio someday. Wanting to find where I fit, I continued my search. (In later years, I'd end up on four or five of Murphey's albums, including playing on two of his hits, "Wildfire" and "Carolina in the Pines.")

I did my first recording session that summer. I had no idea what to do with the chord chart they handed me, but I pretended to follow it. I always had trouble counting and watching measures go by, and keeping up with the music, and I still do at times. But by just listening, I figured out that if you hit a wrong note, it sounded like it, so don't! The Wrecking Crew's Mike Post was making a recording of Doug Kershaw's "Louisiana Man." I hadn't heard of Kershaw yet, but Post was a big deal in the L.A. music scene, and I thought this recording might get me on the radio. It didn't. My next session was for Richie Havens, who was doing a bluegrass version of "Rocky Raccoon." I never got to hear that either, but kept hoping that somehow there would be airplay in my future.

By that time, I had played several shows with Penny and our friend Mary McCaslin, and had observed that both of them laughed and sang beautifully—and took their music seriously. It was important to them, and they really meant to be good. I tried to be as good as possible, too, to make as few mistakes as possible, to play as fast as I could when that was needed, and then to slow it down to find the heart of the song, and listen to the lyrics. It seemed to me that the playing should never distract from the song's message. Those women wanted to make records as much as I did, but I did not want to be just a backup guy. Still lacking confidence in my playing, and not being a singer, I kept practicing and searching for nice instrumental sounds to backup other's vocals.

About the same time, Bill and I heard about a place in northern Virginia where the islands floated and you could get lost in its ever-changing environment. It's called the Great Dismal Swamp, and it inspired an instrumental song we wrote together that year.

My brother actually got into the music biz as a way into movies. Bill and I used to eat lunch staring at the Paramount Pictures studio gates. Sitting in Bill's car across Melrose, watching stars go in and out of Hollywood's inner sanctum, we dreamed of what it might be like if we ever got inside. We saw Elvis more than once. One time, as the

King drove away, he actually looked at me and flicked his finger. I knew we could get along; I'm sure he wanted to talk, too, but he had to get to lunch over on the *Paradise, Hawaiian Style* set, so he rolled on down the road.

I was reading film books and playing music while Bill went to USC film school. We played together sometimes, and his wife, Alice, sang harmony. The biggest gig we had as the Fall River Tarheels (my first group!), was in Newport Beach at the smoke-filled Sid's Blue Beet, where we made fifty dollars a night—each! The bluegrass-loving crowd did a great job of holding up the bar, and the ocean air helped cover up the funky aura of stale beer that permeated the room. We also played the Golden Bear and Troubadour, but Bill's passion was not found on stage.

Our mainly bluegrass menu had songs from Jimmy Martin, the Dillards, Scruggs, the Stanley Brothers, Keith and Rooney, and the Carter Family. Our "Dismal Swamp" became one of my signature pieces in my career. The most important lesson I learned during those months was to never sleep on a pool table, but I knew better things were ahead, even if I didn't know where to find them.

During that pre-NGDB summer of 1965, Bill and I drove to Nashville delivering diesel parts to some of my dad's clients—but the real purpose was to see the Grand Ole Opry. The show was sold out when we arrived that August night, but I was able to peer in through the open back windows on that melting-hot southern evening just in time to see Lester Flatt announce, "Earl an' I'd like t' bring out Mother Maybelle Carter to do the 'Wildwood Flower.'" The place went nuts. I thought, *Someday I will meet those people, and someday I will record with them.* I had another goal: to one day play on the Grand Ole Opry stage.

———————

One fall day in 1965, the owner of the Golden Bear, Del Kaufman, asked if I wanted to loan him $2,000 to help hire Bob Dylan for a concert at Wilson High School. After listening to my pitch, my dad cosigned the note that got me the two grand. I'd made good on other loans, like for the toy airplanes, and he went for it. The show sold out four weeks later, I paid my father back, and I bought a new banjo with the $1,800 profit I made. Bob bought me a banjo! That felt good, and I liked that side of the box office. Although my dad had told me early on, "I think you're going down the wrong road with this music thing," I knew he was now feeling better about that road.

In 1966, Les Thompson, my former bandmate from the Moonshiners, had just moved into the embryonic Nitty Gritty Dirt Band as it was evolving at McCabe's, where I was then teaching banjo. He called one June day and said, "You should get in this group we're putting together! It would be perfect. Jackson [Browne] has played the few shows we've done, but doesn't want to be in a band." I knew all the guys in his forming group—Ralph and Kunkel, Fadden and Jeff Hanna. All fellow McCabe's hangers-on, all trying to learn Doc Watson licks, Carter Family music, Lovin' Spoonful tunes, or Jim Kweskin Jug Band songs. We acted the part of cool young musicians, emulating people we thought we'd never even meet, much less record with.

Jeff had told me he was impressed when he saw me cover for the Greenbrier Boys' banjo player who couldn't make it one night to their final sold-out show at the Golden Bear. That was my biggest show business opportunity to date. In the packed Bear, I felt the full power of performing in a respected band, but it was a one-night stand.

I taught "Dismal Swamp" to Les and the other guys around the gathering table and enlisted them to back me at the Topanga Canyon Banjo and Fiddle Contest that July, which was the only contest I ever entered. It was our first performance as a group, and since I won, it seemed pointless to try any more contests—or bands. With the invitation from Les, I moved into the NGDB in its third month, believing this might get me on the radio. I liked Jeff's voice and quirky sarcasm, too.

As I headed to the Paradox stage in Orange County a week later to play with my new group (the fifth one), Jackson came into what passed for the dressing room.

"Hey, John, listen to this song." He started singing, "Well, I've been out walking / Don't do too much talking, these days . . ."

"Where did you learn that, Jackson? And where'd you get the words?" I asked.

"I just made it up tonight," he said. "Words and everything." It struck me then that we could actually write our own meaningful music and lyrics. This was the first time I had heard an original song with words that were written by someone I knew, and I think I was the first person to hear it. The words were shockingly good. "These Days," known now as one of his classics, was beautiful even then, and it was obvious he was headed to success his own way.

That night had a major impact on me. I thought maybe there was to be more than "Dismal Swamp" in my future. I played with NGDB that paradox night, doing a song we did fifty years later on television, "Truthful Parson Brown." It was Jackson's last show with them (he did about five), and the band had finally finished forming into the one that would make our first album. Once Jackson became successful and famous—which took a few years—Jeff and Fadden would usually state he had been an "original member" of the NGDB. That Les and I had a band that also led to NGDB they never mentioned.

When the Dirt Band got underway, after the banjo contest, I started setting up rehearsals and sound checks, and drove us around in my Chevy Nova Supersport. I convinced my brother Bill to manage us. He had been working with a couple of other acts, hanging out in Hollywood, learning the music business and trying to sort it all out as he also continued looking for a way into the movie biz.

Then 1966 and 1967 were big years on the personal side. Just as NGDB was picking up steam, my wonderful sister Maureen died after a two-year battle with lupus. She was a pal and I was her buddy for many years. A couple times when she was having convulsions, I had to lay on top of her and cram something in her mouth so she wouldn't bite her tongue. The ambulance would come and take her to the hospital again. I was really glad to have the banjo then to escape to. Her last ambulance ride was to UCLA for a month-long stay in intensive care. I frequently took the night watch, and after driving up from Orange County or Long Beach, I would sit up with her. My mom would be there in the daytime. (We had a temporary apartment down the street from the hospital that month.) One day, as I was leaving after dropping mom off for her shift, Maureen called me back to her room.

She weakly reached out and held my hand, looked me right in the eyes, and said, "You know I love you, don't you?" I nodded and said I loved her too. This wasn't something people in my family said too often, except for my mother who made up for everyone else. I didn't cry in front of her, and I went to McCabe's to give some lessons.

After arriving at McCabe's, I canceled my lessons for the day, sat in the back room, and waited. About an hour later I was called to the phone. I knew. It was in her goodbye eyes. Someone on the phone, I can't remember who, told me, "Your sister is gone." I went back to the back room and played my banjo for her for a while, crying through "San Antonio Rose." She liked that one best.

My own life was moving in a new direction. I'd dropped out of college, got out of the draft, and left the safe haven of the Magic Shop to start a band and live in Hollywood with my mates. I had found a house for us in Beachwood Canyon that was dubbed the Dirt House. I was part of something. All those life lessons from the Magic Shop and working for my father were to come into play.

But outside my own triumphs, the Vietnam War was heating up, with body counts reported on the television news every night. Like in golf, the lower score was the winner. We were winning every day, the government said. They also said the Russians had six thousand atomic warheads aimed at us, ready to launch at a moment's notice, after which we would have about a forty-five-minute warning until we'd be nuclear toast. When told we had eighteen thousand pointed at *them*, I felt safe and at peace. I bought a special pair of sunglasses and a beach chair just to be ready to watch the show from the roof of the house, but that never came.

2

The Real Thing, the Big Show, Rock 'n' Roll!

The hip, Hollywood music night club the Ash Grove (now called the Improv) had become the Nitty Gritty Dirt Band's second home. This dark, smoky, 240-seat music room drew all the underground musicians in the area who were looking to find their place in life. Many of them found it here, and we were among them. The Ash Grove's small restaurant area in the front had a kitchen where we could make our own sandwiches when we played or rehearsed there—if not playing or rehearsing, we'd still try to talk the owner, Ed Pearl, into handing out some free food. It was here that I met and played with many musical greats. One summer night in the 1960s, while hanging in the dressing room with one of my idols—the gold-toothed blues legend Lightnin' Hopkins—I asked him why most of his songs (about 95 percent!) were in the key of E. He said, "You can spend your whole life lookin' around in E and never find all of it. I'm still a lookin'." He found a lot.

At the Ash Grove in December 1966, during rehearsals for our ten-day opening run with great guitarist Merle Travis, a guy from Tulsa in a blue suit asked us if we wanted to sign with a record label. I told him we had just signed with Liberty Records and were making our first album. He asked to stay around to watch us for an hour or so, and so began my lifetime friendship with Leon Russell. He liked the food, too. His star would rise soon.

We recorded our first album that winter at Steiner's Eight Track studio, which housed the first 8-track machine in Hollywood. We were right next to the Capitol Tower on Vine Street, two hundred feet away from the Capitol studio where, three months earlier, we auditioned for Capitol and were turned down.

On February 7, 1967, around one in the morning, I was driving down Sunset Boulevard coming up to Vine Street with the radio on loud as I flipped through the stations. One of our songs, "Buy for Me the Rain," (with strings arranged by pre-Bread David Gates, as his first L.A. job) was out and supposedly on the radio. At 1:03 AM the KRLA jock said, "Here's a new song by that Nitty Gritty Dirt Band! 'Buy for Me the Rain!'" I almost drove off the road! I went to the All Night Ranch Market, spent all twelve dollars I had on food, took it back to the Dirt House, and told everyone "We're gonna be rich! I just heard 'Rain' on KRLA!" Written by our folky friends Steve Noonan and Greg Copeland, that song became our first hit.

Soon after that, my father saw me on television, and heard "Rain" on the radio, with me playing that banjo he had bought me. He felt better about my passion for music. The band was only eight months old, and I was only twenty-one years old, and still, we wondered why it had taken so long. But my American Dream was underway: I heard my banjo coming out of my car speaker. From then on, we were in the music business. The next step, of course, was our first promotion tour across the country, much of which was done in a bus (but one that only had seats, no bunks, yet).

"It will be good exposure" is what you are told the first time you want to step on a stage. Then you start hearing the phrase, "It's not a money thing." Even after a few years, you still find yourself playing for free because of said "'sposure." A hit record is good exposure, but often not a money thing. Along that path to the hit, an inexperienced artist is told that anyone who helps make the hit happen (or "hitmakers," with whom you are hoping to be involved) is doing you a favor.

In that early year of "Rain," the egos did flare at times. After all, we were on the radio now, and were allowed, expected, assumed, and deserved to be treated the way other "hitmakers" were treated. One time at a radio station, I grumbled out loud, "Why are we here?" like the pricks we could become. I was lucky that an important lesson was there for the early learning.

On the wave that was building off "Buy for Me the Rain," came that first lesson in Promotion 101 for the class of 1967. After driving for what seemed like two-and-a-half hours into a forest destination outside of Washington, DC, a little building with a radio tower pumping out only one thousand watts emerged.

"It's small, but important," said Harvey, our first promo man.

We skeptically strutted into this podunk station with our first big, national hit breaking the *Billboard* Top 30 Pop charts. I thought it a waste to go all this way to a DJ in the middle of the East Coast boondocks forest, but we acquiesced to this jump through the hoop anyway. In the control room, we got ready to tell this small-time, nothing station lies about how great it was to be there. After all, I had grown up in Hollywood and had heard jokes about out-of-the-way places in the sticks like this.

While he played our song I sat thinking, *Well, yes, it's great to be on the radio . . . but where could this possibly lead?* As we waited, I started scanning the studio walls. There were so many publicity photos and snapshots that I could not see the actual wall. They all had handwritten comments such as, "Great to meet you," "Thanks for all your help," "Great to come back and see you again," "You made it happen," "You got me started," "You're hot . . . thanks for lightin' the fire," "You're the best," "WE got by with some help from you, friend," etc. All those press photos had been signed in person at the station by the Rolling Stones, Glen Campbell, Herman's Hermits, the Jackson 5, Jim Morrison, Frank Sinatra, Frankie Valli, the Beatles, and many, many others.

As we came out of "Rain," live over the airwaves, the DJ said, "Well, DC, that's the West Coast's Nitty Gritty Dirt Band and their first hit! What have you boys got to say to the East Coast?"

I jumped at the chance to speak and meant every word: "It's great to be here! Thanks for the airplay and for having us out! You're the best! Can we sign one of our photos for you? Would you want one to put up on your wall?"

Lesson learned.

Strange days lay ahead that year. On that trip with us, my brother saw a band in St. Louis called the Allman Joys and convinced them to come to L.A., where he would get them a record deal. Two weeks later, Gregg and Duane Allman moved into our NGDB Dirt House in Beachwood Canyon, as a place to park for a few days that lasted six weeks and then found their own places and started working as the Hour Glass.

That May NGDB finally got our first big, out-of-town, headlining job: playing a week at the Multnomah County Fair in Oregon, with Sonny Moore and his Roustabouts as our opening act. It was very exciting to go to new territory, and it was all new territory then. With "Rain" on the radio and our band only a year old, I headed out to change the world, five strings at a time.

Once we got to the misty Portland airport I learned that the only vehicle available that could take us and our instruments—a flatbed truck with no sides—was actually a mile away. As the only one old enough to rent a vehicle, I became the band's road manager that day—and I carried out that job for the next eleven years. I showed up back at the airport an hour later to pick up the impatient band and our gear, all of which we placed carefully in the middle of the flatbed and up front in the cab. The farmer's mailbox that the truck took out on the way was a casualty of my youthful foolishness. That was the last rock 'n' roll destruction I did.

During one of our three-a-day fair shows, one of the guys in the band announced, "The next song is called 'You Only Hurt the Ones You Love,' or 'Who Put the Sand in the Vaseline?'" An old guy in the front row laughed so hard, and pitched forward so fast, that his false teeth flew right out and landed in the dirt in front of him, making a little dust mushroom cloud. The promoter, who already hated us, said,

"This is a family show! We only put class acts on here, so keep it clean," and demanded our contracted sixty minutes and that he wouldn't "have any more trouble."

Our "classy" stage was next to the racetrack. Horses ran past the left side of the stage every twenty minutes, filling the air with dust. That wasn't the worst part. The blaring public address system for the race had speakers pointed right toward our audience. That audience ranged in age from eight to eighty years old, with very few in between. As we played from the other side of our little dust bowl arena, we heard, "They're off and running! And in the lead is . . . ," mixed with midway announcements, ride noises and screams, and carneys barking "Winaprize! Guessyourweight! Winaprize!" That made the sound mix, let's say, competitive.

Sonny's Roustabouts were his fifteen dogs, and he was always yelling at them. A hyper Sonny barking orders, combined with super-hyper dogs barking back and running around, made for a hyper "family" show. We waited our turn for their big finish. What was his show's climax? The littlest dog would take a leak on center stage, which signaled that we had five minutes to get on stage while they mopped up the puddle and Sonny put his dogs back into the bus that they all lived in. A class act.

While waiting backstage between shows, I'd try to learn how to play the piano and chat with Sonny. Every day he said to me, "I had long hair, like my poodles," seeming to forget he already stated that fact the day before. "I was the first with long hair. Everyone has it now," he whined. Once, between shows, he invited curious me to tour his circus-odor filled, fifteen-dog bus. He excitedly said, "Say, looky here," and pulled out an eight-by-ten, nicely framed photo of a "good looking" German shepherd.

"This is Gretchen, best dog I ever had. She was a great lover, too." Shifting his glance back and forth between his lover and guest, he added, "Got her ashes in the back. Wanna see 'em?" I really didn't want to know any more about his One Dog Night adventures and begged off to head back to the piano; I was trying to get good enough to record with it someday. It was obvious there was a lot to learn about show business. By letting me on his bus, Sonny made me feel like I was actually a part of it, and I loved that. I hopped off Sonny's bus but would climb aboard many others that were to prove equally as crazy—only without the barking dogs.

Our crowds started getting bigger at the clubs. The Dirt Band was hot. Shortly, we had a show at Birmingham High School with a lineup of others with their early hits. Appearing with us, during what I saw as a "Dirt Band show," were the Doors, Jefferson Airplane, the Byrds (with Chris Hillman), Buffalo Springfield, the Association, and the Merry-Go-Round (some groups didn't last). None of the bands were huge yet, but we were all becoming part of the fabric of what would make up an important part of pop music in the years to come.

It cost six dollars to get into that show. The crowd that packed the high school football field expected a hot show that hot June summer night in 1967. Valley girls—a mix of long-haired hippie girls and "mod" girls sporting bouffants or beehives and the Twiggy look—surfers, and hippies were all anxious to get their money's worth. The Dirt Band was set for eight o'clock. I couldn't wait to get finished and get out. I had seen most of the other bands before, and that night, high-voiced Bill Monroe and His Blue Grass Boys were at the Ash Grove. There was no way I was going to miss the man who created the genre and gave bluegrass music its name. A true showman, he always wore impressive suits and a great big hat. I skipped out on all those young bands working to be the new real thing to see a cooler, older guy who already was.

As most things in L.A. were about twenty minutes away (now thirty), I made it to the club by nine thirty, just as Monroe's second set started. Ed Pearl saw me coming in and cornered me to ask, "John, how would you like to sit in with Monroe?"

"Of course, but little chance of that," I answered. I wasn't in Bill Monroe's league and assumed Ed was joking.

"Well, I told him you'd be here. He's going to call you up in the middle of this set. Be ready," Ed replied.

This now-nervous, Orange County kid was going to sit in with a genuine music legend, someone I never thought I would even meet! I never had any use for the smorgasbord of drugs available back then and to come, as nothing in the world could have got me higher than this. Monroe called me up. I played Earl's "Shuckin' the Corn" to the packed house and it killed. Monroe was pleased, saying, "That's a'mighty fine pickin'." It was a great night for me. Little did I know that Ash Grove night Monroe would jam with me twenty years later in a Zurich bar. But we'll get to that later.

In those early days, it was easy to get down about how tough the showbiz game was, and how the road to the top was a constant struggle. I probably hadn't changed my strings more than a couple dozen times and thought of myself as well weathered. It was my good fortune to come across a "newsman" whose circumstances brought me back down to earth, and who still inspires me anytime I start feeling sorry for myself.

The first time I saw him, I was starting a seventeen-hour day of work and travel by heading to LAX airport on a foggy morning in the fall of 1967. I spotted his twisted body bent over the front of his motor scooter, with stacks of newspapers precariously balanced in the baskets on the front, sides, and back, as he headed uphill on La Cienega Boulevard to Sunset Boulevard at about ten mph, at sunrise. He looked like he could barely hold on. I knew nothing about this guy, but the mere sight of him instantly drove home the point that I had it pretty easy, that I was fortunate to do what I did for a living.

Back home the next week I saw him again, outside Ben Frank's restaurant on Sunset, a few blocks from La Cienega. This eatery served the best breakfasts in town, and the clientele was a microcosm of Hollywood: agents, managers, soon-to-burn-out rocker hippies, and leftovers from the alcohol daze, all having breakfast, getting ready for the day in that city. You could hear people going on about how they "really got fried last night," over their eggs and bacon. These days, of course, those people just say, "Oh, no, I can't eat that. It's fried."

He didn't make the news, nor even write it, he just delivered it, and his route took him by Ben Frank's daily. I bought from him several times, but I am embarrassed now that I was too embarrassed then to talk to him, with his broken body and stumbling walk. He also had speech problems, a somewhat foamy mouth, and eyes that wandered randomly. He could talk, with difficulty, but few tried to make conversation. It wasn't that anyone made fun of him, but few engaged with him as a human being.

I must have seen him at least half a dozen times over the ensuing years, chugging up that hill on La Cienega at sunrise, already working. I wondered when and where he got those papers, and how he managed it all. I wondered if he knew that I'd held him up as an example of determination, of how anyone who worked hard could make their way in America. I quit whining, and I never forgot the lesson that he never knew he taught me. Later, people from that era said things like, "Oh, yeah. I remember him. Poor bastard. His name was Steve. I always gave him an extra buck or two."

Steve actually had access to the offices of the most powerful people in show business. He sold papers directly to the heads of the major talent agencies, *Billboard* magazine, law firms, and record companies; his access was a kind that few in town had, and all wished for. He also had something from all of us that most of us didn't for each other: respect.

———————

NGDB did about ten concerts with the Doors. I thought Jim Morrison put on a good show, but I don't think he thought it was a "show." He was moody and acted very "important." No one could speak to him as he slumped to and from his dressing room. The other musicians were nice, though. At Hartford's Bushnell Auditorium he refused to leave the dressing room until his mother was out of the building. Such a nice boy. Maybe he knew how silly some of his sick attention-getting antics were, and knew she would tell him so. Maybe he just didn't get it. Maybe I didn't. Hollywood got part of it: his act was a money machine for the time, selling a lot of tickets. It was depressing, controversial, and offensive, as if it were important to be so. Get 'em while they're hot, get them while they offend, and then, when they're not, say goodbye. Jim Morrison thought he was strange, but he'd never met Sonny. In reality, his was just another show, another act for agents of the Hollywood music machine to sell to promoters. It is a safe hypothesis that if the Doors were still around, they would be having a great run at all the Indian casinos.

You let your drug abuse burn you down, Jim, but the Doors produced some great hits and some bona fide classics, especially the one my dear friend Jose Feliciano got hold of. Later that year, Jose called to see if I could drive him to Irvine College for a show. (They weren't called concerts yet.) Thinking we were going to a little coffeehouse, I was amazed to see fifteen hundred people waiting in a gym, all paying to see him! Unbeknownst to me, his version of "Light My Fire" was burning up the charts. I sat in on a couple of songs at the end of his show, and "we" got a standing ovation. I remember that show vividly because that was the night I made it my quest to get that kind of response from a crowd on my own. (Six years later, Jose's "Feliz Navidad" would become one of the most played Christmas songs in history.) It was Jose who suggested to me that I play other instruments besides banjo, so I got a mandolin, not knowing if it could put me on pop radio.

Jose's "Light My Fire" did better than Morrison's. I find it interesting that Morrison made much less of an impact on the world than did a blind Puerto Rican guitar player from New York with more vision for and dedication to his music than Morrison ever had.

After our run of dates with the Doors on the East Coast, we went out with Bobby Sherman. Morrison's impact on music history might be more enduring than Sherman's, who was a Birmingham High 1959 graduate, but Sherman's audiences left happier. At our first of a dozen Sherman shows, we were almost getting booed off stage. The Sherman fans were so intense. Like Morrison's, they had waited months for their idol, and we had two weeks of shows to get through.

One difference between the two crowds was that three-quarters of the Sherman audience was driven to the concerts by their mothers, and the other quarter was those moms. Bobby's audience, girls between nine and sixteen and their mothers, was ready, willing, and wet (we assumed) with tears of joy. He was a great teenybopper performer, and you could see his smile from the back row. It seemed he had little footlights implanted in his lower jaw, and he knew how to use them. When he sang "Julie, Julie, Julie, do ya love me?" he made every girl in there feel like she was Julie and he loved only her.

It was again at Bushnell that we schemed to burn our way across the north with Sherman to final victory. First, we learned to ask, after almost every song, "Are you all here to see BOBBY SHERMAN?" Then, after letting the resounding high-pitched thunder die down, we'd say something like, "Here's one of his favorite songs!" More squeals. We got pretty good at this stuff. Jeff would say, "Before we bring Bobby out, HE wanted US to make sure all of your flash cameras are ready! Get your cameras ready, and on the count of three, everyone click at once!" The flashes from three thousand flashcubes lit the room like daylight, followed by thousands of teener squeals of delight. "BOBBY loves that!" More squeals, another song. At the end of our set, which was now finally going over well, we tested the flash one more time, and let them know, "Bobby is ready to come out . . . let him know you're here!" Not that this band of hippies from SoCal was ready to stop worrying, but now that we were almost getting encores from the Bobbbbbyyyy Sheerrrrrrmmmmannnnnn audience, did *we* suck?

I asked Sherman one night if he minded the constant screaming that got louder when each song would start. "Well, I know something they don't," he answered. "I'm not a very good singer. When they stop screaming, they'll find that out, and my career will be over. I figure I've got about a year-and-a-half run, and I'll make the most of it." As he predicted, he ran that teen horse as many laps as he could, and last I heard he became a dedicated LAPD officer in Southern California. I hear he goes after that with as much zeal as he pursued teenybopper stardom, and he was great at the job I saw him do.

———————

Jimmie Fadden and I had some great times on the road, more earlier on than later. We did the grunt work together: moving equipment, loading, setting up. I continued to get the rental trucks and cars, go to the airport, and pick up the band gear. Sometimes a station wagon would do. By late fall of 1967 we made it to New York City, and to our first New York headlining gig: a week at Paul Colby's Bitter End in Greenwich Village.

We were playing cheap, staying cheap ("They change the sheets every day—from room to room"), and eating cheaper. I discovered it was cheaper to rent a limo than a car. We took two limos the day of the gig, loaded with us and the gear.

It was exciting in the musically alive 1960's Village. I took chess lessons from a grand master, ate pizza and dogs, and played in Washington Square like Dylan and Seeger had. It was November, and I called my mother on Thanksgiving Day. I was missing her and the usual big dinner spread. She asked, "How are the crowds?" just like she always did, and I let her know all was good. I told her I had to get off the phone because my Thanksgiving dinner was about to begin, and hung up. With just enough money for two of New York City's famous Nathan's hot dogs and a Coke, I was happy and thankful—and the next day we would get paid.

Our first time on *Johnny Carson* came that week. The show taped at 4:00 PM, so we had time to race back to the sleazy Hotel Earle between sets that night to catch the broadcast. We ran into our cheapo room just in time for Bob Newhart's intro, "And now here they are with their new hit, 'Buy for Me the Rain,' a new West Coast band . . . the Nitty Gritty Dirt Band." We looked fine in our 1930s outfits from Goodwill (the entire band's wardrobe cost less than twenty-five dollars). National television is a great rush, even to this day. We realized that something like eight to ten million people were seeing us at the same time. To reach the same amount of people playing at the Bitter End we'd have to play two sold-out shows a night for twenty-two *thousand* nights—every night for nearly sixty-one years.

The opening instrumental section sounded fine. Then Jeff started singing . . . and no one heard a single word. His vocal mic was off, and it remained that way until the last verse. We wordlessly dragged back for the last set. But when I called Mom, she said she thought we looked good.

Back at the Bitter End, Woody Allen was doing guest sets, opening for us on a couple of nights. What a riot he was! He was trying out some new material, and he was killing with it. One night, out on the sidewalk in front of the club for a little peace from the wall of laughter before our next set, I confirmed that I was not really "one of those long-haired hippies" of the era. I know I looked the part, but those genuine, hard-core hippies had a different kind of attitude, often worsened by being stoned.

A normal freak (you know, a regular hippie) was lurking around the front door, checking the place out, peering in the window, and he asked, "Hey, man, what's goin' on in there?"

"Oh, it's a music club," I replied, "and right now a comedian is on doing some really funny stuff. He's great, and—"

"A comedian, huh? Whaddyamean . . . a guy that tells *jokes?*"

"Well, kind of, yes," I tried to explain. "He's just funny . . . makes people laugh, really funny guy, talking about 'things.'"

"Is it free?"

"No, about four dollars to get in."

"Well," the freak said firmly, "I don't pay no one to make me laugh. I laugh when I want to. For free! What a rip-off!" He drifted off, mumbling and griping down the sidewalk, looking for his next little rebellion against the establishment.

I couldn't relate to most hippie types, even though people generally perceived me as one. I think that's why I sought out stage costumes. I wanted to dress up in something that would separate me from my real life when I was on stage. Maybe it was something I picked up from my earliest performances at Disneyland. Starting with pin-striped, double-breasted, 1940s suits, to hippie, velvet bell-bottoms, briefly to turtlenecks, then to leather, I did the best I could with no money. I liked looking like I was a part of something special that others were watching. As I went through different styles over the years, it was always in search of something that would fit the instruments' sounds or the performance as well as something that would make me look like I was different from the audience. It's hard to explain, but I just wanted people to see me, and the band, as unique, and to remember us like that.

As the engagement at the Bitter End came to a close, I had to figure out our exit plan from New York. We had tickets to fly out of JFK in the morning, but Paul wouldn't let us leave our gear in the club overnight, nor would he come down to open up early so we could load out. Giving us a key was out of the question, so Fadden and I piled all our road cases and gear on the street in front of the Bitter End and slept on it until it came time to leave for the airport. We made friends overnight with the street people and drew some funny looks when I said we were just waiting to land a record deal. "It's going to be great! Women, limos, and free food!" We waited through the cold night until around seven in the morning, when the two big black limos I'd ordered pulled up. We loaded our stuff up, and away we went, telling the disbelieving street people of Greenwich Village, "Well, looks like the deal went through!"

During this time my father lost his business. He had built his diesel equipment business in the 1950s by buying surplus military hardware cheap at government auctions and then reselling it around the country. He dealt in things like GM diesel injector cores or bearings or engines and all the parts for them. Sometimes he would buy five hundred units of something for fifty cents each from one branch of the service and sell it to another for twelve dollars apiece! He knew every part number, its worth, what he should pay for it, what he would get for it, and where to get it. It was a great business at the start, but it slowly began dying in the late 1960s, as surplus supply dried up. One of his main suppliers was shipping him good things from Louisiana in the mid-1960s but did not tell him where all the great stuff was coming from. I think he sensed it was shady, but went ahead and dealt with him anyway.

What was going on was that my dad was unknowingly buying stolen government property that would arrive in Long Beach after a "good old boy" deal was made over the phone with the seller. For some reason, the seller didn't want invoices. After about a year, the FBI started investigating. His supplier had been stealing from a government base in Lake

Charles, Louisiana! The FBI tapped our phones for two years. We could hear them breathing when we'd call his office from our house. I would sometimes say, "I know you're there. Would you like me to bring you some coffee and a donut? You the same guy from yesterday" and they usually hung up. It was during this time that my mother also ran the NGDB "fan club," which included mimeographing newsletters at my dad's office and sending them out to fans on our growing mailing list. I had to hide my mother for a year as she was listed as an officer of the corporation and could be brought to testify against her husband in that manner. My dad lost his case.

We knew about his weight problem and stress, but unfortunately did not know he also suffered from high blood pressure and severe sleep apnea. His snoring would shake the walls. While awaiting his appeal, in September 1967, at fifty-two years old, he died at home in his sleep. It was just a year after my sister died. My family (now Bill and his beautiful wife, Alice, Mom, and me) would lose the house, as well as my father's fifty-two-foot boat, all the money, sixty acres of mountain land, and two cars.

3

Paint Your Wagon,
a.k.a. the Big Break

In spring of 1968 I was sitting in Bill's office at 8833 Sunset Boulevard, which was the double-glass elevator building right on the happening strip that was a block from the Whisky a Go Go. My big brother was doing his showbiz thing while I ate lunch on the floor. This was a daily ritual of my showbiz education. Bill looked up from the *Daily Variety* he was intently reading and exclaimed, "Aha! This is it!" like he had just located the Hope Diamond.

"What is 'it' Bill?" I queried through a mouthful of sandwich.

"This ad! It's perfect! We can get this," he declared.

How could the ex-president and the other member of the Space Rangers Club get Hollywood's attention? He read aloud: "This is the last week for auditions being held at Paramount Studios for a film version of the Lerner and Lowe Broadway musical *Paint Your Wagon.* We are looking for musicians to play the part of the 1840s miners' band!!"

The nation was still covered in the shadow of gloom after the recent assassination of Robert Kennedy at the nearby Ambassador Hotel. The Dirt Band played that same room the night after he won the primary, at a graduation party in June for four different high schools. In those days, no one would have thought to cancel. We walked to the stage, right past the taped off area where he was hit, did our show, and left.

In the days after, I remember wishing for something that could come along and clear away the dark cloud we were all still under, and here it was. Bill's actions reaffirmed how fortunate NGDB was to have him working with us: he called and got us the audition! We had to be at the Paramount lot in a couple days. I couldn't believe it! We're gonna be big! I'd get my revenge on those dog-pile-on-McEuen guys. I knew someday I would go inside those gates with my banjo, and not delivering pizza. We just didn't know how to get it done—until now.

So a few days later, there we were, actually going through the gates at Paramount, onto the lot with a drive-on, on our way to the big time. Staring bug-eyed at the huge sound stages, we set up in cavernous Stage Number 3 to audition in front of Alan Jay Lerner and Joshua Logan. It was big enough to put our house in it, and held memories of the great films that were made there. (Lerner had written lyrics and scripts for some of the classics of American musical theater; his songs have been sung in every corner of the world and in plays that live on and on.)

The NGDB was now Jeff, Fadden, me, Les, Ralph, and we had recently added fiddler Chris Darrow (whom I had watched in my Disneyland years). Lerner and Logan listened to this bunch of guys who couldn't read music, who together knew only twenty-one songs, and thought about how they could fit us into their $20 million picture. They had huge showbiz power behind them. I thought, *They won't want us, even though we're perfect for this.* Lerner and Logan kept whispering to each other as they watched us going through a few songs. Their heads nodded both ways—affirmative, negative, affirmative. And . . . we got the job!

Lerner kept pointing out, "This will be a big break for you boys." He told us, "You have two weeks to get ready to leave for the set. We'll fly you into Portland, then to Baker. It will be about three months up there." During the couple of weeks that we were preparing to stay at the Oregon location, I got up the courage to ask Kae Taylor, the eighteen-year-old whom I was hoping to marry, if she and her twin sister (Rae) would like to come up to the "big movie set" and work craft service. She said yes! I had met them the year before, on NGDB's first tour. She and her sister were standing outside a Salt Lake radio station watching us do our interview. I went out and invited them to that night's show. Her great smile could be seen from across the room, and she looked perfect. I didn't think someone with a beautiful face like hers would talk to me. She did. This was a bigger deal to me than that concert.

Using negotiating skills I picked up from the many youthful ventures from mistletoe to magic peddling, I worked it out with the company: the girls would fly to Portland, and then take a free charter (arranged with the craft-service guy) to Baker for their jobs. To see the one I wanted to see, I had to invite both.

On location two weeks later in Baker, Oregon, my twenty-two-year-old brain hatched a plan: get an Air Stream trailer, park it on the set, and invite the Taylors to come live with me in it in the forest. This would give us more time to hang out and avoid that seventy-five-minute bus trip, each way, to and from the mountain set. I rented the trailer before the girls came up, towed it to the trees, and prepared to spend the first night on my own.

All was great until about midnight. It started as a small noise, then seemed to get bigger. It was a scratching, dashing, crawling noise. And it was under the bed! At three in the morning, in an old travel trailer parked in the trees in the middle of the wilderness, with every light on that I could find, I looked like a madman junkie digging around for his fix. I now had the unseen noise trapped behind the couch, and I'd opened the trailer door in case I needed to make a quick escape. I jerked the couch up into the air, and there was the predator, rearing back on his hind legs, readying itself for action. Then, that ferocious killer chipmunk jumped past me and landed in the middle of the living room, next to the open door. It turned toward me to attack, but then, at the last moment, looked at the open door to freedom. At the cue of my Orange County–rebel yell, he jumped, as if shot from a cannon, at least ten feet into the dark to safety, and escaped. Since my night's excitement was over, I went to sleep in what now looked like a pile of laundry and discarded furniture assembled from a Hunter Thompson home-improvement show.

With everything in place before the girls' arrival, the next morning I went to the production supervisor's trailer to let him know my plans. He listened as he paced back and forth and puffed harder and harder on a stubby showbiz cigar, filling the production office trailer with smoke. I thought it was going well.

"Are you nuts?" he exploded. "This is a major Paramount Pictures production, and you want to bring twin, eighteen-year-old Mormon girls up here to live with you? On my set?" he screamed. "This is just what the press looks for. Have you read this script? This picture would get shut down so fast we—let me put it this way: NO!" His point was made. To bring a couple of beautiful, fresh-scrubbed Mormon girls up to the middle of the forest, fifty miles from town, with three hundred lonely guys running around, and only Jean Seburg to look at, would have been asking for it. Especially since this film was about two guys buying one Mormon woman.

The first few nights we all ended up in the Baker Hotel—in separate rooms—with the rest of the cast. A week later, I rented a two-bedroom house out in the country, down the road about a mile or two, for us all—Jeff Hanna, Kae, Rae, and me—to stay in. How Jeff got a bedroom, I can't figure out to this day. The girls took the other bedroom and I ended up on the living room couch. We were all just pals. *Music from Big Pink* by the Band and the Beatles' "Hey Jude" had just come out, and Jeff and I were engrossed in them—and the girls—nightly, after being on the set every day.

Kae and I had not yet gotten physical, but there was a lot of "aaannnticipaaation" that we would somehow come together. We'd stay up late listening to records or staring at each other, holding hands. I had never known it could be like this, and I was swept away. We neither knew nor cared what each new day would bring, and were simply having the time of our lives.

Location shoots attract intense and memorable characters—we had one stunt man from the original silent *Ben-Hur*, and the guy who got hung in *In Cold Blood*. *Paint Your Wagon*, a wild and wooly Western, seemed to draw a particularly odd assortment, many of whom were destined for fame, or infamy. During the making of the movie, my path would cross with some I would get to know. Some would go on to fulfill their destinies as I looked for mine, with varying levels of recognition, success, and failure.

Author/producer Alan Lerner constantly scratched both arms, elbow to wrist, but continued to say, every time I saw him, just as he had the day he hired us, "This will be a big break for you boys." But after a month on the set, it seemed he might have meant a big vacation. One memorable day he was working out a new song with the music supervisor Joe Lilly, who wrote the theme music to *I Love Lucy*. It was exciting to see them so enthusiastic about this song. They stayed in that wardrobe tent for several hours hammering away on a piano, and ended up with a usable song called "No Name City" for the film. It was a good lesson that even the pros with track records had to work at the last minute and deliver under pressure.

One character was Larry Schiller, a guy with a camera trying to convince us, a month into filming, that Kae, Rae, and the band would make a good story for *Look* magazine. *Sure,* I thought, *fat chance—slim chance, same thing.* Blah blah, hype hype. *You, like me, just want to impress the girls.* Overweight Larry would order three large Cokes at a time and seemed hell-bent on proving that the drink really could make a person hyper. At that time, he seemed to be the epitome of a particular Hollywood hype: a loud talker, a bragger, someone who could never deliver on big promises. He was the last person I thought could reach the editor of *Life* magazine, Henry Luce himself. In the days before Google, before everybody talked to everybody, I simply couldn't believe this guy talked with the most important man in magazines. Then I found out Larry actually had shot more than a dozen covers each for *Time, Life,* and *Look*. He did incredible work for Luce, and talked with him regularly.

One day he said, "I talked with *Look*, and they approved the story." Its publication was to be sometime the next year. We had to finish the film first.

Filming went *very* slowly. Three months would turn into four. Sometimes they'd only get ten seconds or so of usable film shot in a day.

Waiting in Tent City all day for a shot to be called could have been fairly boring, but I managed to amuse myself by going back in time on this perfect period set. Set designer John Truscott won an Oscar for his work on *Camelot*, and he'd been given free rein to do whatever he wanted for this film. Even the never-to-be-seen-on-camera store interiors were period perfect, with antique books, lamps, everything—things I learned later were taken home by those in the know. The town had faux tent restaurants and hotels, and muddy streets with horses hitched in front of the faux tent saloons.

I loved everything about it. After all, it had only been a couple years since the best time in my life, in period clothes in Disneyland, and I felt comfortable in the grubby look and feel of the mid-1800s. People would sit around the tent hotel playing cards in costume, wearing guns, playing old music; at times, it felt as if it was actually 1849, especially the day the Baker sheriff arrived.

The arrival of police cars was pretty hard to ignore on this 1800s set. They showed up around high noon one day, and got everyone's attention. A few minutes after the cops showed up, the first assistant director blares out on the PA, "Jim Johnson, report immediately to the production office." Thirty seconds later, following a loud rustling sound in the tent hotel, a guy looking like Billy the Kid tore out of it, jumped on a horse, and took off up the muddy street toward the mountains, slightly ahead of his trail of hot checks. Two hundred extras, looking like period hippies, cheered him on. The car posse mounted their steeds but made it only about twenty yards in that mud. They gave up their wheel-spinning chase, again to cheers from the crowd. They never got their man.

One character actor looked like a preacher from out east. This up-and-coming young actor was well liked among cast and crew, and carried himself like a professional. Heber Jentzsch was thought of as a good actor who could handle a few lines, and he was fun to be around. He even sang well. He seemed dedicated to all parts of his craft and appeared to have a goal of earning recognition for his acting. He achieved the recognition part, at least, but not on screen.

Heber spoke often on the set about a new way of looking at life, a philosophy he was getting into, and he tried to interest everyone else in it. It was some wacky idea about how we all came from another planet and, well, it was the 1960s, and people were searching for meaning. There were few takers at the time. I never got the idea of it all, but I wished him well. I think his acting career ended right after *Wagon.* Years later, in 1982, Heber Jentzsch became president of the Church of Scientology International. Maybe his acting career started again then, but he disappeared by the mid-1990s.

When you watched Vegas-slick, nice guy Tony Colti sing, you felt as if you were watching a newly inducted Rat Pack member. He acted like he had a spotlight on him all the time. No one had to ask him to sing, that I remember. But, eventually he would go up to his room, to that special part of his suitcase, and get the treasured gold microphone he carried on the road for such occasions. He'd turn up at the Baker Hilton (the sarcastic nickname for the old Baker Hotel) lounge and when someone would play the piano Tony would get up with that Bobby Sherman smile and gold mic. Folks said he could sing "just like Tony Bennett or Johnny Mathis." But then, we already had Mathis and Bennett. I never heard of this Tony after *Wagon.*

Flying in an old Korean War–vintage, *loud,* twin-rotor, Sikorsky chopper to the set in the forest hadn't been in any of my fortune cookies. Nor was dressing daily at seven-thirty in the morning as gold-rush miners in 1849, but it was a rush. And I was lucky, as the chopper beat the ninety-minute bus ride—you could sleep until 5:50 instead of 5:00.

On our forty-fifth day on set, we finally met Lee Marvin, one of the truly big movie stars of the time. Marvin was the Tommy Lee Jones or Sylvester Stallone of his day. It was a big rush for us, but his Marine reputation had us on edge. Marvin was known for his supermacho roles; he was generally thought of as a tough guy who you definitely wanted on your side. As we set up to film the night scene for "Hand Me Down that Can of Beans" scene, in which the NGDB played the miners band on a wagon, we saw Mr. Marvin coming on set. I use "set" loosely because by now we were all focusing our lives up in this mountain wilderness where Tent City had sprung up and where every-thing looked like a California miner's camp from the previous century.

It was our first big scene in two months. Location sound readied playback for rehearsal using the music we'd recorded months earlier in Hollywood. The lights burned hot; the camera was ready. Just before the director said, "Action," in walked Mr. Marvin. He drunkenly stumbled up to our wagon stage and stood facing us with a defiant stance. With legs spread, hands on his hips, and feet in the mud, he silently eyed us intensely, one by one.

His first words to the group, in a not-so-mock drunken daze, were, "Do you . . . boys know . . . when . . . they raised . . . *the flag* . . . over Iwo Jima?"

Certain that the wrong answer to his Marine history question would send us packing, the band's panicked eyes all met, and we started to mumble some probable dates to each other. Tired with our grasping, he finally gruffed, "Hell, I mean the song! Give me a G chord." And he sang an old World War II song called, "When They Raised the Flag Over Iwo Jima." And we exhaled. We kept our jobs.

To break up the monotony a little, sometime around the third month of shooting I organized a benefit concert to raise money for Baker High School. Getting cast members involved was fun, especially classical singer Harve Presnell, who sang "They Called the Wind Mariah" in the film. Several extras had the PH Phactor Jug Band, and the Dirt Band was a lot of fun. And Heber was part of it, too, as a guitar-picking folkie.

Two months later, on location in the middle of Tent City, we finished our three minutes of film and headed home. The shoot date for the *Look* article was set for late October, and we ended up in the magazine the next year.

I visited Larry's house to get some shots of the band and the girls. Schiller was the first person allowed into Sharon Tate's house to shoot the grisly Manson massacre photos. I saw these exclusive photos, three-by-four-foot blowups of all the Manson victims, hanging around every room of his house. He lost his family over those wall displays, but we ended up in *Look* magazine with Ted Kennedy on the cover. Later, Lawrence Schiller wrote and produced a television film based on Norman Mailer's book *The Executioner's Song,* which was written about murderer Gary Gilmore. Then he was in the front row of O. J. Simpson's first trial and wrote *I Want to Tell You* with O.J. He also later produced a film about the Jon Benet Ramsey story.

4

It's Over—Breakup—
to the Next Level

Things were changing for a lot of us. The Hour Glass just did not
work. Two albums later, after being frustrated by the realities of
the record business in L.A., all but Gregg left California to return to
the southern comfort of their Florida home turf. A few months later
I went to Gregg's Hollywood apartment, at the Mikado on Cahuenga
Boulevard, to record a song he had just written, "It's Not My Cross to
Bear," on my portable two-track machine. Merel Bregante and Larry
Sims played drums and bass. A month later, Gregg convinced me to
get the pink slip for the car Bill had bought him to get around L.A.,
to "settle a traffic ticket." He then sold the car that day and bought a
one-way plane ticket to Jacksonville, Florida. Brother Duane had been
calling, telling him about a new band. I had helped the Allman Brothers Band get started that night. One of their first songs was "Not My
Cross to Bear."

Three months after the *Paint Your Wagon* shoot, Jeff didn't want
to play with a couple of the other guys in the band, and it was easier to
quit than fire people. After four albums, a pop hit, a couple of movies,
and lots of TV shows, we were done. It was the winter of 1968.

We had our last band meeting in Bill's office, at the 8833 Sunset
Boulevard building. We all talked about how it had "been a good run"

and what we were going to do next. Les asked the last question, which got some stares: "Does this mean we're not going to practice anymore?" At least we ended with a laugh. Not wanting to be in a band without Jeff, I started looking for work.

Jeff and Chris played a few months with Linda Ronstadt; Jimmie got a job in a clothing store next to the Troubadour (his only other job); and level-headed Les worked for his dad and later became a very successful goldsmith. Ralph got more into acid. I started digging deeper in my music, and collected unemployment for five weeks. I didn't like doing that.

During this NGDB I-hate-us, I practiced with pre-Eagles Bernie Leadon with the hopes of us doing a bluegrass album. Rehearsing in that off time with Bernie was great, but the bluegrass we played did not seem radio friendly. He went on to play on *The Fantastic Expedition of Dillard & Clark*. I thought it ironic that my banjo mentor Doug Dillard got Bernie. Then Bernie recommended me for a job and I found myself auditioning in crooner Andy Williams's pristine Hollywood office on La Cienga. I felt like a banjo joke waiting to happen when Andy put Stevie Wonder's "For Once in My Life" on his record player, and asked me to play along on banjo. The job prospects seemed dubious, and just when I started to think about packing it in, Andy interrupted in the middle of the song. "Perfect!" he said. "Be in Vegas next Wednesday for rehearsals for a month's run at Caesars Palace. Oh, the drummer is the great Jim Gordon. I think you know him." Gordon had played on some of the early NGDB recordings, along with some other Wrecking Crew players. With my confidence flagging after the breakup of my first real band, this was a sign that maybe I didn't suck because I had something that was very difficult for musicians to find: a job. (And not just any job, but one with $1,500 a week and free food, and a room at Caesars!) I had played Caesars in 1967, during a monthlong run with NGDB opening for Little Richard, but this was better. I had a room in the hotel this time! And I was making four times as much as with NGDB in 1967. I had made it! I was making as much as Steve Martin, who was writing for the *Smothers Brothers Comedy Hour* at the time. I felt successful.

Rehearsals went fine. I mostly couldn't read the music charts, but Gordon helped me through them. Also twenty-two years old, Gordon was making a lot of money as one of Hollywood's top Wrecking Crew session drummers, but he was bored with constant studio work. I sat right in front of his kick drum onstage and our friendship grew offstage as well. When we cruised the Vegas Strip in his new Mercedes during the day, I felt like part of a junior Rat Pack myself. Every third song that came on his car radio, he'd say, "That's me," and it was true. Once, while rocketing down a desert road with his radio at combat level, we hit 143 mph. Jim yelled, "Not enough power! Shouldn't shake like that! I'm takin' it back!" Not much later, he would play drums and piano on "Layla."

Two weeks into the monthlong run, Caesars loaned Andy the Palace's yacht. Andy had to bail on the cruise at the last minute, leaving his lady friend on her own with me and Gordon. Maybe she was just being polite, but when Claudine Longet coyly said, "You do the suntan lotion on me, then I'll do you," it made me hotter than the Nevada sun. The calm waters of Lake Mead didn't assuage my fear that this situation could lead to my doom. Hey, she was the boss's girl! And he knew other kinds of bosses in Vegas, if you know what I mean. A mental image flashed through my mind as I touched her hot back: a barren desert, dead me in concrete shoes, standing on a shallow fresh grave, with a little banjo-shaped marker inscribed "HE PLAYED TOO FAST." Basking in her coquettish Frenchness all afternoon, I decided to steer clear of getting rubbed on, then rubbed out after I finally got her lotion rubbed in. But, I did take my time to decline her offer to "do me." I retreated to my room to practice instead, as I still felt a little musically over my head in this more-than-three-chords gig.

I also got to observe the Osmond family that month, since they were opening Andy's show. They were very dedicated, although I am not quite sure to what. Was it a career in music, or using music to promote their religion? The kids were nice and hard working. But they were very sheltered from the real world. Except for Marie and Donny, their knowledge of music came only from rote learning. The other brothers were good performers and worked hard at it, but Donny and Marie had deeper talent, which became evident over the years.

Right after the Vegas gig ended, I was hanging out at the Golden Bear watching Poco (who were then still called Pogo after the cartoon character, until creator Walt Kelly sued them, which forced the name change). The crowd was going nuts over Jim Messina's hot guitar, with Richie Furay and Randy Meisner singing. Everyone particularly loved watching and hearing George Grantham singing from the drums. By chance, Jeff was there, too.

Having played with Jeff for four years and on four albums, I had come to value his growing knowledge of a wide range of music, his improving voice and harmonies, his lyrics, and most of his song choices. At the same time, there were differences between Jeff and me—in performing style and creative ambition—that had started to come to the surface even before he dissolved the group. I didn't pay attention to those differences at the time, but they would become more pronounced and problematic as time went on.

We looked at each other at that Poco show and said, "Let's get the Dirt Band back together and find a singing drummer." Our lives were about to change. At that moment, I felt like a new "founding member," and this time I called Les. Les wanted to quit working for his dad; Fadden wanted to quit the clothing store; I wanted to get on the radio again and play behind Jeff's voice and Fadden's harp.

We had heard about a guy named Jimmy Ibbotson who had been gigging around L.A. after coming to town from Philly. I went knocking on his Laurel Canyon door with Jeff; he opened it just a crack. We announced, "We're the Nitty Gritty Dirt Band, and we wanted to see if you would like to join us." A disheveled Ibbotson looked us over and said, "I can't deal with this right now. Give me a minute," and shut the door.

We stood around a few minutes, then he reopened it, invited us in, and told us he was a big fan of "Rain." He had heard of us before he had left Philly the previous year, drove his Dodge Dart to L.A. to get in a band, and get on the radio. He was intimidated and shocked that a band he was aware of wanted him. They sang a couple of Buddy Holly songs and it was an instant, obvious, exciting match. Soon, we began rehearsing with our new singing drummer, whose strange quirks and personality would materialize over the years—but then, who wasn't, as the Doors said, a bit strange in those days.

Wiry Fadden often adopted the air of a crusty old sailor. He thought himself a real ladies' man, projecting the air that he had a lot of what all the girls wanted. He had a similarly cocky attitude about his harmonica playing, which had been great since his teenage years, and brought that to the drums that he would take up for this new chapter. He knew the success he wanted wasn't selling clothes. (Before *Wagon,* my brother asked Jeff what he would do if he bought him a set of drums. Jeff said, "I'd throw them off the Santa Monica Pier." But after *Music from Big Pink,* drums were OK . . . and we all wanted to make a successful album.) Fadden was usually friendly to fans, but he could be difficult to work with, acerbic to those close to us, and throughout the years he never seemed to understand all it was that made us—and him—successful. He never missed a show or complained about working and always gave it everything he had.

We rehearsed in Long Beach for five months at Les's dad's juke box repair place for what would become our fifth record, *Uncle Charlie & His Dog Teddy.* One day, Jeff came in and blurted out, "Last night I heard a song on the radio about a dancer guy with a dead dog, by some guy with two first names! One was Jeff!" Ibby, as he liked to be called, excitedly shouted, "I have that in my record collection, in the trunk of my car!" Under his Dart's spare tire was his entire collection: one dirty, rust-water covered 45 of "Mr. Bojangles" by Jerry Jeff Walker. We all waited while Jeff took it to our only record player, which had no speakers, and listened intently in the back room to what was coming off the needle. Jeff took down the words and then taught it to us. We tried out "Bojangles" live at the Troubadour, and it killed. It was an incredibly exciting time in the life of the band.

An exuberant young songwriter was hanging around our dressing room and kept saying, "Hey! I got some songs! You wanna record some of my songs? Can I play some for you? They're really good! I think you'll like them!" He had never been recorded. That week, in my Laurel Canyon living room, I made a seven-song demo of nineteen-year-old Kenny Loggins and his guitar, and we added four of them to the album. I felt like I was contributing to the group dream by bringing in songs and arrangements, and two of my favorite singers and other bandmates were doing the same. Our country rock, Dirt Band–style was forming: I brought in bluegrass and eclectic sounds; Jeff gave us folk music; Fadden contributed his great harp skills and, occasionally, his electric guitar; Ibby shared his rock edge with his half-time drums (he was a natural drummer with the best time of all of us); and Les killed it on bass and mandolin. It was all coming together. I tried to get Jeff to sing one other Loggins demo song that was perfect for him, but he said it sounded too much like a hippie song and wouldn't be a hit. We had had the first shot at it in 1970, but others would later pick up on "Danny's Song."

Timing was in our favor, as just before the release of *Uncle Charlie* we were at the premieres of *Paint Your Wagon* on both the East and West Coasts, and back in the press. That was paving the way for the new NGDB, and the audience was out there, waiting. They didn't know it, but we were coming. The NGDB star was about to come out of its coma.

Our recordings of Kenny's "House at Pooh Corner" (his first song, featuring Fadden's perfect genius guitar lead) and of Monkee Mike Nesmith's "Some of Shelly's Blues" had their lives on the radio with Ibby singing lead, and almost made the top ten. I was excited about that because "Shelly's" started with frailing banjo right on top, and loud. Bill produced and mixed it hot. I had done it—put the banjo on the radio again as an integral part of a hit. I was in the dream. Next came mandolin on "Bojangles." The records of bluegrass mandolin genius Jesse McReynolds inspired the "cross picking" I played on that.

The record company then told us "Bojangles" would be the third single. The band all agreed: putting out a really long song in three-quarter time about a dancer with a dead dog would be the end of our career. Jeff even got some of the words wrong on the record, thinking the phrase "spoke right out" was "smoke ran out." Hey, it was the 1960s, it had to be "smoke," right? "Bojangles" would kick off a whole new phase of our career. Sometimes it pays to listen to others. (Jeff could have learned that lesson better. I could have, too.) I wish Fadden had played on it, too, but that did not work out.

With no idea of what lay ahead, I found myself playing and again road managing the band. I started reserving rental cars, flights, and hotel rooms—and counting money again. We hit the road and headed to the East Coast.

From Orange County/Long Beach to Hollywood, we finally made it to Carnegie Hall. We opened for Mr. Bill Cosby, in the middle of a two-week tour with him. He knew music and asked me to show him how to saw a simple Cajun bowing pattern on the fiddle, on two open strings. Every night Cosby would open for about ten minutes, then bring the band out for our show before his main set. With him onstage to introduce us, he'd say, "Hey boys, welcome to the stage. Here, let me get you started." He'd pick up my fiddle and do the bow sawing to kickoff "Jambalaya" and then he would exit, giving the audience a nice segue into something they likely did not want to see. (I always figure that with most audiences only half of the people wanted to come, and they brought the other half. If you are the opening act, it's safe to assume nobody came to see you, so you need to find a way to keep them interested.)

Barely out of the box as a new band, Carnegie Hall was a very big night for us, but after sound check Cosby came in to the dressing room to add fuel to the fidgets. He said, "I'd like to have an old friend sit in on a song with you."

"Great! Who is it? What's the song?" I asked.

"Just a regular twelve-bar blues type of song, and he'll fit right in. Probably in the key of E. It's Dizzy Gillespie. He'll do fine."

After "Jambalaya," Cosby came back onstage and introduced Dizzy. The crowd went nuts as the horn man walked out. I had not yet felt what it was like to be onstage with a longtime icon other than Bill Monroe, and I never forgot this reaction. Standing dizzy in Dizzy's standing ovation, it felt like we were in an old, faded, black-and-white photo with yellowing edges on some old showbiz agent's wall, from some forgotten show, where a famous horn man sat in with some unknown band ("Yeah, buddy . . . that was a great night . . . shoulda been there . . .") and I was the guy that was out of focus.

I had trouble remembering what an E chord was when those puffy cheeks were blowing his historic notes right beside me. But, "we" went over great. I wanted to thank Cosby after the show, but his dressing room was locked. It was an evening like many that sounds like a fantasy or a fabrication, but that's understandable. Sometimes my whole life feels like that.

———————

After the last show with Cosby, it was almost time to leave the Big Apple. We had to do some promotion for the record first. We desperately wanted "Bojangles" to hit the Top Ten. By its sixteenth week, it had moved on the chart from number eighteen to number fifteen, then to number seventeen, but then back up, and looked like it would stop at number thirteen. The record company told us that since it was not being played on New York's WABC, it would not get higher nor be in the Top Ten. If WABC didn't play a record, there was no Top Ten, because no WABC meant no BCN in Boston, no WLS in Chicago, and no play in Hartford or Philly. They were all critically important stations that followed the lead of WABC. You've never heard anyone say, "We have a Top Thirteen record!" They suggested we play a Manhattan Catholic girl's school, and people in the know told us that could help with getting on WABC and to our Top Ten quest. We listened. We had no idea if this was going to help us make it big. Well, it wasn't very complicated. Rick Sklar was WABC's music director and programmer. His daughter was a student at this school. *Aha.*

I couldn't really believe that other musicians had to do this, but we said yes, and headed to play a Friday show at noon in the lunchroom at this private, junior high, Catholic girl's school. Still wondering if a school gig like this had really helped anyone, a sister came into our classroom/dressing room to see if we needed anything. Trying to hide my skepticism, I said, "Good morning, sister. I was wondering—who else has performed for your girls?"

"Well, hmmm," she pondered a bit, and answered with angelic naïveté. "This year we have been blessed with the Jackson 5—boy, they can dance!—then Aretha Franklin, and John Lennon, that very nice British boy. All very talented. Are we not fortunate all these nice people want to entertain our girls?" She paused. "Oh, and last year Mr. Paul Simon, he was a nice man too, and—" Thankfully, someone interrupted at this point and I could beg off, saying, "Oh . . . thank you. We have to get ready for an important show now."

The next Monday it was time to drive the equipment to Denver with roadie Gary. We headed out of town as WABC announced, "Here's a new song by the Nitty Gritty Dirt Band, 'Mr. Bojangles.'" It kept heading up the chart, for a total of thirty-six weeks, and made it to number nine on the *Billboard* Pop charts. Lesson learned.

Our time in the Apple over, it was time to head west.

I have driven through hundreds of small midwestern towns, often feeling sure the people walking around were actors who were set up to portray small town life for me. This was probably a holdover from my years on Disneyland's Main Street, where everything and everyone was staged. Even in Manhattan, it seemed everybody had an assigned role: the guy playing drumsticks on the sidewalk at midnight; the three-card monte game on a cardboard box, with the card dealer harvesting the green from out-of-town greenhorns as his shill canvasses the crowd for cops; the tourists doing the post–World War II kiss in Times Square; the guys who run the store in Times Square that was "Going Out of Business!" for the past twenty years; and the Stage Deli waitress who barely has time to take an order, doesn't write it down, looks preoccupied, then brings your food before you know it.

But now we had to get to Denver, and I was just as excited to play the part of a truck driver on the road. Roadie Gary, a heavy smoker who looked like a low-rent version of Joe Namath, and I took off in our twenty-foot Ryder rental, heading west on the bumpy Pennsylvania Turnpike to our 1970 debut in the Mile High City. As we bade adieu to New Jersey's refineries and their smell, I reveled in the knowledge that I was living my dream from when I was an Orange County teenager. The road fog had not yet set in, and I loved it, all of it.

Vietnam was getting hotter and occupying more and more radio airwaves every day, and after dodging all those bullets, I was listening more for the new band—our band—on the radio as we drove across the country. Carnegie Hall in the rearview mirror; our destination was a Denver club called Marvelous Marv's. With tiger-skin wallpaper and the look of a Vegas lounge bar, it seemed an unlikely venue for us hippies, but all were excited to be opening in another new city.

Outside Indianapolis, chatting away to the hippie hitchhiker we had picked up earlier, a strange knocking noise started coming from under the hood. I checked the engine temperature gauge, figuring that was something a real truck driver would do, like banging the tires with a heavy stick—"bumping," they call it. I'd bump mine at truck stops without knowing why, but the other drivers did it, and it made me feel more accepted in the drivers-only section, in spite of my long hair.

The gauge needle was nowhere to be seen. I knew that was wrong and pulled over at a rest area to check it out. The engine kept making the knocking noise even after I shut it off. As the hood went up, steam billowed out like Old Faithful. The '60s hippie hitchhiker yelled, "Cooolll!" I rushed to let Gary out of the back of the truck's box. It was about 116 degrees back there with the band gear. (He needed to lose some weight anyway, and had already dropped a couple pounds since Jersey.) He'd been banging on the door for the past hour.

When the steam cleared, I saw that something big had unattached from the engine, and now was hanging with the remains of some belts that were wrapped around, and through, metal stuff.

It has been said a real roadie could make a carburetor—or just about anything else—from a roll of duct tape, guitar strings, and a Dr. Pepper can. I set out to prove how a clever young man could solve a problem like this one. After twisting several wire coat hangers around what later was identified as the alternator, I put it back on its broken mount, and held it in place by this wire web that was anchored on various engine parts with ample duct tape. Although I was cockily confident that the repair would hold and get us back on the road, I felt compelled to get approval from an actual semi driver. The rest area offered one: a definitely Deep South, crew-cut trucker mounting his 18-wheeler, after having just completed the mysterious bumping tires ritual.

I approached him with, "Sir, while traveling to Denver we have had a truck problem. We hope to obtain your professional opinion as to if this problem has been addressed properly before continuing our journey."

Now, this was the *Easy Rider* era—summers of love, and all that. It was only a couple of years since others of my ilk had graced Woodstock. Wordlessly, the lanky, white T-shirted trucker, who was emitting strange growling sounds, suspiciously eyeballed this hippie's shoulder-length hair. Heeding the noble call to help a traveler in distress, he gradually dismounted his rig, and ambled silently over to inspect our not-so-easy-Ryder rig.

He looked at the engine. He looked at me. He looked back under the hood. He looked at me—or just my hair—again. He looked at the ground, his head slowly going from side to side, a small frown of disgust forming. He looked up at the sky and probably thought of that day's Vietnam body count.

Still not saying a word, he peeled his tight T-shirt sleeve down his tattooed arm, took out and lit a Marlboro, took a long wishing-he-was-home drag, and rolled the box back into his sleeve. After another long skyward stare, drag, exhale, and sigh, he looked at the repair one final time. Then, he looked not exactly *at* me, nor in my eyes, but around me, to the sides, without actually looking at my bearded hippie face, and he kicked a rock and offered his well-considered opinion.

"Sheee-yit." He walked away without another word, probably asking himself, *What is this country coming to?*

"That means it doesn't look good?" I counteroffered, as he silently sauntered off to work his American dream, leaving me with mine. Maybe it was a compliment?

Figuring that it wouldn't hurt to try, I started up the truck. The ensuing noise is hard to describe. If you go to that kitchen drawer where you keep silverware and turn it upside down in the sink, or to the cupboard with the pans and throw in an exploding glass bowling ball, you'll get a fairly accurate idea of what it sounded like—only it was louder as it all ripped apart. *Now what?*

A Ryder outlet five miles away answered my distress call. We transferred the load to a new truck and were back on I-70 in less than two hours, with eight hundred free miles for the inconvenience! Laughing about good fortune sprung from bad, we hit the road. Then the passenger's side-view mirror started rattling, shook, clanked off, and disappeared. Gary and the hitchhiker looked at me as I looked at where the mirror had been, as if it were still there.

"Well, at least we have one good one left," I said, and reached out to adjust the now even more important driver's side-view mirror. One little push and it joined the other one, leaving us blind behind in the east, but we were headed west. As mileage to Kansas City and St. Louis started showing up on road signs, we drove into the setting sun. As night came on, I'd see the new St. Louis Arch!

Four hours after the Arch, after arriving in K.C. with no money to proceed, I called Big Brother Bill, to ask what to do. "It's nighttime. Go to bed. Call me tomorrow," were his only words of comfort and advice. We had heard "Bojangles" three times by then. With no cash left, I had to cash one of two emergency checks for seventy-five dollars with the now-parting, northbound hitchhiker. That covered Denny's, gas, goodies, a room with a shower, a snooze, and all was well. The hitchhiker kept that check about nine months before it cleared.

During the next day's collect call to Bill, I asked him to wire one hundred dollars ahead to Topeka, where we'd stop on our way to Denver. Two hours and ninety miles later, there was no cash waiting at the Topeka Western Union. I begged the agent, "Please, we need to get to Denver for a gig. When the cash arrives, send it on to Hays, Kansas. We'll pick it up there."

In Hays, two hundred miles and three hours later, there was still no money. I asked, "Please, we need to get to Denver for a gig. When the cash arrives, send it on to Goodland, Kansas. We'll pick it up there."

Although the next town—another 140 miles down the highway—was smaller, Western Union was harder to find. The good lady running Goodland City Hall told us, "Go down the street past where the Kroger used to be, go left where the new co-op is going to be built. It's behind where the old post office was, right past the red light. Can't remember the street name." Goodland had six streets, and a lot to keep track of what with the new telephone pole that was going in soon, and the street paving a block over last month and all.

With just enough cash for one gallon of gas and two cups of coffee, we waited across the street, nursing our drinks, awaiting financial deliverance. What we learned in Goodland was that it took four hours for a transfer; I'd only given it two. About an hour later when all seventy-eight dollars of the cash arrived, we learned about the deducted transfer fees. But all was great! We got more food, filled the truck, bought goodies, and had eighteen dollars left over for Denver. At the Colorado border's truck weigh station, we learned about state road tax. The guy took sixteen dollars and told us we could drive anywhere we wanted in the state for a week.

With "Bojangles" in the top twenty (we heard it two more times while we chased our Western Union money across Kansas) and two dollars in my pocket, we headed to meet up with the rest of what had suddenly become a hot, chart-topping band. As I drove into the clear air of Denver for the first time, the dazzling Rockies filled our view, and "Bojangles" came on again and filled the truck cab. I felt on top of the world. It was one of the best feelings to know we had made this trip in record time and had a hit record.

The band greeted me by whining that they had a hard time finding the hotel, rather than thanking me for my efforts. I had them fly in the day before. But my mandolin was on the radio, Jeff's voice was perfect for that song, and life was good. I remember thinking they had missed out on a hell of a cross-country adventure. I never did beat covering that much distance in forty-four hours as we did on that first trip from Jersey to Colorado.

This was the kind of situation in which I thrived. I could feel like I had some control and was really accomplishing things: getting all of us around, saving money doing it, never missing a show, taking care of business. The others never mentioned any of those efforts, nor offered thanks or appreciation, except for Ibby occasionally, when he was in a good mood. We had already seen how Ibby could have two moods. It would be a few years before the third one showed up.

None of us could have predicted how much Colorado was going to mean in our lives. The audience was great and we knew we would return—someday. That day, it was back to L.A.

Right after those successes, in late 1971, Jimmy Messina invited me and Jeff up to his house to hear a new demo he recorded with Kenny. While driving away, Jeff told me, "Anyone can write a song like that— 'Your momma don't dance, your daddy don't rock 'n' roll.' Tell him thanks, but I don't want to do it."

Messina told me, "Well, Loggins and I will put it out ourselves and see what happens." It might have been around then that Jeff earned the nickname "Dr. No," but you can't make a singer sing a song he doesn't want to do. At least, I couldn't. I guess Jeff didn't think it was a hit. I think if Ibby had heard it we would have done it, but Jeff was already trying to keep a tight rein on him. In retrospect, I think I am glad we didn't do it, but there was never any doubt to me that it was a hit. Sometimes I wish I had been the one choosing the songs for them to sing. I might have chosen what Jeff and Ibby picked anyway, and added others that could have made a career difference. But, that is the frustration of having "a band," and hindsight sometimes clouds the present. I was glad to get NGDB to play some bluegrass instrumentals and I loved playing on most of the songs he and Ibby chose. Six months later, Jim and Kenny were chartering Lear Jets and we were still in rental cars—with me driving. You can't accomplish as much with "no" as you can with "yes." But a few charter flights were to show up for us.

I worked hard at music, with a simple goal: to be as good as possible every night. I was thrilled to sense a crowd digging the show and always hoped for good reviews. Some bandmates, however, often seemed to have other opinions about a good review. Months after Denver, in a Shreveport Holiday Inn the morning after a show in 1972, I was having my breakfast alone after checking us out, just before driving us to Monroe, Louisiana, when Jeff strutted in. The local paper had reviewed our show the night before, and Jeff threw the town's newspaper at my eggs with the pleasant greeting of "Here's another one of your fucking reviews!" and stomped out. The reviewer loved NGDB and liked what I did, and wrote about it, mentioning only me by name. I hoped for good comments; I worked for it. I wish Jeff had understood it was a win for all of us. This happened often, and as far as I knew, bothered only Jeff. I got in the quiet car and drove us to Monroe for that night's show. My mom loved the review.

5

From Cowtown to Circles

The second time we played Denver, we skeptically gave in to a guy begging us to play some ski town at a place called the Aspen Inn Club. A ski town? What's that? (Already an avid skier, Les loved the idea.) The Dirt Band was the first national act up there in 1971 for a ten-day run, and it changed our lives. People lined up outside for every show, two times a night. Steve Martin opened for us, and lots of strange people showed up to see the band with radio records. The Colorado crowds were great, and gave us a sense of what a great place this would be to live, as we all were burned out on L.A. Everyone but Les took skiing lessons and went after the mountains like a dog on a bone. It was a new life! For some reason, Les had often been made fun of by the band guys, but never did that unto others. In Aspen we found out what a great skier he was, and no one made fun anymore.

I had just married Kae the previous October, and our first kid, our daughter Noel, showed up pretty early—a couple of months "early," actually. We made an impulsive decision to move to Colorado, spurred by the craziness of not being able to reach each other for two days after the 1971 Sylmar earthquake in the San Fernando Valley by where we had been living in Laurel Canyon. We moved the next week.

I drove the packed Ryder twenty straight hours to our new life in Denver and met Kae after she flew in with the new baby. Jeff drove with me and his stuff, too (he was now married to Kae's twin sister,

Rae), and took his turn driving for twenty minutes north of Phoenix. That was it for him. Driving wasn't his strong suit.

On arrival, I gave Kae the $500 I had left, saying, "Here's the truck keys. Find a house, move in, turn in the truck, buy a car. I'll be back in nine days, after New York City." It wasn't fair to her, but I had to work. We had another *Tonight Show* to do. This time the lead vocal mic was on when we did "Bojangles." Miraculously, at twenty years old, she did everything I asked, and told me about it in great detail when I got back.

That winter of 1971, with our second baby's arrival imminent—our first son, Aaron—the very pregnant Kae stayed in Denver while I ran up to Aspen to work. I told myself then that we never missed shows, and I worried that I needed to keep getting paid, but I now can admit that I was more afraid of the birth. It was also the week that Bernie Leadon was rehearsing with his new band, the Eagles, at another Aspen club. People said they were going to do well. I was happy for him.

I have some life regrets, but this one is huge: I missed Aaron's birth. I got notice of my second child's birth just before a show. "It's a boy." I called Kae to "congratulate us." Don Henley had sent a telegram that got there before my call. I sent one after that.

We'd play Aspen for a week to twelve days a few times a year, and would get rooms for a few extra days. I arranged free skiing for all. We had a few great years of everyone skiing and becoming mountain people, but then the town began to change. We should have seen it coming when they started putting in traffic lights. Movie stars came by, along with television producers, and money people. A lot of musicians—some already known and some to become famous later, like John Denver and Jimmy Buffett—sat in with us, as did other players who hung around town. The greatest skier I ever knew, and also the first Vietnam vet I got to know, Duane Arnold, would show up at many of the shows. Duane was pretty much always drunk and having fun. He liked to ski naked and take blind jumps at night. I learned from him that more happened in Vietnam—life there was even crazier—than we could imagine or understand. His wife divorced him because he kept waking up around three in the morning and shooting his .45 at the bedroom window. He had his reasons.

––––––––––––

With the Denver area now the new home base, we would regularly fly out of Stapleton to head anywhere the agents would send us. Bill moved to Aspen to build a studio and start Aspen Recording Society and develop his empire. Kansas City developed a reputation as the hip place to play after the Cowtown Ballroom opened up and quickly got famous. We headed there for its first show and became regulars.

We packed the Cowtown every time and would be led to the stage from the upstairs dressing room by Old Smokey yelling, "Make way! Comin' thru! Make way!" This "old man," a retired Kansas City fire chief, commanded respect with his authoritative fire chief hat, flashlight, and gentle ways. (Back then, Smokey was the oldest person any of us had seen out at night.) He snaked his way through the packed house, waving his huge flashlight, with us trailing behind. "The band's hot, and ready to play! Step aside!" Smokey was something we rarely find now: authority you can believe in.

The Cowtown Ballroom, previously a roller-skating rink, was supposed to hold about seventeen hundred concertgoers. But packed onto the skating floor and in the upstairs balcony, the crowds through which Smokey ushered us to the stage were more like twenty-four hundred, crammed in like sardines. Beer, heat, smoke from various weeds, sweat, loud music, applause, and laughter all mingled together in the hot air of the ballroom—aahh, the good old daze. It was a crazy crowd of great people. If that had been the peak of our performing experience, it would have been enough to have called it a great career. The Cowtown audience became the stuff of legend among musicians. Anytime we crossed paths with friends who had played there, they spoke of it with reverence, as a date you'd circle on your touring calendar. We proudly played there more than any other band, and did the last show before the club's demise. We recorded an integral part of one of our best live albums, *Stars and Stripes Forever*, with that great audience there.

On that last September night in 1974, I walked out with the promoter Stan Plesser after we surveyed the place one last time. The sweat of a couple thousand people lingered in the air, and the floor was littered with their trash. The scene was changing. It was sad to see this place go. I pointed at a sign, a relic of the old roller rink days, and asked, "Think anyone will miss that?" Before Stan even finished nodding his approval, I had that little green sign off the wall and under my arm, proudly taking home something I value as much as a Grammy.

ALL PERSONS GOING UPSTAIRS

MUST HAVE

A SKATING FEE TICKET

except parents with children

All the "kids" were there without parents at the shows. It was a celebration and NGDB was the reason!

Kansas City was to become our conduit to the Midwest, and a place to hang out for a day off. Great food, nice people, a convenient downtown airport—we passed through often and Missouri became like another home state. I felt accepted there as our music was spreading and people liked what I did. Now wearing leather clothes and long hair, I was usually thought to be from the bayou or Kentucky backwoods. I'd left the Orange County nerd far behind. At a time when pedophiles were played by preachers, politicians played by crooks, drunks played by pilots, I played my way in to showbiz disguised as a mountain man.

It was great to be big in the fly-over states, but success there didn't matter much to the influential trendspotters on either coast. A classy, high-profile gig can solve that, besides leading to other great things. One winter month in '71, NGDB opened for Rowan and Martin at the Las Vegas Riviera Hotel, which held promise for a solo idea. We headed to showbiz mecca, where that gig became part of my own personal showbiz quest. We would somehow pack a forty-five-minute set in the twenty-six minutes allowed.

Sha Na Na didn't exist yet when we did our "'50s routine" ("Goodnight, My Love"). Jeff hadn't chickened out from it yet, and it always killed. He was at his best as a stand-up comic for about seven minutes. The NGDB played the part of a '50s band with Jeff setting it up with his great monologue (captured on the *Stars and Stripes* album). It was flashy and "showbizzy" and always got an encore. The bit required me to do a few minutes solo (while other guys changed costumes) and I could briefly recapture part of my original pre–Dirt Band dream: to do something good solo in front of a large audience. When performing alone, it felt like there was more at stake. Whether it bombed or it worked, it was entirely my responsibility. It worked.

I'd throw a few one-liners into my unusual banjo medley, followed by a deadpan, "That really cracks me up," which would get a bigger laugh each time I said it, just like it did at the Magic Shop. As with a good repeat gag, by the fourth time, all I had to say was, "That . . . really . . . ," do a quiet chuckle and mouth the other words, and the whole audience would be laughing. It worked great, and it was mine. I convinced dapper Dan Rowan to watch one night, with a definite purpose in mind: if he saw it go over like it usually did, he might be convinced to again have me on their wacky, wildly popular, hit TV show of the era, *Laugh-In*, as a one-liner guest. (NGDB had been on the second *Laugh-In* back in 1967.) It went great, the room laughed loud, and he was convinced that, yes, if given a chance, "that really cracks me up" could be another big national catch phrase, like Arte Johnson's "very interrrressstingg." Dan said he'd arrange it.

I flew out to L.A. weeks later to wait my turn at NBC's Burbank Studios, thinking this was my chance to go straight "to the top of the toppermost," as John Lennon used to say. They were getting it together for another season, which was perfect timing for a new bit. In the dressing room at 9:30 AM for the 4:00 PM call, I waited for fifteen seconds of fame; I was ready. In my Dirt Band leather and practicing my script, I thought this could be my big break. The studio was across the hall from the *Tonight Show Starring Johnny Carson,* and I thought that soon I could be there, too. I was home. My destiny was being fulfilled. Somebody liked me!

While pacing the dressing room and practicing the line for a couple more hours, I had second thoughts: If it became super popular, would I be known only as the guy on *Laugh-In* who did that "cracks me up" line? Then, maybe no one would take my music seriously. What if this national fame meant the end of a music career! I kept pacing. I also knew I'd never be able to support a family on the band money alone, so I told myself: *It will work! And, there might be a chance for more than just fifteen seconds! Maybe it would lead to fifteen minutes of fame! I could be a part of this hit show, then I might be able to spin it off into a series, and a book, and then the album.*

The knock came on the dressing room door, and an unknown voice finally summoned me back to reality, "Mr. McEuen, stage call. You're on."

The director had me stand on a mark as three NBC camera jockeys corralled me in an arc with their rigs. Rowan, Martin, the director, the producer, the executive producer, and ten others—my non-smiling audience—stood waiting. The tension mounted, and Rowan said, "Do the line."

Facing the fourth wall, I intoned, "That really cracks me up," and waited in the silence.

I said it once again, then a third time, with different inflections; then one more time, emphasizing "That." Finally, going for the slow burn, I tried it once very slowly, "That . . . *really* . . . cracks . . . me . . . uupp." The only thing missing was laughs.

The director turned to Rowan and said flatly and loudly, "You flew him out here for this?" and walked away. My fifteen minutes were up, and had lasted about three.

I asked the fleeing director, "I guess that means I'm done?" The director slowly turned, glancing back briefly at Dan. Rowan's smiling, closed mouth and nod of "yes," with his sad puppy eyes pointed at me, answered my question, and the director went back to his silent, slow, determined retreat, like a disgusted cat leaving a dish of unsavory food. His nonanswer answered the question, and Rowan concurred: "Yes, you can go home now."

I said, to no one in particular, "That really cracks me up," and, of course, *everybody* cracked up. But it was too late. I still think it could have worked.

———————

Steve Martin, now managed by my brother, would open for us in those early '70s daze. It was tremendous fun to watch him transition from a struggling comic with Magic Shop jokes to a guy with his own material who would leave everyone breathless with laughter. Often, he'd sit in with us, dressed in a Hawaiian shirt, and do the mambo while singing "Girl with Emphysema" to the tune of "Girl from Ipanema": "Tall and tan and warm and lovely the girl with emphysema goes coughing, and everyone she coughs on goes . . . uuuuuuugggghhhhhhh." I knew he was on a new path when he said things like "I dream of a land . . . where all men are free! . . . And some women."

The wrong kind of snow started coming down year-round by the mid-1970s and made it difficult for me to hang out with the guys. I was never into coke nor any drugs, nor the play that evolved around it. Aspen was more fun for me in the pre-coke years. When that insidious drug of the rich came in, it was like the traffic lights—it brought a lot of things to a stop. Let me be Frank.

Frank, with a capital "F," was the code word for this dry snow. Whenever one of the dealers was coming to deal, the word would spread with a typical conversation:

"Did you hear about Frank?"

"No. What did you hear?"

"He'll be coming by tonight."

"What time is he supposed to get here?"

"I'll be meeting him in my room after the show. You want to see him?"

"I owe him some money. Can you give it to him for me?"

"Sure. Yeah, he said you owe him about seventy-five dollars, and I'd be glad to give it to him."

"I'll come by your room after he leaves and see what he had to say."

This would inspire me to play songs in the dressing room like this one (to the tune of "Arkansas Traveler"):

> Hey, stranger, where's this road go?
> Been here 15 years, hadn't gone anywhere yet.
> Hey, stranger. How long does a pound of coke last?
> A lifetime, if you use it fast enough.

And nobody would talk to me.

Or, when turning down the offer to turn on, I'd say, "I'm already on." When I would say, "But, I like it when you do it," they'd ask, "Why is that?" I'd answer, "Because it cuts down the competition." And again, they'd turn their backs on me. I told them that stuff should have been illegal.

We learned a lot then, but for some it took a while. I hope we learned that when someone is doing something stupid, it's best to take the risk and tell them. If the friendship dissolves over it, maybe it wasn't really a friendship. Life is too short to help others make theirs shorter. I also believed that whatever got in the way of the music was a serious problem that had to be avoided. But then, sometimes, to paraphrase someone, my fookin' attitude may have gotten in the way. The magic that was to become the Dirt Band just might have needed all those things that happened, good and bad, even the ones I didn't agree with.

My choice to stay away from drugs evolved into sometimes mocking the users, or just stewing in my anger that my life away from family was being wasted because of all the drugs around. Athough I never heard anyone say, "No more coke for me, thanks," we were working. I grew aloof from it all, and from the guys. I didn't care what others might do on their own home time, but road time, show time? My view was that the minute you left the house for the road you were working for the show and the audience. If you did not do your best shows, you would be wasting your time and the audience's, and abusing the privilege that this line of "work" represented. From what I saw, drug and alcohol use while performing *never* made people do their best. Sure, there would be some laughs, but it rarely felt like genuine fun. I felt the same about pot and work, and still do in general—but then, I have hired Willie Nelson and others a couple of times.

It always seemed there was something to learn from everyone. I learned from crazy Vietnam vet Duane. He would jump on stage and sit in with us, bashing acoustic guitar chords on "Jambalya." One time, his bare hand was getting cut up so badly thrashing the strings that he was bleeding profusely on my guitar. I pointed this out to him and he looked at me with a big grin and said, "So?" He kept right on going, ripping the skin from his fingers with a smile. He might be the only one I have known who earned being stoned.

Near the end of one Aspen run, roadie Gary told us that Monica Mancini was riding with him in our equipment van to the next show, in Walla Walla, Washington, to "hang out." With all of the recreational things a rich, good-looking, twenty-one-year-old chick with the name Mancini could have at her disposal in early '70s Aspen, she did whatever she wanted. I had booked flights to Spokane but I hadn't booked rooms, yet. I just drove us to the college gig, after stopping for a leisurely lunch, and ambled to an arbitrarily chosen motel around two in the afternoon. In those days, you could do that. I walked into my randomly chosen room to be welcomed by a ringing phone. We hardly knew where we were, so I was shocked someone else did. It wasn't the front desk.

"Hello. You are with Nitty Gritty Dirt Band?" a mystery voice sternly said.

"Yes. This is John. And you are?"

"This is Henry Mancini. Where's my daughter?" I could hear the high-voltage concern in his voice.

"Monica?" I asked. "She's with our roadie in the truck. They should be here soon. Can I help you with something? What's the problem?"

"Let's start with transporting a seventeen-year-old across two state lines." I sensed the end of our showbiz life was near as the *Peter Gunn* theme started in my head. Usually good on my feet, words were failing me. Our music career might be dying in the flames of their burning lust. I told him all I could (with the *Pink Panther* theme replacing the *Gunn* tune in my mind). I explained that she had told us she was twenty-one, and filled him in, as discreetly as possible, on how well she fit in with all her adult activities. She would be taken care of, I tried to assure him. I didn't tell him how my knees were shaking.

"You have her call me the minute she arrives. Good-bye!" He said it with emphasis, and slammed the phone down. No longer able to keep my charade of calm, I began speculating on how the story would play in the news: "Dirt musicians in jail for trekking a juvenile celebrity babe up Moon River across the country into a Patty Hearst–lifestyle . . ." I spent the time waiting for the truck to show up thinking about what else I might do for a living, now that the show business career might soon be coming to a close. I also tried to imagine the different things one could make with prison food.

When, a long hour later, the equipment van finally pulled up, chirpy Monica hopped out, apparently without a care in the world.

"Monica," I announced, "your father called. He's a bit upset about your excursion, and wants you to call him. *Now.*"

"Oh, Daddy!" she chirped. "I can take care of him. He just worries too much . . . and . . . I know how to handle Daddy. Everything will be just fine. He just hates I'm old enough to make my own decisions." This sweet Valley girl didn't even question how he had found us.

"Call now," I repeated with emphasis.

She made the call. "Hi, Daddy. This is Monica. Say Daddy, I was going to call and—"

She was obviously silenced from the other end. I imagined his fatherly talk covered soon-to-be-ex trust funds, vanishing free rooms and ski passes in Aspen, details on to whom he would now leave the Jaguar, the beauty of working her own way through school, and maybe how he was going to send us up Moon River. Every few seconds she dutifully responded, "Yes, Daddy," and her voice became a bit lower with each "yes," and slower with each "Daddy."

Monica hung the phone up, turned to me, and said, "Will someone please take me to the nearest airport?"

As she shipped off, one could almost feel music maven Mancini's potential curse lifted; I never knew if he did anything to us, and we didn't lose our record deal for a few more years. I think Monica was accepted back into the bosom of the family. But then, we never did get another job in Walla Walla.

There were plenty of other jobs thanks to our hits from *Uncle Charlie*. Loggins's "House at Pooh Corner" and "Some of Shelly's Blues" had hit the top twenty in many markets, especially in Kansas City and south of there. Things were possibly too good, as the thought of chartering a plane seemed suddenly reasonable, at least sometimes. Calling up and ordering a plane to take us somewhere did give me a feeling of accomplishment or pride. The results were never predictable.

A few months later, at New York's La Guardia Airport, the 10:00 AM forecast showed a storm front racing us to our date at a television station in Toronto. We wanted our current remains to remain living, so we buckled up without being told. With Canada only "an hour or so" away, we didn't think the trip would be too bad. Wrong.

When we asked why the five rattling passenger seats were so loose, the Cessna's cocky, over-confident pilot laughed and yelled back, "They come out. Slide right out. This is usually a coffin hauler, but every now and again we'll haul living passengers!" Ha ha. We flew up there just ahead of the storm front without any problems.

After taping Ian and Sylvia's television show, we returned at about five thirty that evening to the seats of the moonlighting hearse to head back to New York. We thought the storm had abated—until we got back in the air. The two-hour flight became three frighteningly bumpy hours through heavy snow. It was a great relief when the unmistakable lights of Manhattan broke through the clouds to finally appear in our windows. Flying in a casket hauler in a snow storm was not my idea of how I wanted to go, neither to work nor out of this life.

On our final approach into La Guardia, following I-95 over the George Washington Bridge, the control tower came on our radio, blaring our plane's call letters.

"Cessna 405 B 32J, divert your approach. A plane on your tail has landing priority."

A bit of silence followed, but not a change in course.

Again, we heard, "405 B 32J, divert your course. You do not have landing priority. A plane on your tail has priority. Respond."

No response. No change. No blood in the Cessna's passengers' faces as we listened intently to every crackle in the hearse's radio. Fadden, sitting next to the air-hearse driver, leaned over to the pilot and said, "Aren't those your plane's call letters, the numbers the tower is calling? Did you hear them?"

"Did they call me? I didn't notice," said our pilot, who was moonlighting from his usual 727 gig and obviously thinking of how he could make a house payment with the extra income from this charter.

The tower came back with: "Cessna! Divert your approach! Respond! There is a seven-two-seven on your tail with priority! SEVEN-TWO-SEVEN BEHIND YOU! DIVERT! You are not cleared to land!"

Finally realizing it was his plane, he banked like a kamikaze and dove straight down into Harlem. About four seconds later, our rattling seats showed how much more they could rattle. Our little aircraft shook as the 727 roared past us. We could see the fire in its engines and the passengers inside, and felt the full power of those jets. With a sinking feeling, I wished I'd been to Harlem before this, as we were apparently going to be living there briefly. Our genius pilot recovered from the dive, circled, and again headed for La Guardia, confirming his landing clearance this time.

The tower came on and sarcastically announced, "Cessna, you're cleared to land . . . if you think you can make it."

As we deplaned, our foolish flyboy told me, "Uh, I forgot to make it part of the quote. I need to collect the La Guardia landing fee. It's $750; you can pay it directly to me." I told him he could look to find this cash in the dark place where the sun never shines, and if he didn't find it there, how much fun it would be to see him in court. Never heard from him again. I felt bold and brave that night, after being scared enough to require a shower.

We weren't conscious of it at the time, but with all this work and all the great music we were making, the band was generating some real momentum that was pushing us toward a truly legendary album we had not foreseen. But first we had to get to Nashville. I still hoped to record with Earl Scruggs someday.

6

The *Circle* Album

I n the late 1960s and early 1970s, pop radio was playing everything
from Joan Baez singing Phil Ochs's "There But for Fortune" to Flatt
and Scruggs's "Foggy Mountain Breakdown" (the theme from the film
Bonnie and Clyde), followed by the Beatles and then Aretha Franklin.
"But first, here's 'Close to You' by the Carpenters." The folk boom had
quit booming, but the song about "four dead in Ohio" from Crosby,
Stills, Nash and Young brought the country together. Well, part of it,
anyway. With the Vietnam War raging, America felt more divided than
ever. The public was still reeling from assassinations, marchers were
recovering from gassings and beatings, and churches burning. Nixon's
bombing of Cambodia plunged the country even deeper into the turmoil
of dissent. The president was lying (some things never change), but we
had shows to do and a hit on the radio, so . . . everything was great.

By late 1970, the three radio hits from *Uncle Charlie* had us out
touring all over. In 1971, two months after the first show at Cowtown
Ballroom, one fall night on the road in Nashville would change our
lives in a way that none of us ever imagined. Fadden and I were setting
up the band gear in the Vanderbilt gym for our first Nashville concert,
and my mind went back to 1965, before NGDB got started, when my
brother and I had driven to Nashville to see the Grand Ole Opry. It was
sold out that melting summer night, but I peered through the opened
windows in the back north wall just in time to see Lester Flatt tell the

crowd, "Earl and I would like to bring out Mother Maybelle Carter to do the 'Wildwood Flower.'" The place went nuts. I thought to myself, *Someday I will meet those people*, not really thinking it was possible. Most people under thirty didn't understand the Opry—or even know of it—since most of the performers there were the "untrusted ones" over thirty. But if you liked bluegrass and real country music from before 1960, then the Opry was the high church—and it was housed in the Ryman Auditorium, which actually was an old church.

The college stage crew who were helping us kept saying things like, "We heard Earl Scruggs is coming tonight" or "The Scruggs family will be here for the show." *Fat chance*, I thought. *Why would the creator of bluegrass banjo come see some young picker or his band from California?*

We continued setting up, excited to be in Nashville. I was hoping our show would be over in time to see the Opry, from the inside this time, and that I might catch a glimpse of Earl again. I knew Earl had "long-haired sons," and that he had recently spoken and played at the Washington, DC, peace rally. He was one of the few country icons who bravely spoke out against the war, and there was a chance he might have heard our hippie-bluegrass music. But, come to a Dirt Band show? That didn't seem plausible.

Later, in the dressing room, for yucks, I put my banjo way out of tune and played Earl's signature song, "Foggy Mountain Breakdown," in as poor of a parody as possible, and told my brother Bill, "I'd better get ready—Earl is coming." Yeah, just like "Dylan is coming," as the hippies often said.

A knock on the door slowed the banjo cacophony. Playing worse with each step that I took toward the door, I said cynically, "I bet it's Scruggs, ha ha!" I opened it to stare out at the entire Scruggs family: Gary, Stevie, Randy, Louise, and Earl. Earl grinned and said "Hi." I stammered, "Oh, shiiiiit . . . just a minute," and closed the door and tuned my banjo. It was like when Ibby first saw Jeff and me. "Hey, Bill. Guess who's on the other side of this door—right now," I said.

I explained the joke as they entered laughing, and they seemed to get it. To change the subject, I worked up the courage to ask Earl to pick one on my banjo; before I finished the question, he had calmly put his picks on and he tore up "Fireball Mail" the best I'd ever heard it. Humble Earl made my night when I asked his reason for coming to the show. His response was to say, "I wanted to meet the boy who played 'Randy Lynn Rag' the way I intended to." (I had recorded this song of his, a hot instrumental breakdown, on the *Uncle Charlie* album.) Earl's friendly boys had played that album around the house. This was huge for me. My music mentor had come to see me, and I, for once, felt like I must have accomplished something of note. Earl had also heard our songs filled with banjo, mandolin, fiddle, washboard, accordion, dobro, acoustic guitars, tight two-part harmony—and liked it! Thanks to our fans for making the record popular enough that it made it to Earl's ears. *His sons had played it for him.*

A few months later in L.A., I met Merle Watson—son of the incomparable guitar flat-picker, North Carolina's Doc Watson—when I went to try to meet Doc at an after-show pickin' party. I didn't meet his father that night, but I got to know Merle as we watched the gathered disciples drooling over Doc, and I told him I planned to ask Earl to record with us.

Merle, also a big fan of our *Uncle Charlie* album, told me he had played it for Doc. His dad thought it was "good" that a group with "radio songs" used banjo, mandolin, harmonica, acoustic guitars, and accordion (the only electric instrument on "Mr. Bojangles" was Les's bass), and he liked a lot of the other music on that bluegrass-laced pop album.

That next spring, Earl and his family (The Earl Scruggs Revue) performed for a week in my home turf of Colorado, and our friendship grew. It was that June, while driving Earl back to his hotel every night after their hot club show at Boulder's famed Tulagi's (run by Chuck Morris), that I finally got up the nerve to ask the question I had been thinking about for months. I stammered, "Earl . . . I was wondering if . . . if you think you might . . . or would want to . . . or would consider . . . if . . . you think it could work out . . . if . . . uhh . . . uhh . . . could you, I mean, would you record a couple of songs with the Dirt Band?" His immediate answer of "I'd be proud to!" made it difficult for me to go to sleep that night, because I didn't know where that could lead. I remember looking in the rearview mirror to see Jeff's eyes wide with excitement about Earl's answer.

Alone at Tulagi's two weeks later, Doc was about to play. Merle got very excited when I told him about Earl's answer, and he anxiously offered to introduce me to his dad. He eagerly added, "Daddy needs this. The folk thing is dying down and he's drawing fewer people. This could expose him to a whole new audience!" That was my hope for both Earl and Doc.

So, with more courage than I had two weeks earlier, and after Merle's warm introduction and hearing Doc's positive comments on *Uncle Charlie*, I said, "Doc, we're making an album with Earl Scruggs, and would love you to pick with us." Doc, a solidly built and square-jawed mountain man, played with assured confidence, but he was a humble and inquisitive man who listened attentively to everyone's story. He asked about another one of the *Charlie* tunes—"Clinch Mountain Backstep"—and was impressed that I was the banjo player on that. Doc lived close to Clinch Mountain. He loved to talk about music and its history.

Doc carried himself in a way that never gave away his blindness. In fact, I like to think that Doc saw a lot more than many sighted people can. After his enthusiastic "yes," I immediately put him on the dressing room phone with my brother Bill, and it was determined that we would proceed. I had already asked one real music hero if he would record with us, and now another, and they were both going along with it!

Driving home happy and excited through the crystal clear Colorado night, I thought back to that Garden Grove night when my dad said about Doc, "Now, how a guy like that gets on television I'll never understand."

After that night in Boulder, Bill and I talked about who else we would want to be involved. Maybe Merle Travis, another guitar hero, for sure . . . maybe Jimmy Martin! . . . and we'd need some fiddlers . . . Earl's wife, Louise, said she would ask Maybelle Carter and Martin.

Bill called Merle Travis the next day. Thankfully, we weren't total strangers to Travis; in our sixth month as a band we had spent ten days opening for him at the Ash Grove, playing two shows a night, and had had a great time. Travis said he always wanted to meet Doc Watson, and came on board.

Next, we needed money to make a record. Bill and I met with the United Artists Records president, Mike Stewart, and with the credibility and momentum of three chart singles from *Charlie* (thanks to Ibby and Jeff's song choices and vocals, I felt), we knew he would hear us out. He sat there listening to the pitch for twenty minutes, with his finger in his nose the whole time. Not a word.

I told him, "We've been playing colleges for the past year and a half, for thousands of people, and they always ask, 'Where is that banjo music from?' And our core audience, about five to seven years younger than us, has never heard of Hank Williams, Buddy Holly, Earl Scruggs, Doc, Travis, or Roy Acuff. They definitely don't know Maybelle. With our following and the power of this music, there would be a lot of buyers." We finished, and Stewart grudgingly said, "I don't know if I'll sell ten of these—a *double* acoustic country-bluegrass-folk album? But, you guys are so passionate about it, I'll put up the money."

Mike approved a budget of $22,000; we set off to make an album, even if we didn't know exactly what it would be. We knew it would be good. This money was to cover tape, studio time, hotels, food, musician pay, travel, etc., and was probably less than what's budgeted nowadays for catering for a Madonna or a Rihanna video. In the pre-NGDB years, I had spent hours listening to Doc, Earl, Jimmy Martin, Maybelle, and others. It had crossed my mind that I might someday meet these people, and now I would.

Three weeks in, we told the band what was formulating. Though Jeff and Fadden had thought it good that Earl "might play on a song with us," until then, Bill hadn't mentioned the other additions that we, with Earl's help, had secured. I don't think they had yet grasped the importance of this opportunity—but even then, they rarely liked my ideas and they didn't know Jimmy Martin's music yet. Given my growing struggle with Jeff about anything that I suggested, I was relieved when early skepticism changed to excitement as it all came together, and especially when Earl said it would include Maybelle. As always, Ibby was excited to do anything. I know it would not have had a chance if Jeff and Ibby had not chosen the right songs that led to *Uncle Charlie's* radio successes.

As it came together, I booked rehearsals, hotels, and logistical things as usual. Bill handled the studio booking (Nashville's Woodland Sound Studios) and decided to bring his favorite engineer from L.A., Dino Lappas.

I asked Earl to secure a few fiddlers to cover various styles envisioned for the album. I called to see if he had found the right guys. He said, "I found one man: Vassar Clements." I had never heard of Vassar, and asked if he could handle all the styles. Earl, always a man of few words, answered emphatically, "He'll do." It was the most underspoken, yet definitive, praise one could get from Mr. Scruggs. I had been listening to Vassar for years without realizing it, as he was on many albums by all the greats I studied. I'd loved his unique abilities from afar, and now I was going to record with him! Though we didn't have a bass player yet, we had other things requiring our attention. We still had twenty-one shows to do—which I had to advance and handle—before getting to Nashville, and the band had a growing list of songs to learn. Now that we had a great canvas, they all came up with ideas of what we could paint on it. It was great. We were all working as a team.

We got to Nashville late on a hot, August Saturday afternoon, on the day before we were to start a week of rehearsals, and only six years after I saw Flatt and Scruggs at the Opry. Earl took Bill and me backstage at the Grand Ole Opry that night to meet the bass player, Junior Huskey. Junior was thought of as the best stand-up bassist in town—any town—and told us, "I cut my teeth on a lot of these tunes Earl has been telling me about. Always wanted to record with Vassar . . . and Martin . . . and Mother Maybelle, too . . . and especially looking forward to—oh, just a minute." He stopped talking in order to focus on the ending of a song he had been backing Ernest Tubb on, live on the

Opry, during that whole conversation. After watching for and hitting Tubb's last note with him, he turned back to us. "Looking forward to pickin' with Mr. Travis, too. I'll try to do a good job for you boys. See you tomorrow at rehearsal!" He was obviously the right man. He'll do. And, I really had to pinch myself. I was backstage at the Opry with Earl Scruggs and no stage pass was required.

Staying at Earl's house during four days of rehearsals (now about seven weeks after my initial invitation), playing music all day and Ping-Pong most of the night, made me think I had died and gone to picker's heaven. One morning I awoke in a daze, with the smell of bacon wafting in from the kitchen, accompanied by the faint familiar notes of "Bugle Call Rag" that seemed to be coming from a cloud. The notes rolled slowly, smoothly, softly, along with the bacon, bacon, bacon. Then through my bluegrass-tinged fog, I heard Earl say, "John, yur eggs are ready," as he sat on the edge of Gary's (his oldest son) bed, serenading me with a banjo wake-up call that he played without his picks on. His quiet grin told me everything was OK.

Over bacon and eggs, Louise quietly laughed, telling us, "If Earl was on TV and played 'Randy Lynn Rag,' Gary'd get up and stomp out of the room. . . . He was mad, and would say 'Daddy never wrote a song for me!'" So, I named an instrumental I wrote for the *Circle* album for Gary: "Togary Mountain." (In 2009, I arranged for Gary to help Steve Martin write "Daddy Played the Banjo" while I was producing Steve's album *The Crow*.) Then, after rehearsing a day each with Jimmy Martin and Travis, we were ready, without knowing for exactly what.

And so the sessions began. On the first day, modest Merle Travis knocked his songs off in one or two takes each, and before we knew it we had his four songs in the can and were ready to do more. As a musical pioneer whose picking style is emulated by thousands and now bears his name, Travis's everyman appearance and humility masked his iconic stature. Next, Earl played Carter-style guitar (the way Maybelle had pioneered) for "You Are My Flower," with Jeff and Gary Scruggs on vocals. As usual, Jeff nailed it. Only about five or six hours had gone by, though eight were booked, so we played back the seven songs of the day. Playbacks were magic. Already it felt like we were listening to a historic recording—only we were on it.

We were all a little bit nervous at first, but soon after rehearsing and then recording that first day it became apparent these folks were such fans of each other, so the Dirt Band calmed down. They accepted us almost as equals, as qualified to record with them. It might have been the mystery of our pop-chart success or because we knew a lot about their music, which they clearly didn't expect. We were there to make music—their music. When Jeff leaned over Doc's shoulder for harmony on "Tennessee Stud" and "Way Downtown," with Fadden's harp chunking along and me on frailing banjo while Ibby was singing or playing guitar, we really were making an "old record."

By contrast, we were ready for the flamboyant Jimmy Martin, who is the man who put color into bluegrass. The often-drunk Martin was known to put down his musicians on stage if they didn't play well enough, or to fire people on stage during a show, and was definitely a ladies' man, which he wasn't shy about announcing. In the pre-NGDB years, Bill, Alice, and I had spent months playing as a duo/trio called the Fall River Tarheels in clubs around L.A., and about a third of our songs were Jimmy Martin's. These moments in the studio meant more to us (and Les, as we had also played his music in the Moonshiners) than I can express, though the others weren't aware of his importance until later. "He is the best" it was said, most often by Jimmy himself. But he was right. Martin let us know when we were doing it right, and especially when we were doing it wrong. I picked so hard on one song that I broke the bridge on my banjo.

It was a great time for all. Louise Scruggs told me years later that she ordered Martin to "not blow it," as he was known to push people a bit far. He pushed us just far enough. I realized then just how good of a businesswoman she was, as her reputation of being tough was known even by me. Years later, Jeff and Fadden realized how lucky we had been to have recorded with all of them. Ibby and Les knew from day one. Jeff became good friends with Jimmy Martin. I was always a bit jealous of that, but glad for Jimmy at the same time.

This amazing roster of players, though unknown to the pop-music mainstream and our audience (but all masters of their craft), came together for the first time on the record. Dobro player Pete "Oswald" Kirby, better known as Bashful Brother Oswald, was a real treasure. Os had a sound that was distinctive. The man made the dobro cry, as if his sensitive soul came out through his instrument. As his sideman, Os had long been in the shadow of Acuff. Bill and I wanted to put him in more of a starring position, so we recorded a few of his instrumental tunes. In the process, it came out that he was illiterate. He signed his contract with an "X." Oswald also did not know the notes of his strings, nor how to follow a chord chart, but he played with more soul than any of us. In the middle of a session he put on new strings, and when I asked if he needed a G note to tune up, he responded, "I don't reckon which one that is." But, when he put his bar to his strings, he made sounds like no other. Later my mother would say, "Who is that man playing the dobro? And why is it when I hear him play, it makes me cry?" Many got that feeling.

Although he looked like a Georgia state trooper, Vassar Clements was the most open and generous person you could meet, and when he played, he played from the heart. He spent time working out parts with Fadden and me, loved Ibby and Jeff's singing, and picked up the guitar for the solo in the middle of "Honky Tonkin'." It sounded like a *real* old 1948 hillbilly-jazz record then! Like most of the cuts, it took just one take, and we were done. Fadden did a great job singing it old style, too. He sounded like an old-time street bluesman.

When I asked Bill how long we had before we were to cut "Lonesome Fiddle Blues" (Vassar's signature tune), he said about two hours. That was just enough time to learn a D-minor song in G tuning (standard tuning for a banjo), as I wanted to do something that had not been done before: play rapid melodic notes in a minor key without a capo. It had a lot of new notes for me, but about four minutes into Vassar showing me his magical, memorable melody notes, Bill popped out in the hallway and said, "We have to do 'Lonesome Fiddle' now." I wasn't ready. But, surrounded by the magic of Junior, Vassar, Randy

Scruggs on guitar, and the band, I made it through. The strangest thing was that I didn't play my solo's end lick like I wanted to, and instead jumped to a couple of different notes sooner than I meant to, but it sounded better than what I had planned! It later took a week to learn my own solo from the recording.

Bill's foresight to have the tape running constantly at three-and-a-quarter ips (inches per second, for those who don't remember) made it possible to catch all the banter between songs, the run-throughs, and whatever was happening in the studio. The master ran at thirty ips, and took a lot more tape, with each reel good for fifteen minutes. It was the three-and-a-quarter ips tape that captured the *Circle* album magic, and preserved what these great musicians were actually like as people, as they talked between songs about the sessions and life. It also made possible one major goal of Bill's and mine: to get the first meeting of Doc Watson and Merle Travis recorded for posterity. It was indeed exciting when Travis walked in while Doc was recording. He went over to Doc and was about to start chatting. From the control room (where the mic controls and mixing is done on the other side of the glass), Bill excitedly motioned to me, so I cut them off and pushed a mic in front of Travis, then stepped back to watch a little American history unfold as they met and chatted respectfully like old neighbors. We happily found out later this part of the recording meant a lot to many people and made them feel like they were in the room for the historic sessions. It was the icing on the *Circle* cake.

The "instrumental day" was, of course, one of my favorites; I had learned my craft as an Orange County teenager by listening to all the tunes we had scheduled for that day, and I was about to become the first banjo player to record with Earl Scruggs! We started with "Soldier's Joy," with me frailing (an old-time banjo style also called "clawhammer" that involves brushing the strings with bare fingers more than picking individual notes); Earl playing three-finger (now called "Scruggs style," where each string is plucked individually with the thumb, index finger, and middle finger); and Junior on bass. Just the three of us. This was the song I had in mind when I first asked Earl to record with us. Earl loaned me Uncle Dave Macon's banjo, which he now owned, and I could tell this would go well. Uncle Dave, the first star of the Opry, started there in 1925 at fifty-four years old. When he died, Earl bought his banjo for a dollar, and I had asked if I could play it that day. It still had the same strings from 1952, which was the last time Dave played it. To this day, this simple three-instrument song is one of my best recordings, done in one take, and I believe it will stand the test of time.

Then came Earl's "Nashville Blues" and the rest, including "Flint Hill Special," with his most difficult ending lick. They had to do "Flint Hill" seven times until all the players jelled, but Earl played it perfectly each time. That day we also cut "Togary Mountain," which I hoped would keep Gary in the room if saw us do it on television. But, I never could get the band to play that with me.

Recording Maybelle was like traveling back through time. Maybelle never thought of herself as an icon of American music, even though she had been recording for almost fifty years, and made her first Carter Family record in 1927 with Ralph Peer in Bristol, Tennessee. Gentle and unassuming, Maybelle was called "Mother Maybelle" by all, as we all wished she was our mother. And in a way, she was. She taught us a lot—about music and life—and coming from nothing, she had a lot to give. Earl told me that when the music business was ignoring her in 1960, the only job Maybelle could get was as a nurse in a Nashville hospital. In fact, the world was ignoring all of these icons back then. Even the Nashville *Tennessean* paper said, "What the Nitty Gritty Dirt Band is doing recording a bunch of old dinosaurs we don't understand." They sure didn't.

One memorable moment occurred as we were getting started on a song with her. I took a call from a Columbia Records lawyer, who called to tell me, "I've got good news! You guys have approval to do one song with Maybelle Carter." I thanked him and hung up. Bill asked me who had been on the phone. I answered, "No one important," and went to play the mandolin and record our fourth song beside this musical matriarch.

Sitting at Maybelle's feet, listening to this quiet angel asking about things like, "I hope y'all don't mind if I do 'Wildwood Flower' on the autoharp in the key of F-standard," was amazing. She had created many of country music's most iconic songs like "Keep on the Sunny Side." Maybelle always called us "those Dirty boys," which I thought was really an honor. Carter Family songs and her "Wildwood Flower" guitar style had been emulated as long as she'd been performing, and now she was asking us if it was OK to play in a certain key. I would find out forty years later, from her grandson John Carter Cash, that "F-standard" meant regular pitch, as she usually tuned her guitar down a half step.

———————

For us young, West Coast longhairs, the most tense time while recording *Circle* was our nervous wait for the King of Country Music, Roy Acuff, to bestow his blessing upon us and consent to record with us—and to show up. We weren't sure he would. Charlie Collins (hired the week before to be Acuff's rhythm guitarist—for the next thirty years) told me years later that while driving back to Nashville from a St. Louis show, the week before the sessions, Acuff told him, "I don't know what I'ma gettin' into . . . or really why. I don't if they're young boys or old men or what—they're all covered with hair and all." On his scheduled day, the last of the six *Circle* session days, Acuff walked into the studio, not looking happy, and authoritatively said, "Let me hear this music you boys've been recording!" Although even Roy called Maybelle "Mother," he was the oldest performer on the album, and with his authoritative air, he commanded everyone's attention. We all wanted his approval. Bill played four cuts for our Acuff "test." It sounded like the magic old records we'd listened to at McCabe's. The confident, stern-faced King Roy sat silently, formulating his opinion.

At the end of the four-song playback, staring silently at the ceiling, he finally broke his silence with a blunt question. He tersely asked, "Now, just what kind of music do you boys call that?" invoking the same intimidating effect as Lee Marvin's Iwo Jima question had caused years earlier while we were filming *Paint Your Wagon.*

Bill, with his long hair down his back, started answering. "Uh, well, it's kind of Appalachian . . . bluegrass or traditional mountain . . . old timey . . . American folk," stumbling over his words like a California hippie at a KKK meeting.

Roy cut him off. "Hell!" pausing dramatically. "It ain't nothing but country music! *Good* country music! Let's go make some more, boys!" Cheers erupted from all the nervous hippies in the control room. It was a wonderful moment for us all. We went in and started with the 1938 Dorsey Dixon song "Wreck on the Highway," which was a defining country song as its lyrics covered prayer, blood, destruction, cars, whiskey, and death. But first he gave us his "policy" in the studio: "Get it right on the first time, 'cause every time you do it again, you lose a little something. So, let's get it right the first time and t'hell with the rest of them." He was right, and to this day, first takes are still my goal.

Before we recorded "I Saw the Light," Jimmy Martin proudly announced, out of earshot to Roy, "I'm gonna sing this so much like Acuff, you won't be able to tell the difference." I'm still not sure which verse Martin sang. (As a single, this recording became Acuff's first top-twenty radio record in fifteen years.)

Overall, that six days of recording made an impact beyond anything I'd anticipated. Bill and I wanted to capture and preserve the sounds and art of these icons with the band, and in doing so we'd all pay homage to their influence on our lives and music, with the hope it would enhance their careers. The band guys wanted to do the best they could with this immense assignment, and they all did great.

Alice would later do the beautiful calligraphy on the *Circle* album. (She did it on parchment paper and it took her almost two days. Bill wanted to make it look aged, and put it in the oven to singe it. It caught fire and she had to do another one, but this one was put in at a lower temperature—acoustic photoshop!)

At the sessions' end, Roy invited me to come by the Opry sometime to see him, which was an invitation that led to my first invitation to jail. Taking Roy up on his offer one night a few months later, I walked confidently into the back of the Ryman Auditorium and up the same steps that Bill and I and Earl had climbed when we had enlisted Junior. I started wandering around backstage, as is my habit. As any of my oft-embarrassed kids will tell you, I have always had a tendency to walk in backstage anywhere and look around, even when not working there. As I gazed at the stage from the wings, the firm hand of official authority clamped down on my shoulder, as my children had always feared would happen.

"Boy! Just what're you doin' back here? You don't belong back here. Let me lead you outside and there won't be any trouble." The security hard-ass did not like the California shoulder-length hairdo that was so popular among my age group at the time. The truth seemed to be the only way out.

"Well, no one was around when I came in, and I'm looking for Roy; he invited me to come by," I said affably, trying to sound totally at home backstage at the Opry.

"And just why would *Mister* Acuff want to see you, boy?" he scoffed, with an I-wish-I-had-my-scissors stare. The chorus of "O-hi-o" was going thru my mind as I peacefully offered again, "Mister Acuff invited me. I just recorded with him, and he said to stop by, and—"

"Yessir, uh-huh, everyone's recorded with Mr. Acuff. Boy, I suggest you head down them stairs rhaat now, or you'll be g'ttin' in more trouble than you kin handle."

Drained of confidence and now pissed off because I had a legitimate reason to go backstage at the Opry, I headed down the stairs toward the back door. With thoughts of his "boy" comments morphing in my mind into an *Easy Rider* scenario, I flung my fist out with more adrenaline than was necessary to knock the back door open. How was I to know it was just cheap, eighth-inch fiberboard? My fist went right through it, up to my elbow.

The guard's adrenaline visibly soared as he watched this longhair's destruction of country music's sacred door. I tried to pull my arm back through the hole. But, like Chinese fingercuffs, it closed in around my wrist, preventing my escape, and tightening with every tug toward freedom.

"You get yursef free and git back up here now! You won't be free fr long. I got a call t' make so y'all have a place to stay a few days, boy." His point was obvious: my arrest was imminent. Struggling free from the door's trap, I trudged back up the stairs to try the truth again.

"Look, wouldn't you be upset if the great Mr. Roy Acuff invited you to visit him, and someone kept you from doing it? Before you make any other calls, just make one for me, please. Call Louise Scruggs at 868-2254 and give her my name, and ask if she'll vouch for me." (Once Earl gave his to me, I never bothered to write it down. How could I ever forget it?)

Surprised at such a strange request and the number, he made the call. Louise answered. After a few words were exchanged, he said, "You can go," and he sent me on my way. I didn't see Acuff that night. I sure was glad Louise was home. She later became my night owl e-mail and IM friend for many years. I miss her.

A couple years after its release, *Circle* reached the Gold level of sales. I called my new friend Marty Stuart to go with me to Maybelle's house, since he knew where she lived, so I could give her a gold record with her name on it. When I explained, "This means the album has sold 500,000 copies," she responded, "Well, I never knew that many people had even heard those old songs!" Marty assured me she meant it, and that she never realized the impact she had made on the world. (For instance, Duane Allman's daughter told me forty years later that her dad had taught her mom "Wildwood Flower" on the guitar.) Then, true to form, Maybelle asked, "Would you boys like some lemonade?" Then she set the record against the wall.

Within a few years, other musicians on the album weighed in with what it had meant to them:

Earl: "The *Circle* album sure put a spark in our bookings for the Revue!" He was picked up by our agency after that.

Vassar: "The *Circle* album gave me a career of my own. It is great not being a sideman anymore."

Merle Watson: "Daddy has more requests from that album than any. People yell 'Tennessee Stud' at us every show."

Oswald: "Biggest royalty checks I ever seen." Several of his songs from the album generated publishing income.

Martin: "Let's do another one! People know my name now in places they didn't before. Get me on some of them college shows with y'all."

Bill Monroe: Initially Monroe turned down our request to have him pick with us on *Circle*. He only knew we were on the pop charts at the time of the sessions, and that was not his kind of music. He got it later. At a 1975 festival he asked, "John, if ya'll ever do another one of them *Circle* albums, *give me a call.*"

It's given me a great feeling of accomplishment to know that we contributed something to the careers of these greats, but of course, that was mutual. I most likely would not have had a career without their music. *Will the Circle Be Unbroken* has gone Multi-Platinum, and continues in popularity today with a constant presence on the charts; it is the *Dark Side of the Moon* of bluegrass. *Circle* is in the Library of Congress and the Grammy Hall of Fame. Strangely, in the time that has passed, it seems we have become what we were emulating.

I was the kid from Orange County who wanted Maybelle's autograph and a chance to meet and play with Earl Scruggs. Imagine.

7

The Road Can Rule You

Our sixth album sneaked out in January 1972. *All the Good Times*
was the follow up to *Uncle Charlie*, with more country rock.
It produced no radio hits, but got great notices and sold well. *Circle*
followed four months later and began selling hot, right out the door.
This meant we'd have to spend even more time on the road, and now
with two kids, I needed the work because I needed the income. Certainly, nobody needed my being gone so much. I loved performing,
and I loved living out my teenage dream, but I hated the fact that I
loved it so much. I hated missing their birthdays, which happened too
often. (Here's a tip: If you get in a band, you should have all your kids
in January, preferably all the same week. That way, you won't miss
birthdays.) I was worried that the life I was living would make me a
well-known stranger.

I mostly got along with my other three wives: the Dirt Band guys
with whom I shared the road. I was still handling the road manager
chores, and driving without pay or even thanks, but I didn't really mind
that so much because I truly loved the whole experience.

I recall one relentless 1974 nine-show run; we still had four to go.
"Arduous" would be too gentle of a word for what my days were like:
driving, flying, waiting, and road managing it all to get us to some airport or into a car to get to gigs. I was tired and wanted nothing more
than to sleep past nine in the morning, have a simple good dinner, and

go to a movie to get away from it all. The tenth day was a day off and we all slept in late.

In those days, before cell phones, a lot of time could pass between calls to home. Our shows rarely ended before eleven at night, and more like one in the morning if we were in the Western time zone. I didn't dare interrupt my wife's sleep. As the mom of a growing squad of kids, her work day went from around five thirty in the morning to eleven thirty at night. Nowadays, I can call on a cell while driving, or after sound check, or between flights. It was one of many reasons to cherish days off back then. It was time to call home. It had been four days since calling, and the conversation went like this: "Hi! Missing you and everyone! Finally got a day to hold still, call, and hopefully go to a movie and have a real dinner. What's up at home?"

She let me know, and said, "School's closed; over a foot of snow; no groceries, had to shovel driveway and go get gas and food, but car battery was dead; neighbor helped get it started. I have to take Teddy [our dog] to the clinic; Aaron [about two] has jaundice, taking him to doctor after groceries; power went off but is back on now—" She paused right as the anxious band members showed up at the phone booth (remember those?) and signaled for me to drive us to the movie.

I offered, "Wow! How terrible! You doing OK?" Oh, she was pregnant with number three, too. "We've been working every day for nine in a row, and we're going to a movie today on this day off, then get some dinner and the guys just pulled up. Wish you were here."

She responded, "Well . . . YOU HAVE YOUR FUN!" and hung up—hard.

I did not feel at all good about that. Dinner was lonely, but the movie was good.

———————

The hours between shows occasionally got tedious and monotonous, unless I kept my eyes open for something fun, like looking for a bet to make with someone. I'd never trapped anyone into a bet, but there was one perfect time I couldn't pass up.

One day, while waiting for Jeff to show up for a road lunch in Austin's historic Driskill Hotel restaurant, I saw the perfect opportunity that involved my favorite dessert. I called it sher*bert.* The hotel's four-page menu, both lunch and dinner, listed my favorite dessert. And there lay the trap: the lunch menu read sher*bet,* but the next page's dinner menu read sher*bert.*

Having long been ridiculed by Sir Jeff for my Hawaiian shirts, playing banjo in my sleep, and other things, I chafed from his constant chiding. His Lateness made a habit of correcting me whenever I ordered my sher*bert.* I knew Mr. Hanna's ego would get the better of him, and I could win some money off him.

"John, it's sher*bet.* Pronounced 'shure-bay' or 'sure-bet,'" he'd firmly state with a little snort of superiority that implied, *How could you be so stupid?* Supposedly armed with an English major somewhere in his schooling, I'd argued the point with him for ten years. This time, I waited until his eyes were down the menu at the lunch desserts, when they lit up a bit upon spotting my favorite after-meal treat—sherbet. I set the trap.

I said, "Food looks great here. I'm gonna have the fish special, and finish it off with some sher*bert,*" leaning just a little on the "r." Jeff squirmed a bit in his seat as the lunch menu's "sherbet" made his eyes saucerlike, until he finally said, "Well, you should order sher*bet,* that way you'll get what you want."

Feigning my usual annoyance, I waited a few seconds, and sprang the trap. I proclaimed to the pontificator of proper pronunciation, "I'll bet you fifty dollars that on that menu it is spelled s-h-e-r-b-*e-r-t!* Right now! Fifty dollars that it is spelled sher-B-E-*R*-T on that menu!"

His bulging eyes locked on the lunch menu's "sher-b-e-t." Fidgeting, he said, "You're on! You're gonna lose this one." He was gloating over his sure bet. But the guy who also got the words wrong on "Mr. Bojangles" was heading to a loss.

"Turn to the back, dinner menu, dessert page, and read me what's offered for dessert, palzo," I said. He turned, and looked down to the bottom of the page. When his eyes got big as he saw "sherb*ert*," I said, "Pay up."

Hanna blurted out, "Misprint!" and "Wrong!" and "How stupid is that!" and then stated, "You knew that was there! And, it's spelled wrong!"

"Well, I don't care if you think it is right or wrong, the bet was that on that menu it's spelled sher-B-E-R-T, and it is. You're looking at it! You owe me fifty dollars," I said. "And, of course I knew that, otherwise, why would I bet? Think I'm an idiot? Who would be so stupid?"

Jeff said, "Wait! I'll have the waiter bring the box that it comes in out here. If it is spelled 'bert' on the box, I'll pay."

The ever-nervous Jeff started to look a little panicked as the smiling waiter arrived and revealed the dessert's proper name. Jeff got that fish-eyed look again, as the waiter read the spelling of raspberry s-h-e-r-b-e-r-t. Jeff jumped, "The box is wrong! I'm not going to pay!" I had the front desk bring a dictionary, leaving Webster to be the decider. Webster said "sherbert" was fine. Jeff said "Not fair! It's a collegiate dictionary!" He refused to pay, and did so again when I brought it up a year or so later. (With the advent of the Internet and posting this story on my website, Jeff reluctantly paid. It had taken thirty-two years. And, there was no interest.) We were already a couple of old curmudgeons and we had years to go.

Some of the best moments in the early days were connected to being onstage with people we had "grown up" with, from Steve Martin to Linda Ronstadt, Jimmy Buffett to John Denver. When I first met John Deutschendorf Jr., then a member of the Mitchell Trio, at their 1965 Golden Bear show, it was clear that he loved to sing. His voice soared over the crowd even before he changed his last name to Denver, which was the capitol of his favorite state. Known as a relentless self-promoter, he believed in his music so much that in the years after he left the trio, before his breakthrough to solo stardom, he'd go to radio stations asking for interviews based solely on the success of the song he penned, "Leaving on a Jet Plane," which had become Peter, Paul and Mary's only number-one record. I had fantasized about the imagery of "Jet Plane" since hearing it every day from the jukebox next door to the Magic Shop. After running into Denver in a Houston airport hotel in the fall of 1970, with both of us headed to separate gigs, he asked me to come by his room after our shows. There he handed me an album, saying, "They tell me it has a hit on it. It's called 'Country Roads' and comes out next April."

"Well, if you're going to be a big star, I should have you sign it," I responded. He did both, but years later the album was lost somewhere.

Since the late '60s at the Troubadour in L.A. (the Left Coast's answer to Greenwich Village's Bitter End), Linda always drew an eager crowd. With her band, the Stone Poneys, she packed the place. Her plaintive, undeniably great voice on her first hit, "Different Drum" (a top-ten song written in 1965 by pre-Monkees Mike Nesmith), brought people in. The untrue rumor of her lack of panties ensured the front rows would be crowded. (She recently told me she always wore the panties her mother made for her.) Regardless of where I sat, the hair on my arm would stand up when she sang.

One warm winter night in 1970, I'd gone to hang out in a San Fernando Valley studio where Linda was recording. After band tracking for a couple of hours, Linda had to overdub a vocal in the vocal booth where I'd fallen asleep against the wall, which was something I did often. I woke up and started to leave, but she said, "It's OK, stay. I'll sing to you." I laid down on the floor and pretended she was singing a cappella only to me. Hearing her cry her heart out, with the music faint from her headphones, and seeing her facial expressions reflect the words while her hands pleaded the lyrics, I felt—and not for the first time—how special some of the people in that L.A. music scene were. Literally, the hair on my arms stood up. A lot of people were just people learning songs and singing folk music, but sometimes you got to hear a real artist, a game changer. Sometimes you got to work with them. It felt great feel to be in a room where a part of American music history was coming to life. I treasure feeling that I was some part of it.

We all believed that song was destined for airplay, but no one could imagine what was to follow for Linda. "Will You Still Love Me Tomorrow" became a number-one smash. Every record label in L.A. had turned Bill's NGDB pitch down twice before we got a deal. This was the same town in which my brother Bill could not land a deal for Steve Martin. The "geniuses" who ran the record business were often wrong. They got it right about Linda, and eventually about Steve.

Our friendship led to our sharing the billing at benefit concerts in New Mexico and Arizona that were produced by Tom Campbell (from my Disneyland days). After NGDB opened the show, we backed Linda. It was my favorite job as a musician up until then. Behind her, we played our best music; Jeff and Ibby both sang great with her.

During rehearsals in Colorado with Linda we discovered that we had worked up two of the same songs, and decided to make a deal: we would do one, she would do the other. Jeff picked what he thought would be more of a hit, J. D. Souther's "The Moon Just Turned Blue." Linda took Buddy Holly's "When Will I Be Loved." Hmm. She picked well and had a huge smash later that year. Tom should win a prize for all the good he has done. After those early days hanging out and scheming at the Troubadour's bar, in the ensuing years he went on to help raise millions of dollars for many various causes through the benefit shows he put together.

"I see the lights!" Les yelled from the front seat of the little, six-passenger plane. Hank Williams's song from 1947, "I Saw the Light," came to mind. But, Hank was in a car in Alabama when the airport lights inspired him. The lights of the runway meant our bass player, Les, would soon find relief from nature's pressures.

But nature had a different plan. Les shouted, "How long until we land? I've gotta go!" "About six minutes," the pilot replied. "I've gottta peeeeee! Is there a cup anywhere? I can't wait!" Someone scrounged up a medium-sized, clear plastic cup and passed it up to him. Les's relief was in sight—in sight of us all, actually—and came with the report of "ahhhhhhhhhhhhhhhhhh." Feeling foolish, but relieved, we all saw the runway dead ahead.

"I can't stop! Get me another cup! Hurry!" Les pleaded, trying to be heard over our grossed-out laughter. Another cup found its way to his hot cider hydrant. I didn't keep an eye on the changeover, but it seemed to go well. Les stopped, almost topping off the second one, too, just before touchdown.

Now came the hard part: keeping the vessels level during the touchdown and taxi, so as not to spill on fellow passengers or himself. If it were gasoline, it would have been enough to keep a small car running for about sixteen miles, which is about how far away from Les we all wanted to be once we deplaned.

In the terminal, Les had to somehow manage disposal of his personal property. We let him handle his own issue as we walked about thirty feet ahead of him, down the airport concourse, and watched him balance his full containers while laughing like a crazy guy. The restroom was just too far away, and every step only made the rest of us laugh harder.

I am sure some of the passersby wondered why he was dumping hot cider in a trash can.

8

Road Animals: Linda, Bottom Line, Sedalia, Wyman, Russell

We had become road animals, often fulfilling an old saying I made up: the only musician that complains more than one not working, is one who is working. As radio hits and the *Circle* album generated a lot of shows for the band in the early 1970s, we'd hit as many as two hundred cities a year. A hundred daily road decisions on top of new kid arrivals pretty much ensured I'd have no interest in alcohol or drugs; it was hard enough just to think straight. I was faced with the challenge of road managing it all while raising a family in the mountains outside of Denver.

It was a beautiful birth. Andrew arrived quietly and looking happy. I was ecstatic, his mother was exhausted, and I had to go to work. He was considerate to arrive early enough in the day for me to make a solo show that night at Marvelous Marv's in Denver, where I opened solo for the cool Martin Mull. Since we didn't have health insurance, I could now pay for his birth. After the show, it was up the mountain to our home in Evergreen and to the other two kids, to tell them they had a new brother who I would pick up at the baby store with their mom.

Animals loved Andrew. If a dog came into a room with twelve people in it, it would immediately run up to shy Andrew, with its tail wagging. Naturally kind and teddy-bear loveable, by twelve years old

Andrew could quiet a crying baby in seconds. He showed an immense artistic talent for drawing that would, in later years, be exhibited in his chef abilities. His two wonderful sons, Trey and Nile, are a pride and joy to the family, and show all the positive effects of their dad's good influence.

Because I would also set up and do NGDB interviews (an average of two per show), and usually worked at home doing that, my youngsters spent a lot of time in their daddy's home office, playing on the floor and watching me work. There was never enough time at home, and I cherished it all. It was around this time that my daughter Noel drew a picture of her daddy. I was on roller skates with a phone in one hand and a suitcase in the other. I worried about how much I worked, but I had to; our NGDB income was never enough if we wanted our kids to eat well and occasionally have new shoes.

I loved home, but the pull of the unknown always got me back on the road. I felt privileged to be doing what countless others wished they could do. I knew there would be stories to tell—like meeting Paul McCartney or a Rolling Stone or a groupie—and telling those stories gave me the same thrill that I felt while doing magic tricks when I was younger. It was as much fun as performing on stage.

It was always fun and interesting to watch friends and acquaintances from the past grow as they went through their various stages of success and life. Linda Ronstadt and I crossed paths many times after the benefits, but one concert from 1974, at the United States Military Academy at West Point, stands out. I wandered into her dressing room to say "hey" and talk about that night's show. We had seen each other a couple years earlier and she started talking easily, as if picking up where we left off earlier in the day.

"John, I'm about to turn thirty and I forgot to learn to play the guitar," she pouted, as she pondered herself in the mirror, and sat somewhat slump shouldered. "Fat, getting fatter, new zits—I thought that'd stop by now," she moaned dejectedly as she reflected on her reflection. She was not fat. Still looking sexy, and skinny as a rail, Linda seemed unchanged from the early Troubadour days. She never seemed to be taken nor shaken by her success.

I had a proposal for Linda. Though we were headlining, I asked if it was OK with her for the Dirt Band to go on first instead of closing. I did not want to follow a beautiful woman onto a stage in front of the three thousand guys who hadn't seen a woman in months, especially one begging, "When will I be loved?" and asking if they would still love her tomorrow. She agreed to close. The band actually applauded my decision, and that felt good. We did fine. Of course, she killed.

Another time, around 1974, somewhere in the Iowa boondocks, as all of us waited for showtime, Jeff answered the hotel phone, looked at me in amazement, and said, "It's for *you*. It's Leon Russell." I hadn't talked with now mega–rock star Leon for a couple of years. He was calling to see if I could do a session with him, for a friend of his, the next week in L.A.

While waiting for his British friend, whose name I didn't recognize, to come to the phone, I covered the receiver and asked Jeff if he knew who Bill Wyman was. He said, "Yeah, he's the Stones' bass player. Why?"

"Oh, nuthin'," I said. Wyman came on the phone as I looked away and said loudly, "Hi, Bill!" The chat went great. After some talk about music and his Nashville influences, the date was set. I signed off with, "Sure Bill, sounds great. Looking forward to cutting some tracks with you." I wanted to impress my bandmates, but more so, I wanted to feel some shared group pride that one of us was doing something unusual. This was one of many examples of how, except for Ibby's supportive comments, the other guys—Jeff and Fadden—never had much to say about anything I did on my own.

I walked into a Santa Monica studio two days later, nervous as a cat in a dog pound. This was as close as ever I had been to the Beatles, and Bill Wyman wasn't even a Beatle. Before introducing Wyman,

Leon confided that he was "really glad" I could make it. "I haven't been around big stars like this much, and feelin' alone," he said. "And, I've already played my three licks." He introduced me, saying, "John here is the best banjo picker I know. Get it out, John, and pick a tune for Bill. Start with that classical one I like."

That only ratcheted up my nervousness. Now I'd have to oblige by playing the hardest piece I knew, in what could have easily turned into a repeat of that *Laugh-In* audition. Fortunately, it wasn't a tryout, and after "Opus 36" everyone in the control room applauded enthusiastically. Then, after ripping a bit of "Fireball Mail," we headed in to record. Wyman was a cordial host and spent a great deal of time talking about music and even about the Rolling Stones' earlier days. I got to play his famous bass (he was proud of the fact that it was his first one, and that he had paid fifteen pounds for it).

My mom wanted to hear this album later, but some of the songs weren't for moms. "One is called 'Pussy,'" I told her, "and it's not about his cat." Wyman's album, *Monkey Grip*, was his first solo effort, and it was destined for nice reviews and obscurity. But it was a gas, gas, gas to meet and record with him.

After the session, Leon needed to get to an Arlo Guthrie session at Warner Bros. Records' Burbank studio and he asked if I could give him a lift. Although he had commented earlier about not being comfortable hanging out with big stars, he was headlining the sold-out Forum in L.A. later that night. There would be fifteen thousand people waiting for him to get up on his tightrope. But, this was just the way he always was: an easygoing, Southern gentleman needing a lift, with no limo and no hard plans.

Before hitting the Warner Bros. studio, I wanted to shock some relatives with a visit. The adults in my Mormon wife's family never really accepted me because of my long hair—until money showed up. Then they just explained it away with, "Oh, it's part of your business." Like most Mormons I have met, they were only impressed when someone with long hair was raking it in. I heard a lot of "Well, you're in the music business," as if being in the music business guaranteed fame and fortune. With rock 'n' roll royalty in tow, I called ahead to make a surprise stop at Kae's sister-in-law's house where she had stayed in 1969, next door to where Don Henley lived on Aqua Vista.

I walked in and introduced Leon—a trademark icon of hippie-dom with hair flowing down to his waist, dressed to the teeth for his sold-out Forum appearance—and was greeted by the gaping open mouths of her teenage kids.

"Hi, guys. This is my friend, Leon. He's a musician and has a job in town tonight. We're on the way to a friend's and wondered if I we could get some lemonade. It's a hot day." They all knew who this headliner was, as he was all over the radio and in the papers at this peak in his career. The kids loved it, and we headed on after chatting and after he cordially signed a few things for them.

Arlo was pissed off that afternoon, ranting about John Denver's changes to the lyrics of Steve Goodman's "City of New Orleans." John altered Steve's phrase "old black men" to "old grey men," purportedly because it allowed him to claim cowriter credit or because he thought it would get more airplay. Arlo was riled, but it never came to anything. Arlo's version became the giant hit, and Denver's didn't get much attention. I recorded Arlo's ranting; gotta find that tape.

It's always great to see Arlo. He had come to L.A. to be a troubadour at the Troubadour, and left town triumphantly after taking the club's absolutely most beautiful, most sought after, golden-haired hippie waitress with him—all the way back to Massachusetts to make kids. I'd never had the nerve to ask her out. About thirty years later, Jackie, then Arlo's wife, told me she'd had a huge crush on me in the '60s before he swooped her away. I wouldn't have known what to do about it then.

Some stars were just like regular people, but some thought they were the brightest in the universe. It was at a Hollywood party for our record company president—the well-named Artie Mogull—that I took the opportunity to not meet Helen Reddy. In need of some free event food and a chance to get some face time with members of the Hollywood press, I got in line for some dinner right behind her drug-addict manager. He liked to let the world know he was the manager of a "big star," both with his attitude and his demands for the star. He was also her husband. He was scanning the room, and I ventured forth a "hello," to which he harrumphed a standoffish acknowledgment.

With a look of feigned excitement, I said "My name's John. What's yours?"

"Jeff Wald," he coldly responded, not looking at me.

I said, "Nice to meet you! What do you do?"

Drier than the Hollywood Hills, he firmly said, "I manage Helen Reddy."

"What does she do?"

"She's the singer," he said, nodding toward her across the room.

"Oh. Good luck with that."

Her "I Am Woman" was a huge hit that was followed by others, though it was known industry wide that her song was not as huge as her ego. With success, so many became drug addicts or alcoholics, but as I'd picked to not do that stuff, I got my free food and left.

On the road, pickers would sit in with us whenever I invited them. Jeff and Ibby invited many, too, and I think we set the record one night for the highest number of people on stage jamming at the Bottom Line club in Manhattan. There were seventeen people on stage, including Linda. This is where we first did "Hey, Good Lookin'" together. Also jumping up that night were Bonnie Raitt, David Bromberg, John Hartford, Vassar Clements, and others, all hammering out "Will the Circle Be Unbroken" just one more time.

We did two sets that night, and, at first, Jimmy McCulloch from McCartney's Wings declined my invitation to sit in. He didn't know us. But after he watched the first set, and saw the audience go nuts, he asked if there was "still room for one more." Shorter than Jeff, he came out during the second set and stood like a small statue, practically motionless, just backing up a few songs. Then, when I pointed at him for his solo, he jumped to center stage, complete with all the rock 'n' roll stage moves and, like Paul Simon says in his song, "He blew that room away." I called home later that night from the club to tell everyone how much I missed them, but I'm not sure I believed myself, and given the excitement they must have heard in my voice, they may not have either. But I really did miss them when I got to my room.

Although we played various well-known clubs around New York City, out in the docks of boon it was everything from Cowtown to colleges to fairs to Sedalia, Missouri.

A lot of us missed Woodstock, including some who were there. It has been said that if all those who say they were there *had* been there, it would have been five million people. The premise of the 1974, three-day Sedalia concert was to recapture Woodstock's legendary vibe. The early buzz was that forty thousand people were expected; it would be a great time on the racetrack, like we'd all heard Woodstock was. Only this time there was money in it for all. Then it grew.

A week before the show, fifty thousand tickets had already been bought, and more tickets were selling faster than expected. Then we found out people were already showing up before the first day even started. By midweek, over one hundred thousand tickets were sold, half of the ticket buyers were there, and already there was nowhere to park in the town. So they parked everywhere; VWs with hippie signage, pickups, buses, campers—anything that would classify as a rolling party showed up.

Then, on the first show day, another twenty-five thousand to fifty thousand people showed up, in addition to those who had already bought their tickets. To top it all off, McDonalds had to close that first day because it ran out of food. This closing even shook up the hippies, like how if the navy ran out of sailors it would upset an admiral. The very basis of one's existence—food—was compromised, and it made one subliminally uneasy about the rest of the day. (Remember, this was when people didn't complain about McDonalds, but felt lucky to find one. You know, as they say, "Back in the day . . .")

It was *hot*, but word got out that the party was on. They came, and they kept coming. On Saturday, our show day, the official count of 184,000 people was a shock to all. (Some later said it was more like 240,000.)

Street traffic made it impossible to drive to the stage. It became mandatory to take a chopper to the stage if you wanted to get to work. Even the politically protesting musician hippies started to appreciate and accept the Vietnam chopper pilot vets in a way they'd never imagined. The only way to rock 'n' roll was to fly in low and fast, while getting ready to strafe the people with eighth notes. Like a *MASH* run, bands picked up at the hotel were ferried to the backstage landing spot for R & R, then the band that just finished would be taken back to the hotel for a different R & R, and S and D. Let's just say Frank showed up from Aspen. When we played, the *good* news was that the Hells Angels had taken over backstage security. That was the good news, but they were doing a fine job.

And it was *hot.*

We were preceded by guitar great Leo Kottke. When he finished, we were to set up while the Ozark Mountain Daredevils played on the other half of the stage. I arrived early to see Kottke, well before he went on, and decided to go out and be "with the people." I wanted to see what it was like in the middle of 184,000 people who, from the stage, looked like a field of basketballs with long hair. I swam through the crowd to the sound mix scaffolding and surveyed the sea of hot hair, all crammed onto the dusty fairgrounds racetrack, as Kottke started playing. (Leo had covered his guitars with towels. I thought that must help the sound on this huge stage. Or maybe he was sweating too much?)

Wolfman Jack, America's DJ of that time, was introducing the acts. We had known Jack for a while, and appeared on his TV show (*Midnight Special*) many times, and I wanted to see him from the audience. Well, from the sound mix position he was about one inch tall, and that basso saw-blade voice of his sounded like it was coming from someone's car speakers across the field. The sound was set up for fifty thousand or so people, but there were now three-and-a-half times that many. But, it was OK once the bands kicked in.

As the NGDB had Top Twenty hits ("Mr. Bojangles," "House at Pooh Corner," and "Some of Shelly's Blues") and the *Circle* album had recently been released, we were anxious to do our set. This was one place, Missouri, where we knew we could hold our own up against the others like REO, Skynyrd, the Tucker boys, and the Eagles. I headed back to get my stuff set up and felt like I was preparing to get on the *Titanic.* It was an "edgy" feeling of knowing there were simply too many fish in the bowl, and we were getting ready to throw out a few crumbs.

We started off with "Shelly's Blues," a banjo-led song, and being the first banjo on this hot stage in the heart of the baking Ozarks helped get some new heat from this sweltering audience. Our music was hot all the way through, and this was truly one of our best shows of that year. Did I say it was hot? So was the weather.

It was reportedly 105 degrees onstage—with the air moving. Once we added the reflected heat from all the metal light trusses, the road cases, the equipment, and the plywood stage, it made it feel like we were in a giant chicken rotisserie at about 120 degrees.

For the third song, Michael Murphey's "Cosmic Cowboy," I was to play my lap steel guitar. I vividly remember picking up the sun-drenched, metal slide bar and dropping it as fast as I could—it was about 140 degrees. I poured water on it to cool it down enough to hold, then made the mistake of putting my lap steel guitar on my lap and touching the strings. *That* was even hotter! It had been absorbing the sun and, well, the song was going to start so I took a bottle of water and dumped it on it, and was glad it still worked. I understood Kottke's towels now.

The cosmic longhairs' anthem brought the biggest hoot we had ever heard (the lyric: "I just want to ride, and rope, and hoooo-t"), right on cue. Forty-five minutes later, after closing with "Battle of New Orleans," we had won the battle to stay alive, and left to a standing ovation from the 184,000 people. (It's a good reality check for the ego to keep in mind that they were standing all day long, though. It wasn't possible to sit down in that crowd.) I think the cumulative weight the band lost in our hour was about twenty-eight pounds. We left a couple of choppers later; we had to catch REO first. They were great. When the Marshall Tucker Band showed up, Toy Caldwell (their lead guitarist) tried to talk me into doing a line of coke with him as he always did, but I turned it down, as I always did. But, I still sat in with them.

Overall, reflecting back over the NGDB's years on the road, Sedalia was one of the top ten shows for us. Maybe it had something to do with the previous time we played the same fairgrounds (1972), when we opened for the Jackson 5. This Sedalia show was, in spite of heated adjectives above, a lot cooler.

Months after Sedalia, there was the all-important (at least to the work-obsessed) trip from Aspen to Denver on the morning of New Year's Day. I had accepted a job to produce an album for a Japanese singing star of that time named Mike Maki. Ten days in Japan would earn me much needed big dollars, with all expenses paid, but they had to have me start January 2. This meant that immediately after the Aspen Inn New Year's Eve show, I had to pack up my wife and three kids, drop the kids at the house, and then have Kae drop me at the airport for my flight to Tokyo. At one in the morning, we drove away from Aspen and headed for home, which was five snowy hours away, and my plane was leaving at nine. I always reveled in the excitement of it all, but I overlooked the stress that it put on everyone. This frantic trip to the airport, before sunup, to fly to the land of the rising sun, was no exception.

Kae always supported me in these pursuits, which I appreciated more as time went on. Still, I wish she would have spoken up a few times and said, "Couldn't you work it in later?" Although, I probably still would have gone. I had to do something new.

So, on the first of January, 1975, I changed planes in San Francisco and found myself on a 747 to Tokyo with three passengers in coach and only me in first class. As a test, I dropped a napkin. Five stewardesses rushed over and practically fought over the right to pick it up. I jogged the length of my seemingly private charter and felt like a lonely king with a flying concubine that couldn't be touched. What a great day and way to travel! What a long trip! What a shame not to have waited another day.

The plot thickens. On a previous NGDB trip to Japan about a year before, I had become friends with a beautiful, hot, Japanese woman named Mako. When I finally got her to my room after several nights of hanging out, I chickened out—or came to my senses. I had the lust up to cheat, but, after a fumbling, stumbling encounter, thought better of it. Anyway, I passed up the opportunity, with guilt for a deed not done but already too hard to deal with. I said to Mako, "Let's just stay here a few more minutes, and then go to the lobby bar and hang out. Everyone will think we've been doing it anyway, so what's the point? I'd rather not worry about feeling guilty." We hung out together a lot on that first trip and wondered if we would see each other again. Now, a year later, as I headed west into the dark toward the mysterious east, I wondered if she was again in my future. I forgot about that fantasy and fell fast asleep, heading to the land of the rising sun at forty-two thousand feet.

The work in Tokyo was intense: arranging, rehearsing, recording, and mixing, all to be completed in nine days. I learned enough Japanese to get by in the studio, but on one mix day I asked the engineer, "Can you make the bass more 'round'?" It took fifteen laughing minutes to get that point across, as it could not be translated.

After six intense fourteen-hour days in the studio, Mako showed up at the Tokyo Hilton to say hello over my bowl of popping Rice Krispies. We talked and arranged a fantasy night for me to occur the following day, when I'd be off. She had a "traditional" friend (one who liked to dress in a kimono) and a foxy "white" friend from California who hated "white" boys, and was only interested in Japanese men. We set a dinner date for the next evening, and planned a little performance of our own to go with it.

Boy, did eyes light up when we strolled into places for a table—a hot chick on each arm of a tall, long-haired bearded stranger in a white suit, and a geisha (apparently), who was respectfully following ten feet behind with head bowed! In a booth at Biblo's Disco, with all three laying around me, we spent the evening laughing uncontrollably as we tried to translate jokes, simply enjoying our charade. My own concubine!

I was the high-roller that rainy night, a hot guy flaunting his girls while a lot of pissed-off Marines wondered, "Who is that long-haired hippie guy? Look those chicks!" I felt like Rod Stewart with a Jagger entourage.

The two hot ones would each feign struggling for my attention, as the one in the kimono would only get close after we sat down. Then she would fix the tea or arrange the drinks, and I'd pat her on her big bow on the back of the kimono, all for the benefit of our charade.

In the various cabs between bar stops, the girls would talk loudly about the steamy plans for later that night for the eavesdropping driver, so we could judge which cabbie had the biggest eyes of surprise.

They dropped me off at my hotel around five in the morning, after about seven hours of laughing and disco hopping. I was tail-wagging happy and said sayonara in the lobby, with none of the fantasy plans happening in reality. The next morning, it was back to the long, grueling studio days until we finished the record and I headed home.

Maybe you had to be there. It isn't one of those stories that's easy to communicate, and few would believe me anyway. My kids have never heard about it, unless they read this book. But, I did have a great night one hot, rainy night in Tokyo, and came away with no regrets.

9

The Good, the Bad, and the Drugly

We used the Kansas City airport almost as often as Denver's as we crisscrossed America's heartland. We passed through there on our way to a Missouri show that would turn out to truly be one for the books, so here it is.

Usually, promoters would send contracts back to us with a 50 percent deposit, forty-five days prior to the show, with the balance to be paid on the day we performed. This time, the deposit never arrived, and there was no money to pick up when I got there. There we were, in the middle of another muddy field, in the middle of not getting paid at Datolla's Delicatessen and Farm. This promoter was practically a caricature of the Ozark hillbilly and I wanted Lance Smith, our agent, to be present. Lance booked this show—the opposite of the apex of gigs—way below the curve.

I sensed the promoter's flakiness on the phone while talking with him the night before, and I'd called Lance so he could get there in time from Denver. I needed backup. We were scheduled to go on about eight that night, but by five o'clock I hadn't gotten paid, as was required by our contract. I had already decided we'd play without it: the people were there, we were there, the PA was set up, and there was nothing else to do in this pre-cable era. If the hotel had a book called *What to Do in the Area*, it would have read, "You're doing it."

The people were there (some die-hards anyway, called Dirtheads), and had come to see us with the Earl Scruggs Revue and a few other acts in the heat and humidity one could only find in Missouri, or maybe Vietnam. This region was, after all, where most of the training for Vietnam had gone on. This was fitting, since we were just a few miles from a Marine training camp, although thousands of miles from their sweltering battleground.

Datolla's Delicatessen festival site smelled like a farm in the sticks, since it was a pasture on the edge of the Ozarks. Lance arrived around six that night, ready to earn his 10 percent. We went to the promoter's "office" and Lance demanded, "Gimme my band's money, all of it—now!"

The promoter didn't offer much in the way of a reply, saying, "Hain't got no money. Not enough people. They thought it'd rain." (This is one of the standard excuses promoters offer, along with "everyone is out of town" and "they thought it would be too hot.") A cute thirteen-year-old girl was sitting on a filing cabinet in shorts, watching the men argue.

Lance knew the promoter had taken in enough money to pay us, and so he pressed on. He'd come all the way from Denver to prove his worth and he didn't want to lose our dough, his integrity, nor his commission. It was obvious that Lance would not give up, and the guy would not give in. It was not in Lance's duck-hunter nature to call off the hunt, but he hadn't resorted to threatening violence—yet. What we didn't expect was the promoter's counteroffer: He stepped back so he could give a grandiose (a word he probably didn't know) sweeping motion with his arm, and pointed at the perky young girl he professed to be his daughter.

"Take her. She's all yours. I gar-an-damn-tee you'll have more fun with her than ya could with the money anyway. She's yurs. Take her home 'n' keep her a few days. You'll have a good time with her. I have."

Lance did not appreciate this offer to participate in the trade with the guy's daughter. Doing a slow burn, he stood up to his full six-foot-four height, with a few extra inches from his boot heels. He picked up the shorter Datolla by his shirt collar and lifted him above his own bulging eye level, as Datolla's feet dangled. Lance calmly screamed through thin lips into the promoter's face: "Give me my band's fucking money you bastard, or I'll kill you! Right here!"

Summertime . . . livin' in Missouri . . . veins a poppin' . . . sweat runnin' free . . .

Not sure if it was showbiz or the corndogs from earlier that were making me sick, I left to the sound of paper being counted and headed to work.

Twenty minutes later, from my vantage point on the humid stage, I saw Lance walking toward the stage through the steamy, mud-crusted throngs that made up the audience. He sported a Cheshire-cat grin and the biggest bulge in his pants that any man's woman could ask for. It wasn't because of the daughter. He had proven his clout, and gotten the money.

We were starting another frenzied set and all was good in the land. It was a pivotal time; we were making do-re-mi doing what we wanted, as were so many others we knew, many of whom were on their way to stardom and would pass us by. Around this period, those Eagles were catching up to Loggins and Messina; their jet trails were crossing. That was fine. Jimmy Buffett's paradise cheeseburger had not cooked yet, but we were destined to cross his bus's path.

There was something new about the audiences then, too. Veterans returning from Vietnam were starting to show up at the shows. They tended to keep a low profile, but their short hair often gave them away (sometimes they wore longhair wigs). It seemed like most Americans couldn't figure out how to treat these guys. People weren't able to truly reach out to these vets yet, to befriend them and accept them; hopefully by now they have been finally welcomed home, although at this writing, I don't believe that has been done properly and officially, yet. Many have told me over the years that "Mr. Bojangles" reminded them of a good part of America, and that it made them think of home when they heard it long ago in that faraway hell, or that it made them feel comforted once they got back. I understood Aspen's crazy skier Duane better after a few years of talking with vets. They went through hell while I played the banjo.

The interest in drugs, and lack of interest in new music, pissed me off. The "high" shows were usually OK, but between leaving A to get to B, there was not much R & R, and a lot of C. By the mid-1970s, it got boring sometimes—not the audiences nor the shows, but the band. There was little new music, but there were plenty of drug-influenced problems. For me, logistics—looking at the map of America and figuring how we could get from A to B and net enough money—became the most rewarding challenge. Bill had gotten further into managing Steve Martin and the film business, so early on the job of approving concert dates fell directly to me. I was good at it; he usually asked me if we could get somewhere, anyway.

One overcast Denver day, I wanted to test my judgment and told our agent Lance Smith to confirm a few widely scattered shows. The infrastructure seemed built for rock 'n' roll touring: airports were everywhere with adjacent car and truck rental places, and hotels. Once we knocked off twelve cities in thirteen days. I approved a week of what could be called "extreme touring," even now. The five consecutive shows were in New York's Central Park; Grand Junction, Colorado; Anchorage; Phoenix; and Aspen. We spent more than forty-four hours in the air that week, yet made it early to all the gigs. Unaware that I was the culprit, the band wanted to kill Lance—until our paychecks arrived. There was a lot of net, as most nights we were in the "air hotels" at thirty-five thousand feet.

On that first visit to Seward's Folly, I found the last frontier to be noticeably spirited. Anchorage wears out most people from "below" with its pace. Especially during "daytime," when after being cooped up all winter it seems like the winter zombies are out everywhere! People play golf from 7:00 AM to 1:00 AM.

Although we were in Alaska only nine hours the first time, it has been a part of my life ever since. On that first visit, we flew in at 2:00 PM, played at 7:00 PM, and left at 11:00 PM—and made it to Phoenix by noon!

One day before cockcrow, in 1975, our blank stares were packed into a station wagon as we headed to the Kansas City airport from the Manhattan (Kansas) Holiday Inn. No one really wanted to travel the ninety-four minutes to the airport. All half asleep at five in the morning, nobody in the car had any thoughts worth sharing. Our show had ended six hours earlier at K-State and had gone great, but now, as always, I had to get us to the next gig just three hours after getting to bed. I started to pull out of the parking lot.

Suddenly, the normally quiet Les sprang to life, shouting, "Pull over! Pull the car over! Let me out! Let me out! Pull over. STOP THE CAR!"

Not even out of the parking lot yet, and thinking he'd gone nuts, I did what I was told. Les jumped out and started running. I rolled along slowly, in case he just kept running, thinking we'd be better off without his exuberance breaking the predawn calm. But wait! He started climbing the Holiday Inn sign like Spiderman, up to where the letters announced "Welcome, LEVIS." His intensity made us sleepily say our first words of the day in unison, "What's . . . he . . . going to . . . do?" We waited. He maniacally moved letters around on the sign, like the Mad Hatter arranging clean cups. After a couple quick minutes and quick moves, he climbed back down while laughing, got in the car, and we headed on.

We laughed over the next couple of years every time we thought about the small-town Holiday Inn with the sign that morning announcing "Welcome, ELVIS." I'm still laughing, every time I think of it. That really cracked me up.

A couple of side notes:

Steve Martin, who hadn't quite "made it" yet, opened the show for us. Fadden thought it would be funny to put honey on the oranges that Steve was going to juggle. It ruined the end of Steve's great set. It wasn't funny, and it was a stupid thing to do. It would be the only time I would ever see Steve really pissed off.

Philip Anschutz, a student in the audience, would later become the sixth-richest man in America and start Anschutz Entertainment Group (AEG), which would become one of America's major concert/event producers. He told me two decades later the Dirt Band was a huge influence on his getting into show business.

———————

Our crowds varied in size in 1975. We had great crowds in Atlanta, Kansas, and Colorado, and the band had achieved some regional successes on the coasts. Although our home turf of California was the most difficult area to draw, we set the record for attendance at the New Mexico State Fair that year with about twelve thousand people, but followed up the next day on an El Paso baseball diamond with about three hundred people in the not-so-grand stands. Because my mom's first question was always, "How are the crowds?" I called her after Albuquerque, but not El Paso.

As Dickens kind of said, it was the best at times, and it was the worst at times. Some said they were crazy times, but we just did what our job appeared to be: live out other people's fantasies on the road without any, or very few, rules. Mostly, the rules were something like this:

Get on the bus and eat.

Get off the bus and eat.

Get on the bus.

Get off the bus and do the show.

Repeat Numbers 1 through 4.

By some measures, it did get a little oblique. But as the viewpoint of normal got more skewed, it's difficult to judge what you look in on when you are already . . . in. It was normal to not be normal, a justified condition of the times. Along the road that would lead to "Little Rock Connie," I sometimes reached a point of boredom in this traveling pharmacy just before the point of exhaustion, between steps 1–3.

After that El Paso show I was bored (in those days before cable), so around midnight I said to promoter, Steve Part, "Let's go get Gary laid in Mexico." Since we were hungry, too, we woke Gary, who was now our road manager, and asked him if he wanted to get laid while we ate, to which he sleepily agreed. Not having the nerve, nor able to admit to a fantasy of a hooker of my own, I found this a rather noble, safer quest. I was an agent for tush, with no commission necessary. Being a band on a run, we crossed into Mexico at about one in the morning. The promoter and I scanned the market places and the market, settling on an establishment that seemed to smell OK and maybe had washed its dishes that week, so we could get a bite while Gary was served.

Calling up my best Jack Nicholson impression, I found the honcha in charge of the stable and was pointed the right way. I negotiated with the girl's "agent" in this fine eatery, and convinced her our Juan would be quick, and thereby qualified for a ten-peso discount. Having paid the equivalent of fifteen dollars, he headed to the backroom service quarters for her services, but came back not even two minutes later, laughing so hard he could hardly breathe.

We queried, "What? Already?" He stammered an answer out through the laughter, "I need . . . a dollar . . . for . . . the . . . Pecker Checker!" A customer was required to lay his "tool" on the table in front of a nice, gray-haired *abuela vieja* in a white nurse uniform, complete with cap, so she could roll it around on a white cloth for examination. We gave him the dollar. Under her harsh interrogation light, she asked the owner where it had been, to judge from her ninety years of experience if it had fared safely on previous journeys. They both passed the test, and his package went for an adventure that lasted another whole fifteen minutes, while the promoter and I ate between laughs. Gary came out, had a cigarette, and regaled us with his tale of adventure.

As he headed for bed back in the States, our bleary-eyed, coke-head road manager, burned out from too many years on the road, asked, "Was it good for me, too?" We told him yes, and said goodnight with the final parting word we often used after a night on the road: "Next?"

I'm little bit ashamed I talked her down. After all, he was a *roadie*, and should have cost more. Cable TV cut down on this type of night out more than the market anticipated. You'll still pay, but you don't have to leave your room.

The many times I crossed paths with the Southern, good ol' boys of the Marshall Tucker Band, Toy Caldwell (who played all his lead guitar with his big thumbnail) would come by my dressing room to chat and hear my banjo, and usually to ask me to sit in. They were all heavily into coke, and even did lines off the guitar amps during a show. With their ears deadened to the pain of high volume, they'd turn it up even more, to eleven, I am sure.

They liked my banjo and mandolin music, and they rocked; I felt honored to be living the dream of being in a heavy, loud rock band. Their stage vibrated with their volume, making me feel like one of those little players vibrating across the field in a kid's electric football game. Toy invited me to come play on their 1976 *Long Hard Ride* album, which was a great compliment. My constant practice was actually leading somewhere new.

Toy picked me up at the Macon airport for the session, and right after saying hello he asked, "Hey John, you want a toot?" As I again turned him down, he put that five-inch pill bottle full of coke back in his pocket—for a while. It must have been worth $5,000. At the studio, I also reconnected with the dapper and even-tempered Paul Hornsby, who was the keyboardist from the early Hour Glass days and had also lived in the Dirt House when the Allmans first came to L.A.

We got to work. It felt great to be in Macon recording for Capricorn Records. They were paying well, asking for what I thought would work on various songs, and letting me play what I wanted. Only one cut led to trouble—the title instrumental song, "Long Hard Ride." I never feel like a great player, but am confident that I am good enough to cut the mustard, but this was too much mustard. I always play best on the first or second take, and inevitably start to go downhill after that. I was thirty minutes on the downhill side, not able to lock with the drums and struggling to get through the solo. With its naturally percussive sound, the banjo has to be in perfect sync with a drummer using sticks in order to sound right. The sounds blend better when a drummer uses brushes.

He was using sticks, and I was sounding worse with each take. The bass player came out and offered, "John, me an' the drummer, we been playin' together since early high school. He speeds up and slows down on certain licks. You know, rushes and drags. I know right where he does it. I can sit here an' show you, cueing right before the speed-ups and draggin' if y'all like." I was relieved it wasn't just me, and once he conducted, we finished on the next take. The album would win a Grammy.

Though I never did coke, one time in New Jersey I went to their dressing room and asked Toy for a couple of lines. Two days earlier, an abscessed tooth had started to hurt, and by this time I couldn't eat. It was killing me, making it hard to even think, but the show would go on, with or without pain. "Well! Finally goin' ta join th' boys in th' fun! All right!" he said as he pointed at the powder, which was already lined out. I put my wetted finger on a line, and put that powder on my gums where the most pain was and—it started to go away! I put more on, then on the other side of the tooth, then on the other side of my mouth, just in case, and then on my lower jaw. My head felt like a block of wood, and with no pain I had a steak. After the show, one more dab on each side seemed like a good idea, but that was the end of it for me. Eighteen years later, after too many lines, it was the end of it all for Toy.

———————

Now I was just over thirty years old—younger society was telling me I could no longer be trusted. I was up to kid number four, and while

I was thrilled when Jonathan came along, I had to head right out and work more to cover the family expenses. The band career kept building, with the next album, *Symphonion Dream*, under way in Colorado. Linda sang on a couple cuts, and there were some exciting road dates ahead. We were booked in Leon Russell's hometown of Tulsa, at Bob Wills's favorite spot, the historic Cain's Ballroom, which was *the* place to play in Tulsa. Cain's had hosted everyone from Wills to Asleep at the Wheel, to many of the big rock acts of the day.

While collecting our money in the office at Cain's, I asked the club manager how they knew when they'd had a good show. "We count the teeth on the floor when the show's over," he said. It seemed there would be a lot of teeth that night: we were sold out. He saw me noticing a couple of shotguns leaning against the wall, and added, "Yeah, they're loaded, ready to go. No one be messin' with us."

That kind of cracked me up, and I left quickly to see Leon. I'd called Leon and arranged to drop in after the show to record a track in his state-of-the-art basement studio, which was as good as any I'd seen in L.A. Only Les and Ibby came with me.

His Tulsa house was unforgettable, a huge old Southern-style mansion, suitable for the "Master of Space and Time," as Leon called himself. A master he was, and all-knowing, as he proved when I asked to make a phone call. Leon directed me to the visitors' phone: a nice, red, wooden, British phone booth with an actual pay phone inside. Leon knew musicians well, but he never charged us a nickel for the use of his studio.

Around one thirty in the morning, Leon put down a piano and percussion track, and we finished our song, Ibby's "Joshua Come Home." The session's drummer, nicknamed Teddy Jack Eddie, was great. After the sessions, he reverted to his real identity: Gary Busey, with a vaguely Buddy Holly–like persona, well before his breakthrough movie came out. Fadden and Jeff weren't interested, but it was a great night. I do wish they had gone. I couldn't figure out why they didn't, other than they never understood why Leon and I were friends. I ran in to Busey a year later in Austin, and it seemed he had truly become Buddy Holly.

On that night in Tulsa, we cut a great track, made even sweeter by the feeling of being accepted as part of that night's great band. I would cross paths from time to time with the ever-cool Leon, and he would always ask me to sit in on his sets. His songs, voice, and piano are part of American music history, and it felt great to be included. I got the same feeling when I sat in with Willie Nelson. It's still hard to believe that I get to be a part of that.

Later that year my very excited mom called to tell me, "I'm at the Long Beach Arena at Leon Russell's concert. It's sold out; eight thousand people are here." She added, "And you know how smoking bothers me? Well, *everyone* is smoking! And it doesn't bother me at all!" I chose not to explain why. "And, I'm *really* hungry!" I did tell her to stop at Denny's and eat on her way home.

Soon after that, I'd booked a day off in Memphis so the Dirt Band could go see Hoyt Axton with Joan Baez, and to settle a bet with my "bandmates." Drummer Jim Gordon, from my Andy Williams's orchestra days, was in Hoyt's band at the time, and I hoped he would help me win. After Joanie's sound check, I walked over to Gordon and said, "Hey, Jim, long time since Vegas. I was talking to the guys about how you played that great Layla piano solo, and they don't believe you did it. Got a minute to settle a fifty dollar bet? I could use the money."

Although we had not seen each other in several years, he gave me a knowing nod and silent smile, and beckoned for us to follow him to the piano. Without a word, he sat down, looked up at us, raised his hands high over the keys like Liberace, and—as the entire stage crew and cast looked on—dove into one of the 1970s' most beautiful and powerful pieces of music. Finishing to resounding applause, he said he had overdubbed the drums to this iconic song after laying down his piano part. I won the bet, but they never paid up, which had pretty much become the pattern (except for with Ibby, who was always honorable in that regard). And to think that back in Vegas with Andy, Jim was just learning three-finger piano chords.

After Joan Baez and Hoyt, Gordon teamed up with, among others, Delaney and Bonnie, Cocker, Clapton, and somewhere along the line, as bad luck would have it, heroin. That was before he left music—he was removed from the general population when he killed his mother. He is now living in a small room in California. The word was that, while up for parole, he told the board he was anxious to get out as his chocolate pudding was telling him he should now kill his brother. He is still there.

Often, when the schedule did not leave enough time to get home between gigs, I would use Nashville as a place to hang out for a day or two off. I've felt a deep connection to that city since the *Circle* album, and always tried to make the best of my time there. During one visit, I learned that Paul McCartney was in town recording, which was news that was largely kept from the general public. All the pickers had hopes of maybe being called for one of the sessions. I didn't have much hope of that, maybe because of my brother's remark from years before still ringing in my ears: "If the banjo was any good, the Beatles would have used it." Well, to be honest, while I have always maintained that my brother said that, the truth is that I'm the one who said it; this is a reflection of my perpetual insecurity.

Nonetheless, I wanted to meet Paul, so I headed to the studio about eight thirty in the morning, knowing he had a nine o'clock session. Nowadays, sitting in the overcast studio parking lot, waiting for his limo to show would be called stalking. Anticipating an actual Beatle encounter made my heart beat as fast as "Foggy Mountain Breakdown." Paul pulled in at 8:45 AM, having driven himself. He was going to work, after all, and in those days before John Lennon's murder, it was easy to approach him. Walking up to him, I introduced myself, and proudly said I was from the Nitty Gritty Dirt Band.

"Oh yes!" Paul said. "Spencer Davis gave me your album—*Uncle Charlie & His Dog*—a few years ago. A lovely album . . . with the 'Mr. Bojangles' song on it . . . and the bluegrass music was lovely." We chatted long enough to play "Yesterday" three times through, with me offering several opportunities for him to exit gracefully. But Paul just hung out, chatting like two old friends running in to each other after a long time away. He listened, asked questions, and never exhibited that myopic "celebrity eyesight" I would find in so many stars through the years. That one of the biggest stars in the world could convey the feeling that you were possibly a long-lost neighbor is a lesson I've carried with me ever since.

We'd been involved in some benefit concerts for Native Americans, environmental causes, diseases, and other worthy causes. These had mostly been produced by people like Tom Campbell, but I realized that I had learned enough to organize a benefit myself. A big fan, Phil Nash, told me about the need for general diabetes research, as well as the specific need for support in his town of Little Rock, Arkansas. There was a woman named Heather Rhodes who was in particular need whom we could help, while at the same time raising money for their Diabetes Center. It was in that city that we met one of the truly "blue" fixtures of the touring musician's life.

The show sold out after a couple of weeks of promotion, and it brought us a lot of good attention, including one unexpected source. She showed up backstage, an absolutely gorgeous girl in her midtwenties. We never envisioned meeting a groupie like the ones we'd heard about and read about in *Rolling Stone*, especially not at a respectable event like a charity benefit. Her opening introduction was, to say the least, memorable.

"Hi! My name's Connie," she said as she proudly lifted her blouse. "Pretty nice, aren't they?" They were perfect, as was her gorgeous body, but so were the visions of my family at home racing through my mind as I admired her . . . long dark hair. I wasn't about to touch them! "I want to give you the best blow job you've ever had or will ever have," she said.

Nothing had tempted me enough to stray from my happy marriage, but it crossed my mind this time, even more than it had in Japan. I waffled between taking her up on her offer and running away, but Connie eliminated the suspense of pursuit and cut right to the bone. I was startled by her challenging invitation, and admittedly, it felt great that she was coming on to me—until I found out she was coming on to anyone and everyone. Her breasts did feel pre-silicone perfect, but our contact didn't go past that stage. I wasn't up to extending any other greeting.

I offered to find Connie a nice German shepherd, like Sonny Moore's Gretchen, thinking maybe my sarcasm would get me out of the situation. Instead, her eyes streamed with tears, and I apologized for hurting her feelings. It was not my place to judge what "Little Rock Connie" saw as her calling in life. She was bringing a lot of pleasure at no expense, except her own possible humiliation, and she was just trying to get ahead, as it were. It didn't really bother me personally. At least I wasn't pimping for a road manager. There are many ways to be in the world, and Connie had hers. I made up for my comment by setting her up with some of the crew, and a musician, and we developed something almost like an alliance.

That benefit sold out, and Connie later got her jobs done. Everybody was happy. Even though she seemed to embody the Cripple Creek lyric I learned as a teenager—"Girls on Cripple Creek about half grown, jump on a man like a dog on a bone"—we made a truce that night: she wouldn't come on to me (other than showing me her beautiful breasts on occasion), and I would introduce her to some newcomers.

It was difficult, not being secure nor brave enough to say to my wife, "At the benefit, people were really nice. I met this strange girl who really believes in her calling in life. She is like, well, a real pro . . . at least, I'm told she is . . . uh, well she's . . . she says she's a blow job expert . . . or, I'm *told* she is. I've just heard her stories, and we just talked." Somehow, that didn't seem like a good idea and would not have cracked her up.

Later in the year in Eureka Springs, Arkansas, at a mud festival in a forest where NGDB was performing, I ran into Connie again and saw an opportunity to have some backstage fun. "See that guy over there?"

I asked. "His name is Randy Scruggs. Go do your stuff. He's standing right between his parents, Earl and Louise. Lay it on thick."

Connie sashayed over to the unsuspecting Randy. "Oh, Randy. Great to see you again! Are you really randy? How's that big boy doing? Let me do those things you like I'm so good at." She dramatized her come on by running her hand up and down his leg. While rubbing up against him like a cat and tugging on his belt, she chattered away about how she'd be better than the last time, and how he'd never forget it.

Beet-faced, nervous Randy tried to get away from her probing hands, protesting, "I, uh, Momma, Daddy, I don't know this girl. What did you say? You'll do what? Momma, I swear I never met her before." We all remained a safe distance away, watching and cracking up. I could hear the chorus of Randy Newman's "Mamma Told Me Not to Come" in my head.

On one Arkansas trip, our mildly macho, new guitar player spotted Connie backstage and brashly whisper-announced, "Look at that beautiful chick over there. Boy, would I like to . . ."

Knowing he was more bravado than brave, I summoned Connie over and said, "This is our new guitar player, and he'd really like to see your breasts." Before I finished, Connie proudly proceeded to raise her sweater and said, "These?" and placed his hot, horny hand on her perfect pair. "How do these feel to you?"

When I dryly added, "He'd really like to get it on with you, Connie," the guitar player's jaw dropped.

Connie just asked, "After the show? Or is there time before?" He took his place at the head of the line.

Connie had pride. One year, she pouted, "Three Dog Night took me to Roanoke with them. I did thirty-two guys one night, and they had the nerve to send me for KFC chicken after. Now *that* was humiliating! Never again!" She had limits.

Connie had integrity, too. Once, when Little Rock's Barton Coliseum security decided they'd seen enough of her, even though she had every stage pass from any band that had ever played an E chord, they refused her backstage access. She was a woman scorned. The next day in city hall she told a few folks about her history and services rendered to those who came to town. She also shared some very specific personal details of those who had kept her away from backstage. The powers that be shut down concerts for two years. It seems she had a really good memory of various people's identifying peculiarities.

Grand Funk Railroad paid tribute to Connie in their song, "American Band," when they sang:

> Out on the road for forty days
> Last night in Little Rock, put me in a haze
> Sweet, sweet Connie was doin' her act
> She had the whole show and that's a natural fact

Her come-on brought so many comers, Connie once confided in me she was reaching her life goal: "To give more blow jobs than any woman in the history of time." I still declined to take a number in her line, settling for eggs benedict instead. It's said they have something in common with blow jobs: you don't get either at home.

I wondered if Connie's hard-won recognition was something she shared proudly with her mom. I don't think her mom called to ask how the crowds were. To round out her life experience, between concert jobs, she was also a substitute grade-school teacher, carving out a unique professional niche.

Connie showed up at various band and solo shows over the next few years. As AIDS arrived, her business got soft and petered out. She quit "doing" roadies and security personnel and stuck to just musicians. They say some Little Rock politicians knew her too, as another era passed.

Sometime in the late '80s she got her recognition—an article in *Esquire* about her abilities and accomplishments. Her position at the top of her craft has never been challenged. I've never met anyone else like her.

10

The Most per Note
We Ever Made

Atlanta, 1976. The biggest festival since Woodstock!
That's how they were billing the Southeast Bicentennial Bluegrass
festival, anyway. It featured Southern rock bands, hippie country, and
acts ranging from the Earl Scruggs Revue to the Dirt Band. By the
time we landed in Atlanta at 10:00 AM on show day, I'd already heard
rumors that this was a potential big stiff. I told Gary to wait with his
first love, the Ryder truck, at an airport pay phone until he heard from
me, and I raced off in a rental car to the fairgrounds to check things
out—and get the second half of our fee.

From the moment I arrived, it seemed obvious that this promoter
was not going to even make expenses for the food. There were about
seven hundred people, which was maybe a big crowd for a city club, but
picture five hundred revelers at a Mardi Gras parade in New Orleans,
or a thousand folks at a NASCAR race, or twenty-five hundred fans at
the Superbowl, and you get an idea of how empty the hot, dry, Atlanta
Fairgrounds racetrack looked that day.

The promoter stood to lose a bundle, but in this case the agreement
had to be honored. He made plenty of bad moves that made it almost
impossible for the show to succeed, but none of which supported his
not paying us. For starters, his poster did not look right: it was too hard

to read group names. He had not placed radio spots and newspaper ads well, nor soon enough, nor had there been enough of them. He hadn't arranged for any advance media interviews with any of the acts prior to the event, and the NGDB was *hot* that year. Most important, we had given him a summer Saturday, and had to fly in from far away at no small expense. That promoter needed to live up to the contract.

In talking backstage to some other bands, lighting guys, nervous security guys, and finally the sound company, I learned they were all worried about not getting paid. I knew I'd better hurry. I phoned Gary at the Ryder place with specific instructions to come to the fairgrounds ASAP, park the Ryder next to the stage, and then to get out of the truck and slowly light a smoke as if everything were normal and he was totally relaxed. Then I set out to find the promoter before his well ran dry.

The sound guy told me the promoter was meeting soon with some mafiosi who were looking to launder money, which could mean the rest of the cash might be coming. That seemed unlikely to me. He'd already started delivering the sound company $100 cash an hour to keep the PA system on. I hoped logic would be enough to persuade the promoter to pay up, but at the same time, if I was ever going to be a hard-ass, the time was now. I eyeballed the supposed money launderers. I decided they may be criminals but didn't think any physical harm could come to me.

The production office overlooked the fairgrounds from the middle of the horse track, with the stage visible at one end. I introduced myself to the promoter. We made some chitchat and I commented that the bleak crowd looked a little "light."

He responded, "It's not even noon, and people don't get out on a Saturday that quick." Then he went on about how he expected a big walk-up crowd, even though advance sales were less than expected. The promoter threw out some of the usual excuses for a concert that doesn't draw. I listened politely until I sensed it was time to "show me the money."

He started squirming when I told him that if I didn't get the second half of our money we wouldn't set up for the show. We were the main act that night; he knew he needed us. If he didn't pony up the dough and we walked early, so would others. I also knew he wouldn't pay the second half until he knew we were there. With perfect timing, Gary pulled in backstage and parked as instructed, right next to stage right.

"Oh, there's our road man with the equipment truck," I said to the promoter, pointing to Gary's truck. "He'll probably get out and light a cigarette like always." At the smoke signal, we started counting money.

Georgia State Police were starting to show up more on the grounds, looking nervous. The concert was on Georgia state property, with a lot of city employees for crew. They all needed to get their money, and there was none. I went backstage, picked up Gary, and raced off in my rental car to the hotel for lunch, and to let the band know we got paid, but probably would not be playing that night.

I was having lunch with Earl Scruggs when the word came that the show had been shut down, and that everything was locked up inside the fairgrounds by the police—impounded—until the situation of all the unpaid state employees was resolved. Nothing was going to leave there for quite a while, including the equipment of many of the groups. The band had a nice night off, Earl paid for lunch, and we headed out the next day for our next town, as planned. I did call Ryder to let them know where their truck was, and I always wondered how long it took them to get it back.

Gary and I had an easy time checking in the equipment when we left Atlanta, since it was already at the airport. On departure, our flight path took us right over the fairgrounds. I could see the stage, with the Ryder still sitting next to it. It was empty of course. On that phone call, I had told Gary to leave the gear at the airport. I had told the promoter the truth when I said, "Why, there's the equipment *truck* now." I felt good about that for a while. But we all agreed that playing shows was better than leaving without playing, even when we were paid.

It was fun being a problem solver. I sometimes applied that to raising kids, and kept working at making that work. One trick I had to learn early was how to protect my own snacks. Driving with a car full of kids, it was always amazing that no matter how quietly I would open a snack or a drink can, I would invariably hear from the back seat, "Can I have some?" That usually meant I was going to share it all. Divide a small pack of potato chips by six, and be grateful to enjoy your two chips. They always had plenty, but always wanted more. They were kids.

I figured out a trick to keep all my Fig Newtons, which is a cookie that would be more popular if it had a better name. When my daughter Noel was about eight, she heard me opening a package of my favorite cookie and piped up with the inevitable, "Can I have some?"

I handed one to her, commenting, "I'm surprised you like to eat those, considering what they are made from."

"What do you mean, Dad?"

"Look closely at the cookie," I explained, after she took a bite. "People don't talk about it much because they're so good, but it's made from caterpillars . . . crushed up." Looking at the filling, it seemed entirely possible, and to this day she hasn't eaten another one.

I have no doubt that there are things I could have done better, but I loved everything about raising my children, although I regret that I wasn't as well prepared as I might have been. But, who is?

———————

I think there's a rule in country music: if your name is Curly, you either play the steel guitar or drive the bus. We had a Curly for a few trips who did both. Then there was Tennessee Bill, a great name for a bus driver. Aside from the fact that he always kept the bus at eighty-five mph or higher, even on the worst roads, and would never slow down, he was fine. I wasn't.

One bus he called "Old Ready," probably because it always seemed ready to leave the road. When he hit "blue magic"—the high-idle switch—that Eagle bus would fly. High-idle was for when the bus was parked; flick the switch and the engine maintained higher than normal rpms to keep all the systems running. But unlike most buses, Old Ready's high-idle could be engaged while rolling, when passengers are supposed to be standing behind the white line. Dubbed "blue magic" after its little, glowing blue light, it was fun to use *every now and then*, if you held onto something. Tennessee Bill would floor the pedal and keep the hammer down, as they say, then turn on Blue Magic. We could feel the engine revving faster and faster, rpms inching their way higher and higher, way beyond what a normal bus would do.

One night in Virginia in the early 1980s, we were just getting under way after a show. He hadn't yet hit his normal cruising speed when right after midnight our CB crackled with the news that Jimmy Buffett was coming up behind us, southbound on I-95 in his new Silver Eagle. Our friendship dated back to our early days in Aspen when he would sit in with us. He was then still a long way away from "Cheeseburger in Paradise," and not yet the wealthy beach bum/pilot/author/restaurateur he would become. Years earlier, when Jimmy and his harmonica-playing friend opened for NGDB in Hattiesburg, Mississippi, I facetiously said, "Buffett, your harmonica player is so great you should call him 'Fingers!'" They both liked that, and so it was. Fingers Taylor has been stuck with that name to this day.

When we pulled over at a rest stop, Buffett jumped on with us to chat a while as we convoyed to a Roanoke restaurant rendezvous that was about a hundred miles ahead. We hadn't seen that son of a son of a sailor since the Aspen days. As we reminisced about the old days, I thought I knew what was going on in the back of Jeff's and Fadden's minds: This guy had opened for us. Then we opened for him. Now he's playing to five thousand people a night while we're playing to one thousand. I was thinking the same thing. It wasn't jealousy, but an envious feeling maybe. His career was zooming ahead.

Buffett didn't know I had a plan, and after a few miles of talk about buses, the road, and other stuff, I steered the conversation to how fast we could get to Roanoke. His ears perked up. He had a *new* bus. We only had Old Ready.

"You got a nice bus there, Jimmy, but sometimes those new ones aren't as fast as these more roadworthy, older models," I smiled. "You might want to get back on your bus soon, so you won't have to wait for them to catch up with us in Roanoke."

The challenge was made. Buffett countered, "My bus will be there first, waiting. And if it's not, dinner is on me for all of you, even your crew!" We agreed on a truck stop at which to meet, and he got on the CB to tell his driver to make us eat his dust. Tennessee Bill let Buffett's bus get a mile or two ahead. In those first few minutes the tension built, but Jimmy relaxed as he saw what appeared to be an easy victory. The polls may close early in the east, but the race isn't over 'til it's over.

"OK, Bill, hit Blue Magic. We'll be eating free soon!" I yelled.

"What's Blue Magic?" Buffett asked, as Tennessee reached for that high-idle switch. He eyed that friendly blue light and noticed Tennessee taking his foot off the gas pedal. We were at seventy-one mph, and we all felt a little shiver go through the bus frame. Old Ready was like a racehorse waiting in the gate after prancing up and down, champing at the bit. Once the switch was thrown, the power of the light descended down on that old Jimmy 6-71 Detroit Diesel, and we prepared to go to blue light speed.

The needle glided to seventy-three, seventy-four, seventy-five; we were speeding up by one mile per hour about every twenty seconds. About ten minutes into our ascent, we blew past Buffett's bus like it was stalled (at a "safe" 104 mph), and then we hit 109 mph and held out there for around twenty minutes. At this shake-rattle-and-roll speed, even the Virginia hills couldn't slow our soaring Eagle down as we barreled ahead toward our free dinner.

We were well into our reward meals at the truck stop's buffet when Buffett's bus pulled up. Jimmy was already paying our tab. As for Tennessee Bill, to quote an old country saying, "We had to let him go." He drove too fast.

―――――――――――

Food, always a main preoccupation of a bunch of young men on the road for weeks at a time, also helped relieve the boredom of the endless repetitive tasks of road managing: this one needs a window seat, this one needs a room at the end of the hall, that one's wake-up call is thirty minutes before the others, we'll turn in the car at the same airport, we'll turn it in at a different airport, sound check in the afternoon, show at eight o'clock, blah, blah, blah.

As the day-to-day was pretty much the same between stage time (check out/check in/drive/fly/on the bus/off the bus), we sometimes needed to break up that monotony and have some fun. I thought up a good prank, and got everyone to secretly devote a month to a "fatten Jeff program." The plan was that everyone would save part of his meal—fries, pie, toast, muffin, cake, whatever—and pass it over to Jeff, who we knew would gobble it up. Occasionally I'd offer, "Hey, Jeff, can I get you an ice cream?" (I dared not offer sher*bert*.) I even came into his hotel room one night after he went to bed to give him a cheeseburger, claiming that we had bought a bunch and this one was one too many. It was actually the only one, and he ate it in bed at one thirty in the morning, and then went to sleep. Our plan worked. Jeff gained eleven and a half pounds in a month, after which we told him about our scheme. It was laughs all around; we had done something together that was fun. I wished a rehearsal was that easy.

A fast bus can cover a lot of ground, but we didn't always use one. At the same time, having to drive a rental car for six hours and then play a show was exhausting, especially when I was also road managing, checking in and out of hotels, looking after the baggage and equipment, handling the promoters, and everything else. Buddy Holly's tragic plane crash notwithstanding, a charter sometimes seemed the best way to get someplace and maybe also get some sleep. Rather than complain at the time, I took these things as a challenge.

I thought of Steve the Newsman when I had to get us to Fayetteville. I was tired, so I chartered. I should have known it would be an interesting flight day when the six-pack-toting fat pilot said, "Anyone want a beer before we take off?"

After a rambling, crooked takeoff that used *all* the runway, I asked how long it would take to get his old twin-prop museum piece to Fayetteville and was glad to be told it was only an hour and a half. Three hours after takeoff, however, after dodging seventeen thunderheads, we were still an hour away.

"Never seen it like this," was all the pilot would yell back at us, which he did, over and over again as he zigzagged across the Ozarks in his movie-prop vintage DC-3. "Vintage" and "classic" are nice words to apply to cars, but when said about a plane, it just means "old." The lightning was so intense all around us that the last hour was constantly lit up, even inside the plane. We morbidly sang "Will the Circle Be Unbroken" like we were whistling past the graveyard, and hoped for the best. We sat sullenly inside our soon-to-be tomb, channeling Buddy Holly, et al., until the arrival control tower's crackling radio finally came on through the lightning interference: "You are not cleared to land at this time. There is a Frontier plane heading to the runway. Circle the field and wait for clearance."

Even though we would have been happy for him to put it down anywhere, the tower's report brought a little relief. Then our pilot fog-horned back to the tower, "Get that goddamned plane out of the way! I only have five minutes of fuel, an' I'm bringing this bird in raht now!" Four minutes later, our airborne Bubba got his winged pickup on the ground, but by then I'd already decided to rent a car to drive us back. The pilot fueled up, got more beer, and then took off into the storm to head home. I think he made it. Ask me if I care. At least that flight saved us a whole thirty minutes over the drive!

Seeking empathy or some guidance for future travel, I told my brother Bill the story. He took a moment away from managing Steve Martin's career to offer this wise advice: "Don't charter planes." Martin was heating up, and it looked like he was going to break through, even though his early reviews were as questionable as ours. (The *Los Angeles Times* said: "Comedians should be funny.") Steve was killing it, selling out clubs, but Bill was still in search of the record deal. (He soon signed him to Warner Bros. where he would sell seven million albums.) Hoping to increase my solo exposure, I asked his agent, Marty Klein of the Agency for the Performing Arts (APA), if I could open for Steve at San Francisco's Boarding House on his sold-out weekend. Although I would only make about $200 for that week, it was worth it to play one night to a packed audience.

The young Larry Gatlin, who was just starting out, shared my need for exposure and the same booking agent. He and I agreed to share the bill on Tuesday, Wednesday, Thursday, and Sunday; I'd get to open for Steve on Friday and Larry would open on Saturday. Steve sold out four shows that weekend while Larry and I played to crickets and twenty or thirty people on our co-billed weeknights. Our draw was so bad that we took turns headlining (going on last) so the other guy could take the blame for not drawing. We had a great time, though. We both knew better things were ahead—because it had to get better than this!

Steve gave birth to one of his signature bits that week. Before the first show on Friday, he told the light man, "No matter what I say DO NOT change the lights. Don't change them. Leave them up." Steve asked me to be standing right there at the time and then asked me to go to the light booth to make absolutely sure the light man did not change the lights.

The packed house greeted the man with an arrow on his head (one of Steve's early gags, like bunny ears, that were Magic Shop leftovers)— some of them had arrows too—who was helping America out of its Vietnam funk. In the middle of his set, Steve looked toward the light booth at the back of the house and asked, "Say, can you change the lights a little please? A little bluer maybe?" The lights didn't change as Steve went on talking a bit before asking again, "OK, can you change the lights a bit? Not so bright? Bring them down a little?" He paused. "Guess he's not up there." A minute later, he added, "I want the hot dog light and mustard beamer on me now." The crowd chuckled a little, then Steve yelled, "Hey! Are you up there? I am down here doing my job. Where are you? Take the lights down! I need some mood change!" Now he was getting visibly irritated, and still the lights did not change. "I know, I may have said, 'Don't change the lights,' *but I changed my mind.* Change them now, *pleeease!*" Steve's face got red, and blood vessels bulged on his neck.

At this point, the light man was shaking. He turned to me and pleaded, "Should I change them? I think I should change the lights. He seems to have changed his mind. Should I?" I had no clue where Steve was heading with this, but I told the light man emphatically, "Don't touch the faders!"

Steve was now screaming, "So! You think you know more about show business than I do! Well, it's my ass up here! I ask for a simple light change and YOU—" He pointed at the light booth, then paced the stage with veins throbbing and sweat on his brow, looking like he was on the edge of a heart attack. The audience started squirming and fidgeting in their seats, exchanging worried glances with each other, pointing at the lunatic with an arrow in his head, wondering if he was about to explode.

Steve delivers: "SO! IF YOU THINK YOU KNOW MORE THAN I DO ABOUT SHOW BUSINESS, AND DON'T WANT TO DO A *SIMPLE* REQUEST FOR *MY* SHOW BECAUSE *YOU* THINK THE LIGHTS SHOULD NOT CHANGE, AND . . . AND . . ." He paused three long seconds, looking like he was going to climb up the beam of the spotlight and punch the light man out, then yelled, "WELLLLLLL . . . EXCUUUUUSE MEEEEEEeeeeeeeeeeee!" Then, he instantly changed his countenance, adopting a look of serenity like the Dalai Lama, strumming a banjo tune and smiling at everyone like Mr. Rogers. The audience erupted in laughter that continued for two minutes. Some people couldn't breathe because they were seized by uncontrollable, uninhibited laughter, as if they all forgot they were out in public. That really cracked me up.

I've always felt fortunate to have forged lasting friendships in this fickle business. There are a lot of wonderful artists in music and show business; there are many who are great people as well. Ronstadt joined us in a Denver studio a couple years earlier, in the mid-1970s. She'd dropped in to sing a part on "Hey, Good Lookin'" as her star was skyrocketing. Her performance on that *Symphonion Dream* album inspired us all, particularly Jeff and Ibby who never sounded more country. She performed the song later with us on the *Midnight Special* television show, and Wolfman loved it. It was right after that album that Ibby's attitudes became too difficult to deal with—for several reasons, some unknown—and "we had to let him go."

This was just before our historic trip to Russia.

Me as a happy kid at about two years old.
Family archive

Around 1952, I was briefly a cowboy.
Family archive

With my brother, Bill, and pal sister, Maureen, who
I often hid behind, in Shasta County, around 1950.
Geri McEuen, family archive

About eight years old.
Family archive

I didn't like uniforms until they became costumes. I lasted three months, then I moved on.
Geri McEuen, family archive

The first real job, the fun years at The Magic Shop. Steve Martin and I made the same pay: $1.15 an hour. This is my backstage pass to get into The Magic Kingdom.
Personal archive

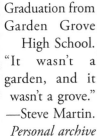

Graduation from Garden Grove High School. "It wasn't a garden, and it wasn't a grove." —Steve Martin. *Personal archive*

Handbill for the first big job for the Willmore City Moonshiners, at the historic Golden Bear in Huntington Beach, 1965. *Personal archive*

My first real band, the Willmore City Moonshiners. Les Thompson on left, me on the right. 1964 in Long Beach. *Personal archive*

Jose Feliciano spent time at my Garden Grove house in 1965, where we played together before going to clubs. *John McEuen*

On the gate of Houdini's burned out mansion in Laurel Canyon, 1966. NGDB's first publicity shot! Left to right: Bruce Kunkel, Jimmie Fadden, John, Les Thompson, Jeff Hanna, Ralph Barr. *John Stewart, from Willaim E. McEuen archive*

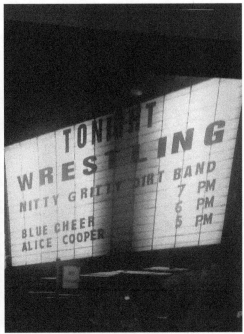

The Jug Band days of 1967. Les on Mandolin, Fadden on tuba, dressing room of So. Cal. Club. *William E. McEuen*

Work night in Santa Barbara in 1967—worst echo ever. There were seventeen distinct echoes of everything. *John McEuen archive*

John, Les, and Ralph Barr at sound check in Circle Star Theater, San Carlos, California, 1968. *William E. McEuen*

Wearing the *Paint Your Wagon* clothes at Hollywood's Troubadour. *William E. McEuen*

Taping the 1969 TV show with the big East Coast radio icon Cousin Brucie, a.k.a. Bruce Morrow, during the *Paint Your Wagon* premiere promotion. *William E. McEuen*

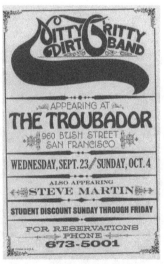

Poster from before Steve broke big, 1973. This is the club Elton John had played in 1970 in the small room while NGDB headlined upstairs. Things changed. *Personal archive*

At the Wheeler Opera House in Aspen v John Denver and Jimmy Buffet sitting around 19 *William McE*

While recording "You Are My Flower" on Circle. From left: John, Norman Blake, Randy Scruggs, Junior Huskey, Earl, Gary Scruggs, Les Thompson. *William E. McEuen*

"Man with voice" is how Roy Acuff referred to himself. From the *Circle* sessions in August, 1971. "Wreck on the Highway": John, Roy, Earl Scruggs, Oswald Kirby are facing camera; Les Thompson with mandolin has his back to camera. *William E. McEuen*

Rehearsing "Nashville Blues" with Earl in studio control room for the *Circle* album. We did it in one take.
William E. McEuen

"Nashville Blues" with Earl. I am wearing the shirt and vest from my *Paint Your Wagon* costume.
William E. McEuen

Listening to playback of "Soldier's Joy." It was one take. I believe I was the first banjo player to record with Earl, an honor I greatly appreciate. *William E. McEuen*

Recording "Soldier's Joy" for Circle. I am playing Uncle Dave Macon's banjo.
William E. McEuen

At the *Circle* sessions with (left to right): Earl Scruggs, John, Vassar Clements, Junior Huskey, Roy Acuff, (engineer) Dino Lappas, Alice McEuen (she did the *Circle* album calligraphy).
William E. McEuen

John, Jimmy Martin, Jeff, and Les (on mandolin) recording "Walkin' Shoes" for the *Circle* album. I had learned how to play from many of his records and never thought I would record with him. We got along great, and he sat in with me several times after that.
Personal archive

NGDB plays Sahara Tahoe Juniper Lounge in 1974, the same week as Elvis. I saw him in the hall twice.
William E. McEuen

Jamming with my banjo mentor Doug Dillard at a 1975 festival in York, Pennsylvania.
Personal archive

I was the greaser. This was before Sha Na Na was widely known. Twelve years later I opened for Sha Na Na at this same hotel in the Sahara main showroom.
William E. McEuen

During "Good Night My Love," at the Sahara Lake Tahoe Juniper Lounge, 1974. Always got encores with that. *William E. McEuen*

At the Boarding House in San Francisco, 1974, shooting a live show that has never been seen.
William E. McEuen

The Boarding House taping with Doug Dillard, John, Ramblin' Jack Elliot, 1974.
William E. McEuen

At the famed Boarding House in San Francisco with Jim Ibbotson, 1974.
William E. McEuen

Playing late in to a 1974 winter night in Aspen with Les Thompson.
William E. McEuen

At San Francisco's Boarding House with Vassar and Steve, the comic, 1974.
William E. McEuen

Festival photo from the "good old daze." Backstage at the 1974 Marin County Bluegrass Festival. This festival happened around the time of the television taping. *Jon Sievert*

With Chip Carter on the first lawn on our way to be the first American band to go to Russia in 1977. *Gary Regester*

In Leningrad visiting the home of a family teaching their child to defect, as they never thought they would get out. They all now live in New York.
Gary Regester

One of five shows to six thousand people each on the Armenian Bike track. Rain did not stop us!
Gary Regester

A "busy" street in downtown Leningrad, 1977, on way to a Dollar Store, but not the type we have here!
Gary Regester

During our Russian trip I did three presentations about America at music schools, a fantastic experience for people hungry for freedom. This music school lecture was in Leningrad before our concert at Revolution Hall, 1977.
Gary Regester

My solo church banjo moment at a 1450 church in Armenia, 1977. *Gary Regester*

Sitting in with Doc Watson in Colorado around 1978 for "Way Downtown." *Personal archive*

I had called my lifetime friend Leon Russell to see if he wanted to go see Doc at the famed Palomino Club in North Hollywood. It got me a free dinner from Leon! *Personal archive*

Opening for Steve in 1980 at Lake Geneva, Wisconsin. My Lear charter to my NGDB date the same night in Fort Smith, Arkansas left the Wisconsin venue at 8:40 PM. I was picked up in Arkansas in a pickup truck, and on stage in at 10:15.
Maple Burns, personal archive

At one of my Rocky Mountain Opry shows with violin virtuoso Eugene Fodor and Donovan in 1983.
Bill Warren

One of the *John McEuen's Rocky Mt. Opry* shows at Red Rocks in Denver. With Chuck Morris I had booked Ricky Skaggs, Bonnie Raitt, and Arlo around 1984.
Noel McEuen, family archive

Somewhere in Nashville in the 1980s, taping a show with Johnny Cash and Merel Haggard.
Personal archive

Sitting in with Johnny Cash and June Carter in Wales, 1986. I played two shows with them that night.
Personal archive

John, Eddie Rabbit, and Gary Hart on the 1987 presidential trail helping the guy who blew his chance to be president—before he got into too much monkey business.
Archive

At the Grand Old Opry, in Roy Acuff's dressing room. I'd just convinced him to introduce Gary Hart to the audience a few days later. *Personal archive*

One of my favorite stage bits, smoke bomb and flash paper . . . leftover tricks from my Magic Shop days. *William E. McEuen*

Some Colorado club in the 1980s, with Jonathan singing "We Belong Together." *Personal archive*

Jamming in Idaho Springs at the Maxwell House with lifelong friend Leon Russell and Edgar Winter, 1988 as we burned through "Jambalaya." *Personal archive*

I'd invited Bill Monroe to a midnight jam after the 1988 Zurich concert—and he came! Jeff Hanna and Carlene Carter jumped up, too.
Personal archive

During shooting in Deadwood, South Dakota, for my second music video, "Miner's Night Out." Jonathan on guitar, Bryan Savage, flute.
Production still, personal archive

Opening for Tanya Tucker, 1994, in Las Vegas.
Personal archive

A festival around 1995 in Carbondale, Colorado, with my son Nathan. *Personal archive*

Every day on the set of *The Good Old Boys* (1995, directed by Tommy Lee Jones) I gave Sissy a forty-five minute piano lesson so she could play live in the filming. She learned it in five weeks. *Ryan McEuen, family archive.*

Five albums together; we'd always jam when our road paths crossed. This might have been the 1998 Deadwood Jam with Michael Martin Murphey.
Personal archive

At Nashville's famed Station Inn one early 1990s night, getting ready to pick for fun. Marilyn came with me and met Vassar for the first time. They were both impressed.
John McEuen

Recording in L.A. for *Circle III*, I asked Tom Petty to come record with NGDB and Willie, and he came! Petty sang on "Good Night, Irene."
Marilyn McEuen, family archive

Danny Farrington, Kevin Nealon, Steve Martin, Nathan McEuen at Kevin's fiftieth birthday party in Hollywood, where I met Brooke Shields.
Marilyn McEuen, family archive

During the Deadwood Jam, Noel in front having a good time. My son Aaron is behind her, holding his daughter, Sydney.
Craig Whitus, family archive

Making a NYC deal in 2004 for Kevin Nealon with the man in charge of Legos.
Marilyn McEuen, family archive

On the set of *Manassas: End of Innocence.* Left to right: Ray Herbeck, the producer, who was my first guitar student in 1965; Ibby; John McEuen.
Courtesy of Ray Herbeck

At dinner in Disneyland Hotel with Russi Taylor—the voice of Minnie Mouse—and my wife, Marilyn.
Noel McEuen, family archive

Levon Helm invited me to his seventieth birthday at his famed Midnight Ramble in his Woodstock, New York, barn. After my forty-five minute set, he did two hours and had me sit in. What a great night that was!
Marilyn McEuen, family archive

At a NYC fundraiser for Why Hunger where I played behind early mentor Pete Seeger and artist Tom Chapin.
Marilyn McEuen, family archive

We try to get to Europe as often as possible. Traveling in Germany to Checkpoint Charlie with Marilyn, 2014. *Marilyn McEuen*

At the wedding of friends John Carter Cash and Ana Cristina. I met John Carter when he was a teenager performing with his mom and dad, June Carter and Johnny Cash. Pictured are Lisa Kristofferson, John, Kris, and Marilyn McEuen. *Personal archive*

With the great David Amram in Kansas City at the 2016 Folk Alliance convention. *Suzanne Ladgene/Elmore Magazine*

Fan/student Hayes Martens gave this wonderful print to me in 2016. Thank you, Hayes! *Personal archive*

11

The Red Brick Road

The commies had learned to party.

Since Alan Freed first said "rock 'n' roll" in 1952, the constant fearful blather from the American Right was that rock music was a Communist plot to overthrow America. To the Soviet censors, it was the other way around: rock 'n' roll was a Capitalistic plot to overthrow Communism. It wasn't a plot, but the Soviets had it right, and the American Right was wrong. I later came up with my own theory: the snare drum was a Communist plot to overthrow music, and it was working well. Why would we spend hours in a studio working so hard to get pristine sound—perfect acoustic instruments, quiet amps—only to have someone crash down on a snare drum every two seconds?

The 1970s saw the rise of cultural exchange between the USSR and the USA, with their Bolshoi Ballet, orchestras, string quartets, and various folk ensembles coming here to perform, while they agreed to showcase American talents. The US Department of Cultural Affairs cleverly committed the Soviets to bring over an American group (specifically, a self-contained band that played music all over our country rather than one that was just a "star" with a back-up band), that was a "democratic musical enterprise." After enough "exchanges"—that is, after enough Soviet artists played in the United States—they had to live up to their part of the bargain and agree on an American band that would fill the description. The Soviets looked at many American groups and came to

137

rest upon the Nitty Gritty Dirt Band, for reasons they never disclosed. It was known after the fact that the American head of the US Cultural Affairs division in Moscow, David Hess, was instrumental in getting our name in their hat. USSR representatives came to see us four times before they finally decided on us. The NGDB, sans Ibby, now had two newbies: Jackie Clark, from Ike and Tina's band, and John Cable, a friend from a Denver group that had opened for us.

I packed my weapons of mass distraction and went to change the world five strings at a time, and I found that from Lubbock to Latvia to Leningrad, the banjo caught people's ears and lightened gloomy faces. Some say the first thaw in the Cold War came in 1977 with a little hot American music by this band of ex-hippies from Colorado via Southern California. We played twenty-eight sold out shows and did a television show that was seen by 140 million comrades.

Let me take you to Russia in 1977: The wall was still up and the Cold War was still hot. Their prisons were packed with people who had tried to defect. There was very little in the way of food, milk, clothes, news about happenings in their country or outside of it, cars, money, apartment space, happiness, security, health care, music, television, radio, or free speech. There was virtually no freedom. It was like "a whole other country" over there.

We arrived late in the afternoon on May 1, with the heat in the air in contrast to the gloomy faces of the smattering of pedestrians. I wondered if they were pondering their ancestors' struggles for freedom, first against the czar, then Lenin, then Nazis, or if they were thinking about the generations of sacrifice that failed to deliver the promised easier, better life. Every day, the Soviet authorities invented more reasons for the walls that kept people in—not just the Berlin Wall, but also the walls of authority and mind control. We were to learn a lot about those warm people and about the authorities under whom they were forced to live.

The staff at Moscow's Hotel Russia (the biggest in the world at the time, with four check-in desks and more than five thousand rooms) couldn't even tell us exactly how many rooms they had. After dinner that first night, we jammed using the hotel band's gear and were faced with the worst instruments I'd ever seen: broken cymbals, broken guitar strings tied together, a Czech copy of a Japanese copy of a Fender guitar, and so on. On our last song, I noticed that a 1960s-era tape deck appeared, just in time to catch us butchering "Will the Circle Be Unbroken." After that, it was time to head to our rooms, but not all of us turned in right away. I could rarely do that, as I have felt that time is running out since I was about twenty-five. There's more out there, wherever the "out there" is, than in a hotel room. I wanted to see more, and I found eager company with the photographer I had enlisted, Gary Regester, who was famous in the business for the hundreds of album covers he had shot. Gary was also something of a Renaissance man. In addition to being an ace photographer, he was a serious inventor and seemed to have an encyclopedic knowledge of a wide range of subjects, especially art. Gary had wisdom that he tended to keep to himself, unless the conversation happened to veer into an area of his expertise, such as yoni egg rituals. I knew from our first meeting that he was someone I'd want to know for a long time. To this day, he has been a lifelong friend. I had found him during one of his L.A. album cover shoots and asked if he wanted to go to Russia for a month with us. Without so much as looking up from his viewfinder he simply said, "Yes. Let me know when we leave. I'll need about six hours' notice."

Sharing my compulsion to visit Red Square that midnight in Moscow, Gary just said, "I'm right behind you," when, after the jam, I pointed outside. We soon found ourselves getting nearer and nearer to the rhythmic *thonk-thonk* of goose-stepping guards, as we watched with amazement at their hourly (*every* hour since Lenin had been parked there) changing of the guard at Lenin's Tomb.

A local comrade citizen approached, offering to buy any American thing Gary or I would part with. "I pay fifty rubles for Hendrix album, seventy-five rubles for T-shirt, two hundred rubles for your Levi's. Come to Freedom Square. You want buy cocaine?" Even though possession of foreign currency by a Soviet citizen would get him a three-year jail term, he continued, "Seven, no eight rubles, for American dollar." The official exchange rate was $1.60 per ruble. The ruble could not be legally exchanged anywhere but Russia (and then only by foreigners). A comrade could not defect with rubles, so if he did manage to get out, he would need to have money from *somewhere*; his own was no good. Foreign currency, especially American dollars, was their ticket to freedom.

I could hear Lenin turning over in his little stone dacha in Red Square, for as the guard changed, so had the people. Gary commented on two *Spy vs. Spy* types, complete with trench coats, following our disparate trio out of the square. Our now-nervous black marketeer and drug dealer saw them, too, and said over and over, "Yes. See men. Much big trouble," as he pulled a syringe out of his inside coat pocket. He frantically crammed the hypo into his pants, apparently not worried about what the needle might hit, then tried to hail a cab. As each cab pulled up, though, they seemed to spot the trench-coat guys about ten yards behind him, and sped away. One even locked his doors first. Then the trench coats closed in on our dealer. One put his hand sternly on our sweaty friend's shoulder, and firmly said to us, "Russia police. Excuse please." This was a little different than the Grand Ole Opry security.

The three of them faded into the post-midnight mist, with the dealer between the two trench-coat guys as our pal emptied his stuffed pockets and was apparently headed for a free ride on the Siberian railroad. All this went on only two blocks from our rooms, scarcely six hours into our first day behind the Curtain. And the night wasn't over.

After returning to the hotel later, we tracked what sounded like faint Dirt Band music to the house band's broom-closet dressing room. The band, whose broken-down equipment we had used, was excitedly gathered around that old tape deck. One would run the tape briefly, then stop it, then they'd chatter, then continue playing it, then stop it again and rewind, all the while listening intently and talking. It was a recording of our earlier jam.

When we asked what they were doing, the drummer said, "Free performance your music has very impressed with us." The performance they were listening to had some scat singing, noodling solos, and an a capella section whenever we got lost, all played on their funny-sounding and hard-to-play instruments. In other words, it sucked. He said again, emotionally, "In your music we hear is freedom of America!"

They explained to us that if a Russian band played an American song, one of the members would report them to the KGB. Always, an unknown someone among a band was an ear and eye for the KGB. If the crowd at a concert became too aroused, danced too much, or otherwise got too happy, the KGB would call the band into their office and warn them to stop that. Hey, it's a free country, isn't it?

So after being in town now seven hours, we'd had two meals, jammed in a club, walked around Red Square, watched a drug bust, talked about music with a local band, got rooms, and headed to bed. Thinking back to 1967 and Sonny Moore's dog act, I knew again I had made the right choice following this music trail. I went to sleep thinking about my wife back home, who was four weeks pregnant with number five, and about how I wouldn't be able to call home for two more days.

The next day we boarded a train bound for Tbilisi, Soviet Georgia, which was the cognac capital of the Soviet Union. Most of us paired up in sleeper compartments à la the Orient Express. In fact, my friendship with the always-amenable Gary Regester solidified that day, as the Soviet tour manager, Marina, looked around to inquire who to pair up with whom. Gary simply said, "John and I are together." The real trip on that train was back where our three roadies had to ride. They endured arguing in five languages, animals, and no water; the tracks even seemed narrower and rougher back there when I briefly visited them. I stayed in my place up front and watched Russia turn into Armenia, which was the only republic that wanted to be a part of the Soviet Union so that Turkey wouldn't gobble them up.

"That's our Mount Ararat," said one proud Armenian passenger, pointing across the expanse.

"Have you been there?" I asked.

"Oh, no," he answered. "Turkey claim as theirs now. They take from us."

After the lunch reception in the Yerevan mayor's office the next day, they took us to a special performance by the Armenian men's choral group that featured fourteenth-century music in a thirteenth-century church. When the choir finished I could not resist the chance to play my banjo inside those historic cathedral walls, which was the first time that had been done, and a chilling event for me. I'm not sure why it was chilling, but I somehow felt part of that building's history.

Wandering the streets that night with Gary, looking for something interesting to photograph, we drifted into a nightclub, where a hot (not) Polish rock band with a lot of lush, European vocal echo held the stage. It was a perfect *Star Wars* bar scene—people from all over the world crowded into this Russian excuse for a disco/club—but hospitality was trumped by reality when we had our first personal interaction with the Soviet secret police.

Gary made himself right at home dancing and enjoying the music, and got great shots of the partiers with his tiny camera. Before too long, though, a friendly looking face came up to him and said, in perfect English with a very proper British accent, "Nice camera. What make is it? Can it shoot well in this low light? So small! No focusing? May I look through it?"

Gary happily handed the man his camera, at which point his English accent turned into a Russian growl. He whipped open the back and yanked out the film, barking, "No pictures!" Then he calmly handed the camera back to Gary, and strode away into the crowd.

After the Red Army stage crew put the piano on the "stage" (a very, very funky platform on wheels) at the Yerevan Velodrome, we set up our Peavey PA and did a sound check to empty grandstands at what would be the sole outdoor venue on the tour. We wondered whether people would show after the sound check, but we began to feel more confident when the surrounding rooftops started to fill with people. Then, the line of people started filing in. For three hours they came, until the place was packed.

The whole country ran on 220 volts, and the voltage converters we brought with us were supposed to bring their power into our equipment at 110 volts. It was there that we found out that their 220 was more like 200, with constant ground problems, and not at all stable. This was the most powerful country on Earth? What we ended up with was usually 98 volts, often sinking as low as 88 volts, which sometimes made our gear heat up too much and ended up requiring us to turn everything up all the way.

It was all part of the cultural exchange, like when I learned in Tbilisi, Soviet Georgia, that they didn't exactly get the concept of take-out food. I had decided to not leave the venue after sound check, and asked for "whatever anyone else is having at the hotel, bring that." Two hours later, a bunch of strange food showed up, all wrapped in newspaper with no plates or utensils. The ink made for a nice seasoning. I ate what I could while the mayor learned how to throw a Frisbee. Both of us were having a new experience.

One of our translators told me that a young man, who had come to one of the shows, wanted to know about banjos and was hoping to meet me. She arranged a visit to his Armenian home two days later. Her friend looked depressed and teary-eyed when I advised him about how to obtain instruction books, records, strings, and a catalog, not to mention a banjo. The translator told me that if this banjo enthusiast followed the advice I'd given, he would land in jail. He'd serve three years for any one of the offenses: importing unapproved books, trying to import without permission, sending rubles abroad, or, if he sent foreign currency, possession of foreign currency.

Two weeks into the trip, I concluded that your sanity couldn't possibly survive if you lived there. Then we had that day off in Tbilisi. The Soviets took the band to a lake for a cookout and we brought along two-alarm chili from Texas. While it was being prepared, we set up the "party" members for a little "cultural exchange."

We carefully demonstrated the "old American custom" of "calling up the chili," which included rhythmically pounding the table with silverware in each fist, while chanting, "Chili . . . chili . . . chili . . . ," until the cook jumped out and hollered, "It's chili!" Then everyone was told to cheer wildly. We hoped they might someday repeat what they'd learned about American/Texas culture and find they were part of the custom of the great American put-on.

After that first two weeks we flew to Riga, Latvia, just after one of their non-publicized meat riots. The policy had been to ship all of Latvia's meat to Moscow, leaving none for the Latvians who had raised it. We found out later they made sure they had quelled this demonstration before our arrival so we would not see it.

A radio guy had come to meet us at the airport and excitedly said that he wanted to have me on his show, and do an interview later in the week. Now, that seemed normal, just like home: come to town to play, go on the radio, talk about stuff. This was one of my Orange County hopes—to reach the people on the airwaves. That deejay vanished, however, and I didn't find out why until later the next week.

I met a Latvian man walking the Riga streets that night who spat on the ground every time he said the word "Russian." When told the show was sold out, he said, "I have ways. They are stupid. I hate Russia, man." He kept his promise and showed up in the second row of the hockey rink where we performed the next night. From him, we learned the hotel was cordoned off, inside a "secured" three-block radius, to keep ordinary citizens away from the Americans. For example, the sign posted outside the always-empty hotel restaurant read "Sold Out" in Russian; in other words, "Your ruble not good here."

Still, one of my life's most emotional onstage experiences happened in Riga. I had learned the old Latvian national anthem on the banjo. For years, playing it there—the song, not the banjo—would bring harsh legal penalties. I had made up my mind to include it in my solo section of the NGDB show, to see what would happen.

The "concert rink" was packed with about four thousand people, with a lot of red clothes worn on the floor level by the Commie VIPs, who were mainly higher-level party members. All the "lower-level Latvians" were in the bleachers surrounding the floor, except for that one Latvian guy I'd met on the street. There he was, in blue and black, sticking out like a sore tongue. About halfway through the solo spot I began the medley: first a folky, frailing, 1880s banjo song; then a classical-sounding piece; then a bit of "Malagueña," with each transition getting nice, mild applause. Then, I gazed around the room, strumming a couple of times, and started the Latvian anthem. About five seconds into it the room exploded with applause. All the response came from the bleachers. The red-clad Russians didn't clap—at all. The Latvians were again free for a few chilling minutes.

In Riga, I lectured at a local university for music students. I talked about how Americans do music both as bands and working with others, I played some different banjo styles, and I met a lot of people close up in a relatively safe situation. Here they could talk more openly, because the purpose was "educational," but talking wasn't so safe everywhere. Anyone who talked with us out in public situations faced the real probability of being picked up and questioned, often overnight, just for having that conversation. Many told us throughout our tour about going through that. To me, it was proof of the State's belief that rock 'n' roll was a capitalist plot to overthrow Communism. But at the lectures, the people spoke out freely.

In this third week behind the Iron Curtain, while still in Riga, we'd had no meaningful contact with the opposite sex, until our stage manager, Leonard, finally convinced Irene, a "dollar store" clerk, to accompany us on our day off on an outing to the Baltic Sea. (A dollar store was one place where you couldn't shop with rubles, as it was a way for the Russian government to collect foreign currencies from tourists buying things with their own country's money. Russians were not allowed in these shops unless you were a party member. Dollar stores stocked things from around the world, at good prices.) Reluctant at first, she eventually warmed up and joined the picnic fun: running on the beach, throwing the Frisbee, and just hanging out with the crazy Americans. The "Russians" did a day at the seashore their way. They slowly walked on the wooden paths down to the water, all dressed in their Sunday best, acting as if they were at a beach funeral. Happily hotel bound at sunset, the weary called it a night early, and waited for tomorrow's flight to Leningrad.

That night, after the beach, Gary and I snuck off to a gathering at the country home of a new Latvian friend, Pete Anderson. Pete boldly approached me after a show and I learned that he was a known underground rock star. Pete loved the music of Buddy Holly, and he dressed like him down to the horn-rimmed glasses. Like a lot of Cold War Europeans, his fashion sense was a strange take on 1950s American cool. Playing his original songs with his band the Swamp Shakers, who had a rockabilly beat, he sounded like he was doing American music with incomprehensible lyrics, but his style was all his own. Pete (who had Americanized his name from Pits) instructed me how to ditch the constant KGB tails we had: get on the 10:00 PM trolley north, go two stops; just as the trolley starts after the second stop, jump off the back and get on one going south; go three stops, get off, and walk one block around the corner from that stop. He'd be waiting there to whisk us away in a car. It worked. We lost them.

At Pete's house about twenty-five miles out in the country (our allowed travel limit was a ten-mile radius of the hotel) waited about eighteen of his friends, all wanting to hear about America. I regaled them with stories about 7-11 stores open all night ("Milk anytime? Such a country!"), motor homes, concerts, traveling across the country freely, and comedians making fun of the president. It was all stuff we sometimes don't even notice, but which seemed fantastical to people born and raised behind the Iron Curtain.

How do you put to music the kinds of things I heard that night? Pete said, "I never be free, but I dream someday I have son. I teach him to defect to America, then, I know freedom." At 5:30 AM they finally agreed to let us go if we'd sing "This Land Is Your Land" a third time, with all eighteen joining in. Only three of them spoke English, but they all knew the English words, and sang loudly as they faced the map of the United States on Pete's wall. I had never felt so close to home, and yet so far away.

When we left Latvia to head to Leningrad, the missing DJ reappeared in time to see us off, apologetically explaining that the KGB had seen him talking with me that first day and had taken him to a hospital for a week of some "necessary psychological tests."

"They told me not need talk with you . . . Needed mental checkup," he said. He had not obtained official approval to talk with us. To avoid any possible embarrassment from an interview, they just locked him up.

Before leaving, our stage tech Leonard went to the dollar store to thank Irene for her company, but she wouldn't talk to him. She wouldn't even acknowledge him, and instead just stared straight ahead as if he weren't there. Pressed by Leonard for a response, tears streamed down her face, and she muttered, "Thank you. Can't talk. Goodbye." She then turned and walked away. We sent in Brant Basset to figure out what had happened.

Although he was supposed to be our constant companion and cultural liaison, Brant would disappear for a day in every new town. His Russian was so good that one night, backstage security threw him out, thinking that he was a local gate-crasher. While watching him argue with the guards, Marina (our non-party, Russian tour manager) said, "His dialect so good, he sound Russian. He must be CIA. But John, everyone must have job." We agreed. With his dour demeanor and the attitude of an apparatchik, Brant could easily blend in with a crowd of Russians.

As Brant pretended to browse, he quietly asked this girl some questions about her response to Leonard. She whispered to him, "When return home beach from trip, KGB took me and question overnight, accuse of planning defect, stealing, black market, said I fired if again talked to Americans." As explained by both David Hess and our tour manager, Marina, the KGB controlled dissidents through threatening forced unemployment, then blacklisting, as being unemployed would make the person a "parasite on society." They would find you after a few months out of work. Then you'd be sent to a minimum of three years' manual labor camp for not holding a job. You would then have a job. You would lose everything you left behind. Everyone knew and lived with this fear. Being sent to Siberia was a reality!

The more we learned, the more we thought, *Get us outta here!* But not yet: Leningrad first, then Moscow, then back to freedom. The five Riga shows had all gone fantastically. Off we flew to Leningrad.

Just before leaving Latvia, two very agitated dissidents gave Gary and me a four-page letter to take to the States, saying it was a "record of Soviet violations of Helsinki Human Rights Agreements: prisoners taken without reason, torture, unreported plane crashes, political executions . . ." They were very excited about getting it to the United States, and they knew we were not KGB. Gary and I took the letter to Brant for translation and advice on how to handle it.

In Leningrad, after we asked Brant how the translation was coming, he said, with a CIA-voice overtone, "It's not your concern. It's taken care of. The government has special files for these things. Leave it to them. No further discussion on this." People had risked their lives giving us that letter and we blew it by trusting our side. I may never know what was best, but I do wish I had given the letter to *Rolling Stone* instead of to Brant.

In Leningrad, we visited the Hermitage, which was the biggest museum in the world. The place seemed to go on forever, like our tour guide: "So you see why we Russians are so proud. All these beautiful art works: Van Gogh, Rembrandt, Da Vinci. The best in the world . . ." Under her breath Marina added, "All stolen from other countries over centuries."

And yet the people sought treasures of a different kind, like Levi's. At the hotel in Leningrad, I asked why the floor lady (every hotel floor had one sitting at a little table at the end of the hall) refused to clean my Levi's. I was told she was afraid she would damage such expensive material (one pair was worth one-and-one-half months' Russian salary). An hour later, I almost traded a pair of Levi's for a small house and a car.

We experienced another of those strangely rewarding moments in Leningrad. Avowed party member and our tour assistant Irena had told us for weeks about what to expect from the crowds in Leningrad. "They not yell loud or clap like people you have been playing for," she said, "but, will like you just as much. More culturally refined in Leningrad. You will get encore, maybe, but not this craziness we have been seeing. Much more respectful." I hoped to prove her wrong.

That night, during our third encore, some sailors, preceded by a screaming girl, ran up on stage to give each one of us flowers. After the girl kissed a couple of the guys, the crowd rushed the stage with hands in the air, clapping along, stomping their feet and yelling for more. It looked like a normal American concert night to us; to the Commies it was absolute pandemonium. (In the USSR, it was illegal to even stand up during a concert, so this crowd's response, in the eyes of Soviet authority, was downright subversive.)

In the wings, getting ready to go out for the fourth encore, I stood next to red-faced Irena and saw her astonished look as she took in the scene. With a sigh of amazement, and a hand by her dumbfounded openedmouth face, she said, "But . . . well, I . . . I never . . . ever thought *this* could happen! I mean, here, *in Leningrad!*"

It was in Leningrad that I again felt both the freedom of America and just how pent up and restricted these comrades were. I did another lecture for music students at a local university, to talk about how Americans record. I described how American musicians would be hired based on their reputation, then show up to a studio and be handed a basic chord chart. I said, "They usually play what they want, what they feel." The students asked, "How do they know what notes to play?" I answered, "They just make it up right then to fit with the chords on the chart; they play what they think is right." As Marina translated it, that freedom comment got a long standing ovation.

The glum faces were lightening up. It again became obvious what a responsibility we had in representing the United States and helping these people feel free and happy, just for a little while. I felt more responsibility than ever in my life for representing a good part of American culture. Whew.

Next stop: Moscow. Or, *Mockba*. A red dawn broke on the taxi rushing to the train station for the Red Arrow. We were anxious to get there, because it meant we could make our third calls to home from the embassy. During my turn, I learned my wife had miscarried alone the day before. It was not an easy day for either of us, but it was much harder for her. I felt terrible, but we had one more week to go.

I had heard that lines would form at various stores whenever word got out that a shipment of some type of goods had arrived. The line would form even though no one knew what it was that had arrived; they just knew that it was *something*. Since they needed everything, they knew it would most likely be good to get in line before whatever it was ran out. I was skeptical.

In Moscow, I saw one of those lines and decided to get in it like a good comrade. Eventually someone in front shouted, "It's shoes. Shoes are here." Someone else said, "I don't know why wait two hour for shoes. They fall apart in month." And someone else grumbled, "Be quiet!"

On our third day in Moscow, we found ourselves in a television studio, preparing to film our show for a Soviet television special. As I was going through the list of songs to shoot that afternoon with the director, he mentioned, "And song eight, Jan sing 'Break My Mind.'" (We had brought our Aspen friend and great jazz singer Jan Garrett with us to represent the female side of American music.) The director, a very overweight party member named Yuri, was referring to the careful notes he had taken when he had come to the first concert three and a half weeks earlier, in Tbilisi. I interrupted to let him know that Jan changed that song to another one. Yuri protested, "But have 'Break My Mind' on list, and must be song eight . . . Jan sing 'Break.'" Hearing that we had decided to replace that song did not make him happy at all. He insisted, "Must do song on list!"

I called Jan in and asked what she would do if Yuri said she had to sing that song. "Well, I'll just go back to the hotel, and he can sing it," she snapped, and walked out. She, like the rest of us, were done with Russia. Yuri was furious. He was now sweating, blood vessels were bulging on his red neck, and his face was turning Commie red. I didn't really care how mad Yuri got and was not going to let him tell us what to do. I had seen enough of the Communist Party hacks, who basically ran the country for their own personal enrichment even though only 3 percent of the population were actually party members.

"Yuri," I started to explain, "there is a difference of cultures here. You see, you are a Russian Communist and you must do what you are told. We are Americans and we come from a land of freedom, *and we do exactly what we want.* She won't sing that song, and I won't make her, and if you yell at her, she'll leave and so will I."

I flashed on a memory of my teenage years working at the Disneyland Magic Shop. Every day at 5:00 PM, the marching band would come down Main Street to the flagpole to bring in the flag. I loved it even more now.

Something told me that I had to let him save face. "So, here's what you can do," I suggested. "Jan will sing 'Georgia,' the one that goes over better anyway, and you can call it 'Break My Mind.' Or, we'll all leave, and let you sing the songs." He went for it.

We saw something amazing at the first Moscow concert, and then again at each of the next four shows there. After about twenty minutes, a few people would get up in various parts of the theater and run out. They would quickly return, sometimes with a different shirt on, and sit for another twenty minutes, before getting up and running out again. *What was going on?* Tickets were so hard to get and so expensive that three or four people would go in together on one ticket, and keep an eye on their watches to get their twenty minutes each. It was "time-share" seating!

The crowds were always great, and their hunger for American music was palpable. It was as close as one could get to the feeling of being in the Beatles, although it wasn't the group itself that generated such excitement. It was American music.

But it wasn't easy. The venues were well built, but other buildings, made of the poorest-grade concrete, felt like they were crumbling around us. They poured at the wrong temperature and used very little rebar. Milk was only available two hours a day. They had very little hope, and even less freedom. They were afraid of the American build-up of arms, and wished that they did not have to do the same.

I missed the United States and my family. I wanted to hear a Brezhnev joke. I heard my favorite one from a guy who would only tell it to me in the middle of the street, with traffic on both sides, in front of the hotel one night. He wouldn't even utter the name "Brezhnev" as he told the joke, since it was literally treasonous to mock the "great Soviet leader." Instead, he indicated "Brezhnev" by brushing his fingers across one of his eyebrows wherever the premier was to be mentioned. For our purpose here, and because of where we live, I use the name (to be said in a Russian accent):

> Breznev was in canoe, middle of lake, with beautiful young Belarus girl, sunny nice afternoon. Accident happen. He fall in water. He went down once, twice, three time. Third time, girl grab his arm, and with great struggle pull him to safety into canoe.
> "My darling! You saved leader of greatest country in world. You saved Soviet Union from chaos. So grateful am I, you I grant any one wish your heart desire!"
> The girl thought for moment and sweetly said, "Open Soviet borders to free travel for 24 hours!"
> Breznev coyly responded: "So . . . *you want to be alone with me.*"

I asked long-bearded, often-acerbic David Hess, who was in charge of our trip from the American side, if our tour would really make any difference. He replied, "Well, if there is a war between the countries, and some Soviet soldier has an American in his sights, and *he* saw one of the concerts, he might think about that concert and what a good time he had, and pause long enough for us to nail him. Other than that, I'm not sure." David was 90 percent responsible for making our trip happen. It had gone over so well that they did not let another American group in for eight years.

Our tour is still talked about today in what used to be the Soviet Union. The great Russian bluegrass group Kukuruza ("corn" in Russian) told me they started because of that tour.

Pete Anderson had told me many times that he was beat up by the KGB who also made threats against his family, who would be punished if he continued. His mother called, begging him to stop playing that American music, as her job in Moscow was being threatened. She did not want to go to Siberia. One night, with his wife in a hospital with their new baby, he was coaxed to sit in with some friends at a club, and basically "blew the room away" with his music. The next day, he went to see the new arrival at the hospital, but a nurse told him, "We had to take the baby downstairs for tests, and he died." When he asked to see the body, she told him, "We have taken care of it." He never saw his son. His wife divorced him. He quit music for many years and went on a ten-year alcohol binge—until Glasnost, when the curtain went back up on his music career.

Pete then enjoyed doing something that had been illegal and life threatening when we visited in 1977: playing his rockabilly music. He did about fifteen performances a month in Latvia and the other Baltic states by the 1990s. Pete was honored as a cultural hero with a Latvian postage stamp of his own.

I arranged for Pete to sit in with NGDB at a concert in Norway in 2010, and later I put him on my XM radio show with some of his fine music. Thirty-four years after meeting him, I arranged for Pete to be featured sitting in with NGDB at a 2011 concert in Kansas for the film *Free to Rock* (released in 2017) about how American music brought down the Iron Curtain in the '80s. I got him on the main radio station in Wichita, KFDI, for an extensive interview with my lifetime radio pal Orin Friesen. Pete was glowing and happy while freely talking about his music and life in the heart of America. Things had changed.

Pete passed away in 2016, having achieved his life's dream of freely playing music he wanted to play. The rest of the Dirt Band rarely mentions any of the Russian trip for reasons unknown to me, but we did America proud. I could not have done it alone.

Though the party members ran the place, their 3 percent could not overpower the power of music. Of course, in the United States, we have worked that out more efficiently: it is only 1 percent running the show here.

I love recording even when I'm not sure what I'm going to do with the music; the freedom of creating something just for its own sake. Months after returning from Russia and realizing more than ever what freedom we had, I worked on some recording ideas at Bill's Aspen studio. While I was always trying to make something new, it took a while, to say the least.

12

Starting On-the-Job Training
Being Towed in the Fast Lane

After more than a month with little communication, I'd missed my family tremendously. Though we felt extreme relief to be back on home turf, we were tired—both individually and as a group. And, by the time we got back from the USSR that summer, NGDB was falling apart again. Jackie Clark left, and for some unknown reason, Jeff got rid of John Cable. It may have been because Cable wrote good songs and played and sang great, and Jeff felt threatened. With the Dirt Band stalled, I started working solo more often, starting with the Oxford Hotel down in Denver. I was heading back in time to when I was first playing solo, two years before NGDB, but that had been in the '60s. I only had about thirty minutes of material. I was scared, not knowing if I could fill the bill, but it went great, I was told. I went home with enough cash to buy good shoes for all six of us without standing in line. Still, I wanted to get back into the record business. I started working on recording for several months at Bill's Aspen studio, but those tracks would not be finished until the mid-1980s. And there was a new NGDB deal in the wind.

My first solo jet charter was also in the wind. I'd booked a big solo opportunity at Hollywood's famed Roxy. But as showbiz does, Mimi Fariña (Joan Baez's sister) called and wanted me at Berkeley's Greek

Theater for a Bread and Roses benefit the afternoon of the same day. There was no way I was going to pass either one up! Seeing it as an excuse to join the jet set, it would be easy:

Leave Van Nuys airport	2:30
Arrive at Oakland airport	3:12
Arrive at Greek Theater	3:35
Play	4:15–5:00

My old friend Hoyt Axton was on the Greek show; his welcoming bigger-than-human hand engulfed mine, and his eyes got as big as his hands when I told him how I'd gotten to the gig. This was a great day.

Leave for Oakland Airport	5:30
Take off from Oakland airport	5:45
Arrive at Van Nuys	6:40
Get to Roxy by	7:45
Play	8:00

Genius sound engineer Bob Edwards met me (for the first time) at the Greek to hitch on the return ride to meet with my brother about working with NGDB. Now a lifetime friend, Bob told me he was impressed that a banjo player had a jet. That cracked me up.

After the Greek set, our little rocket shot straight at the moon from the Oakland runway, right over the hospital where I was born, then made a ninety-degree bank left, climbing over downtown San Francisco. The pilot, silhouetted against the sunset as the city lights were coming on, with his face lit by the green cockpit lights, turned to us and announced, like a cocky Humphrey Bogart, "That's the only way to see that town."

The charter cost me $1,658, which meant I netted about $40 after I paid the band. Doug Dillard brought Ringo Starr that night. That night I felt accomplished.

Within months Steve was taking over the TV airwaves and needed an opening act for his sold-out live shows. He was to become the biggest comedian draw in history. I got to open two of those shows, playing to nine thousand people a night. A while back it had looked like the Dirt Band had a better shot at making it big, and Steve and I had made a bet: the first guy to make $10,000 in one night would win $1,000 more from the other guy, just to rub it in. Now I was grateful that Steve had called off that bet a few months earlier. The fact was that I needed those two days opening solo for Steve Martin in Chicago. I needed the money. Our fifth child, Ryan, had just arrived, and he was just as beautiful as the others. We didn't have health insurance, so again some "birth cash" would seriously come in handy. Raising kids on a banjo budget was never easy, so solo gigs were crucial to supplement the income from the band. Even though I told Lance, the Dirt Band's agent, not to take a NGDB date on a day when I had this solo gig, an offer came up.

"I'll only do it if the promoter supplies a Lear Jet to get me to the Dirt Band gig from the one with Steve that night," I told him, thinking they'd never agree. But they did. I booked the plane, and with my stage call in Fort Smith, Arkansas, at 10:15 PM for the 10:30 PM NGDB show, I figured I could make it. Besides, I wanted to live like a rock star, even if just for an hour.

I jumped off the stage in Lake Geneva, Illinois, just north of Chicago, at 8:35 PM and got into a waiting backstage chopper at 8:37 PM. We hopped over to the little Lear, warming up on the short Playboy Resort runway, at 8:42 PM and were wheels-up at 8:45 PM. The pilot turned back to me and said, "Barely enough room to strike a match on what runway we didn't use for that takeoff." I felt like I was in a fireworks rocket.

Relaxing in regal style in my own Lear, it occurred to me that the reality of the situation was simply hunger. The fifty-five-minute flight to the Ozarks cost about three dollars a mile, but the only food on the jet was two packages of peanuts. I laid them out on the table, forming the letters NGDB, and ate one nut per minute. We arrived a bit early, when I still had two nuts left. It was better than the DC-3 trip. My pickup—in a pickup truck—went smooth, putting me backstage early at about five minutes to ten. As soon as I arrived, I got the message from the band as they were about three miles away in a Holiday Inn.

"Can you tune our instruments?" they'd asked. "We're having trouble getting there, and we'll be a bit late." *Well . . . excuuuuuse meee.*

———————

I had come to admire the Chicago singer and songwriter Steve Goodman from afar. I had heard about Steve for many years, known even then as the Cubs' best fan, but I was still a bit shocked when I finally saw him perform for the first time, sometime in the mid-1970s. He was a guy who could get more response from a broken string than most acts get from a whole set. He would continue singing and change it before the song was over! Yet, Goodman never seemed like he was taken in by his talent. You got the sense that he was just kind of along for the ride. A good man, he was. After seeing him the first time, I knew he was the real thing.

I saw Goodman perform many times and was fortunate to sit in with him several times. He had a simple trick for handling a crowd: he killed. So much so, that when Steve Martin started to play eight– to ten thousand–seat venues, he needed an opener that could hold the audience. I knew Goodman was perfect. At a Hollywood lunch that I requested with Steve's agent, Marty Klein (NGDB's very first agent), I told him that Goodman was the only guy for the job. A few other acts had tried, but they were usually booed off stage. The audience wanted the star. I had done all right the few times I opened, but it wasn't what was best for Steve's show and it didn't really work well enough. I knew Goodman could do it best. Marty gave him a try. Not only did he go over, he often got encores, which was an incredible feat in front of ten thousand people wearing bunny ears and arrows through their heads who came to see the other Steve. Goodman did over four hundred shows with Martin.

A few months later, Bill closed a six-album deal with United Artists for me, Fadden, and Jeff. We added a few hired-gun players to fill out the band, notably Merel Bregante, the first drummer I ever saw play live in 1966 in the Sunshine Company, which was a short-lived group my brother was managing then. He brought along his friend Al Garth (who played violin, sax, and recorder). Both had played with Loggins and Messina for seven years. Our new lineup generated several albums under the name the Dirt Band—a bad name idea with which I did not agree.

I loved the music Al made. He wasn't a bad guy when sober, but after about a Heineken and a half, he became weird Al, and no one wanted to be around him. If you can imagine a cartoon of the NGDB walking anywhere, with one guy who had a cloud over his head, that was Al. Al was plagued by something we dubbed "bad food karma" that flared up whenever we went into a restaurant. He could be first off the bus, the first one seated, the first to order, but he'd always be the last to get his food, whether alone or with the group. His affliction reached its zenith, the best of the worst, one night around three in the morning.

Four hours after fleeing a 1978 gig we were starving and piled off the bus at a crowded truck stop on the rainy Pennsylvania Turnpike. Al sat down first, alone by a fogged-up window, and ordered. Even he knew it wasn't fair to subject us to his karma at this hour. I sat down last, but as it often happened, my meal came out first, followed by everyone else's—except Al's. His chili arrived about the time I finished eating, at which point things got worse. He started grumbling in a stage whisper loud enough for the whole room to hear.

"This is the worst! How can they serve this?" Al glared at us as we laughed silently.

You don't expect fine dining on an interstate at any hour, but in the middle of the night even the Belgian waffle isn't as good as advertised. The dough gets as sour as some of the patrons. For Al, this set a new benchmark for bad, but hunger won out as he continued to choke down his chili, muttering all the while. When finished, he slowly picked up the check that the nice waitress had brought him and defiantly walked over to the cash register, looking ready to kick some ass.

He thrust his check toward her, took off the dark glasses of indifference for emphasis, and declared, "That was the worst food I've ever eaten! How can you serve that here and expect people to pay for it? I wouldn't feed it to a dog! It was so bad, I refuse to pay this check, and, and—" At this point, the smiling waitress calmly held up her hand, indicating for him to wait a second.

"Oh, I'm sorry. Just a minute, sir, I'll be right back." Coffeepot in hand, she walked over to a nearby table where three Pennsylvania state troopers were seated. She bent over smiling to whisper something to one pursed-lipped patrolman while she refilled his coffee cup. He looked Al's direction and nodded, smiled up at her and slowly nodded his head yes.

Like a circus clown getting out of the midget car, the trooper pried himself out of the booth and rose up to his full six foot, five inch height. This John Wayne–looking sheriff seemed to weigh about 260, and he lumbered over toward Al with an air of weary resignation. He petted his holstered gun, as a matter of habit I'm sure, and somehow the strap over it came unsnapped. Al appeared actually to diminish in size as this trooper, looking like an Old West lawman, moved into Al's space. We all saw Al's sad eyebrows go up as he opened his puppy eyes wide in preparation for a confrontation.

"I understand we have a problem with the check, son," intoned the lawman in a voice as deep as it was hard, with hands on his hips. It did seem that one of his fingers kept flicking toward his unhinged holster.

"Well, I, uhh, yeah, I had this chili, and it was so bad a dog wouldn't—" Al stammered, as his brow showed beads of sweat in the cold air conditioning.

"Son, did you eat the food?" the towering trooper asked the silly sax man.

"Well, yes sir, I did, but in many years on the road I can say it was the worst I ever—"

"The way I see it," interrupted the stern lawman, with a wave of his hand, "is you have two choices here: Pay the check and leave, go on your way. Or, don't pay the check . . . and go with me to jail. What'll it be, son?" His voice carried a faux paternal authority and sadness like he was reluctantly carrying out a punishment and acknowledging the moment, while anxious to get it over with. He wanted to end this poor boy's pain.

Al fished out some per diem money from somewhere in his pocket, fumbling as he tried to hide his sax attitude glasses, and started panting heavily as he ponied up the tab. He left, tail between his legs, to remount the bus while we spent the next fifteen minutes trying to stop laughing. On the bus, we greeted Al with comforting comments like, "Boy, *that* sucked," "You got the shaft, man," and "Man, the service was slow in there." We never brought it up after that.

With Al, our duet (my guitar and his violin) of my song "Mullen's Farewell to America" would often get standing ovations. We worked well together that way, and it was a favorite part of that era's show for me. Still, Al showed me something I had noticed early in my career: those who did drugs or drank alcohol simply had more bad moments in their day than I did. To this day, I remain grateful for that lesson.

As my own kids came in to the world, one skill I developed in those baby-raising years was the ability to do a phone interview and change a messy diaper at the same time. Cradling the phone between my shoulder and ear, I babbled about the upcoming show with various press or radio people, while somehow, the kid knew to keep quiet. I could get the change done in about two minutes, and the interviewer never suspected my attentions were divided. Although not starting that until kid number three (as the kid crowd grew so did the need to multitask), I changed diapers until I was brown in the face, but got a lot of interviews done.

The bus had its comforts, but flying offers the chance to meet people, and plane people tend to talk about any and everything. Most of those chats would be forgotten as soon as the plane landed, but you never know when one of them might turn into something more. That happened with one woman I met at thirty-five thousand feet. Our paths crossed unexpectedly, and our night flight would cover a lot of ground.

Married we were, happily for a while, but not to each other. Just a man and woman talking about life. She traveled a lot, too. We agreed that life on the road, and its curves, make the straight road difficult, but more interesting. We talked about the country, travel, horses, and even a little bit about politics, and realized we had a lot in common. She was funny and plainly pretty, and I instantly felt like she liked me for myself, as I did her. It felt good.

After a couple of hours, she said, "I wonder where we are."

I raised the window shade, looked out, said, "Lubbock," and put the shade back down.

She laughed and commented, "Funny! That's a good bit," but I assured her the town below was indeed Lubbock. At first, I thought it funny too, until it dawned on me that it really wasn't that funny because it seemed I'd spent more time in the air than with my family.

The woman was impressed: "You must travel a lot!" I explained that I was in the music business, worked all over the country, and indeed flew a lot. She said she did the same thing.

I had asked the flight attendant to confirm our whereabouts, and a moment or two later, the pilot came on the loudspeakers. "We just passed over Lubbock, Texas, on the right side of the plane." We laughed and asked for some snacks. (It was easy: I could see Midland/Odessa south of Amarillo off to the left, and the lights of Lubbock below us. It looked like a giant Rand-McNally map all lit up.) She asked if I was in a group, and I said yes, and that we played about 180 cities a year. She said she was a singer and did about the same, then asked, "So, you must make records. Think I've heard any of them?" I mentioned that she might have heard "Mr. Bojangles," and that I played mandolin on it. "Of course I have!" she said. "But that was by the Nitty Gritty Dirt Band. Did you play on their record?" I informed her I was a founding member of the group, and heading to a show. "Whoa! You are in the band, and, well, how nice."

Then it was my turn. "You said you sing. Have you done anything I might have heard?"

"Well, 'I Never Promised You a Rose Garden,'" she answered. "You might have heard that." Of course I had. I knew it was a big record, by Lynn Anderson, and told her so, adding that it had sold something like five million copies as a single. She said it was something like that, "Seven million. It's my record. I'm Lynn Anderson." So, about two and a half hours in to the flight, we met again.

That was Lynn, talking not about stardom, but about horses (she was a great horsewoman), loving singing, life, love, the pursuit of living. I was talking about kids, and all kinds of other things, many of which are in this book, like the Japan trip and doing interviews while changing diapers. She liked that. Trading stories covered the next two hours till we landed.

An abiding, albeit periodic, friendship was born, one in which we told each other things shared only with certain trusting and non-judgmental friends. This was the kind of friendship one wishes for, with someone who accepts whatever you may be. I had to admit to myself that this was largely missing from my band experience, and that I was craving that friendship from my own group. I knew this about myself.

A few years later, well after Linda Ronstadt had become a huge star, she came to sing again on one of our records. She showed up at the Denver studio in her pajamas, and again the hair on my arms stood up when she sang. Maybe she wanted to get back on the radio since she hadn't had a hit for, oh, a few weeks. Her vocals on "An American Dream" helped us get another song on the pop chart (number seven in some places), which affected our career in a strange way.

The appeal of Linda's voice was obvious. Jeff sounded like a cross between Jimmy Buffett and Jackson Browne, which had worked great for radio, but in 1979 radio started to distance itself from old groups with funny names. Stations would not tell listeners whose record it was. Once again, we'd disproven our first showbiz review by Leonard Feather in the *L.A. Times*: "Doubtful they will ever be captured on record." Radio just did not like saying the band name. In fact, I don't feel like putting it here, either. Produced by Bob Edwards and Jeff Hanna, "An

American Dream" (and "Make a Little Magic," written by Jeff Hanna and Bob Carpenter) would get us on bigger shows.

In Indianapolis we opened for the Doobies. Before the show, Leonard Martinez—who took over road managing after I had to fire Gary due to cocaine a couple years earlier—came to me and said, "The Doobies road manager won't give us enough stage room to set up right. You'll have to play standing behind the piano. He said it can't be moved!" It's common for the opening act to suffer such indignities, but this was just over the top.

I went on stage to see the guy, and said, while pointing at it, "What a great piano! Didn't think they would have one like that here." (I knew it was theirs.)

"Well, they don't. It's ours. We carry it with us."

"Wow," I enthusiastically said, "all the way from Columbus last night to here?" (I had checked to see where they were the night before.)

"Yeah . . ."

"Man, it went a hundred and seventy-five miles last night and can't go another five feet? That's all I need to work in. Think about it, please." He did. He moved the piano. Nice? Well, during our last song's last few bars of music and our standing ovation, he hit all the house lights and the house music, killing our encore. I hoped to get back at him some day.

We opened for Buffett the next year, and he came into our dressing room to say, "I shoulda recorded that 'American Dream' song! You guys got a hit with it, and it could've been mine!" Ironically, it didn't matter; most people thought it was Buffett anyway. Twenty-three years later, at the 2003 Country Music Awards, Buffett beat *Will the Circle Be Unbroken, Volume III* for Recorded Event of the Year with his Alan Jackson duet. Maybe *Billboard* was right. It was good to see that in all those years he had not learned the celebrity eye trick and was as happy and friendly as ever.

My confidence built with the success of my solo shows, and with five kids I needed more work. I started performing more as the opener for other artists. These necessary shows brought me the personal artistic validation I was not finding in the Dirt Band format. If things didn't work, it was my fault; if they did, I felt great about it. I was fortunate to get on shows with some great talents.

It was strange having a radio hit ("An American Dream") with NGDB around the time I was getting the opening jobs with Dolly Parton, Crystal Gayle, and others. I was the hitless unknown opener from a band with a pop hit that I did not perform solo. The opening sacrifice act does about forty minutes. The audience, waiting for the one they paid to see, often doesn't want to see anyone else. You had to be a good entertainer to survive this slot. I was good at it; I would even get encores. Both Dolly and Crystal would have me sit in on banjo for their encore of "Rocky Top."

Riding on her clean-as-a-pin bus during one week's run in 1979, I asked, "Dolly, what all do you have planned to do?"

She said, "I'm going t'have my own makeup line, star in a movie, and a play, write a song for a movie, and open an amusement park and call it Dollywood. Ain't that cute?" She followed through on all those ideas. She was another inspiration to me in doing what you want to do, and believing in it.

That was most obvious one rough night in Fort Worth on the next run. I used the Dirt Band bus this time, taking four kids and their mom on five dates. That night, Dolly told my son Aaron she would sing "Happy Birthday" to him from the stage. In the wings, while waiting to go on, the cattle stockyard's smell was strong in the inside air, and the announcer was yelling into the PA, "Welcome to the Dolly Parton Show! (*Crowd roar.*) It is great to have the great, mega-star, singer Dolly Parton here tonight! You all want to hear Dolly? (*The audience roars louder.*) She'll be out in about thirty minutes; until then BEER IS HALF PRICE! BUT ONLY FOR THIRTY MINUTES!" The crowd started going in droves to the back bars to tank up, and then he said something so quietly I could barely hear, "And now here is John McEuen."

I wasn't sure people even saw me go on. It was a tough set, about eight minutes shorter than all the others I had done, as there were few laughs and little applause. The Texas-cowboy-beer-drovers were louder than me through the PA. After my set I told Dolly, "This was the worst audience for me. You don't have to slow down your show with Aaron's birthday song, so if you leave it out no worries."

"John McEuen," she replied, "I guess you don't know Dolly Parton. She does what she wants t'do. I told Aaron I'm gonna sing to him, and I'm goin' to sing to him, an' if they don't like it they can just take this red dress of mine and shove it up their ass!"

She dropped two major quiet songs and sang to Aaron mid-show. No one could tell that her stories were a bit shorter and her pace was a bit faster. Giving the impression it was the best night in her life, she took bows over by the stage-left wing after the last song. Her road manager was two feet away, out of sight of the audience. As Dolly bowed, she held the mic away, glanced at him, and hollered, "Don, did you pick up the check?" Don nodded yes. She had been paid. Dolly looked out at the audience, arms of "I love you" spread wide, and said, "Thank you! And good night!" No "Rocky Top," just straight to the busses; we left quick.

The family had now grown to eight, as wonderful Nathan had arrived in 1980 in Salt Lake, only thirty-two minutes after his mother's water broke. Quiet, watchful Nathan, the youngest, would be liked by all. Determined to learn from his older brothers and not repeat their mistakes, he'd learn his lessons well, avoiding most of the pitfalls of growing up. Responsible and grateful, he has the good fortune to be able to remember everything. Nathan showed songwriting skills at eight years old, and to this day continues to pursue a successful music career.

With the house now very full, even more do-re-mi was needed. NGDB just wasn't working often enough, but fortunately, unexpected income would show up.

One Salt Lake day, the woman cutting my hair let me know there was a phone call for me. The United Concerts promoter for Utah, Jim McNeil, was on the other end, offering to pay me $1,000, plus airfare and a room, for an opening gig—but he wouldn't tell me for whose show. He just told me to be at the Executive Air terminal in two hours. So, I raced home to pick up my instruments. I lived for this! The excitement of an unknown show and the chance to make the house payment.

He was covering the airfare by having me hitch a ride on the main act's chartered plane—a fifty-seat passenger Convair 580 that was recently retired from Frontier Airlines (known as the airline with gun racks in front). While awaiting the stars' arrival, I found out, as Paul Harvey would say, the rest of the story. I was replacing the hard rockers April Wine, opening for Foreigner at a sold-out rock 'n' roll show in a nine-thousand-seat venue in Pocatello. Cool . . . kewl . . . cruel . . .

I opened my banjo case during the flight to check something. Two of the fluffy-haired headliners sauntered over, looked in the case, and derisively asked, almost in harmony: "What's that?" So what if they didn't know a banjo from a potato, I thought. The great Idaho audience would appreciate it. I couldn't wait to knock the judgmental smirks off those cold-as-ice rockers' faces. Soon it would be show time, and the banjo would prevail!

The sound check went great. When the doors opened, in came every out-of-work street kid between the ages of sixteen and twenty-two, ready to rock 'n' roll. Show time. It was going to be tougher than I thought. At first, about three hundred people were cheering me on, intently listening to my notes. The difficulty was 8,700 others were busy talking about how much they thought I sucked. The enthusiasm of the guy directly in front of me at the edge of the stage spoke for them. He held his middle finger high, into the spotlight, right about level with my knees. Twenty minutes in one of the cold as ice 8,700 decided to break the ice.

A roadie yelled, "Incoming!" pointing up over the audience. There I saw it, glistening in the hot white carbon arc spotlight: a Jim Beam bottle, turning end-over-end in slow motion, as if in a Quentin Tarantino film, making its path toward me. Time slowed down, like it does for a horsefly or a hummingbird, and I realized their aim was a bit off. Or, maybe their aim was perfect, and I wasn't that bad. I jumped to the left about a foot, held my guitar up in the path of the incoming ordnance, and knocked it down to the stage floor. I followed by lighting the flash paper and smoke bomb on the peghead (a Magic Shop thing and rock 'n' roll parody I did at the time), which won over some of the haters.

McNeil, waving from the wings, yelled, "You can get off! It's OK! You've done twenty-five." But the deal was for forty minutes. I explained loudly, over the twenty-thousand-watt PA system, that the beloved group they were waiting for had in their contract they would not go on until nine fifteen. That was still fifty minutes away, and I had ten more minutes to do. After that, they could go shopping for band T-shirts and stuff. Some more of the fans actually listened, although the finger stayed in place, and I finished. I got paid.

Unable to sleep, at one thirty that night, I turned on the TV. Some folk-music show I barely remembered doing three years earlier was on. I was wearing the same clothes on TV as I had on for that night's show. Most of my stage clothes at the time were my brother's hand-me-downs, as all the money went to the kids. At about one forty-five I turned it off mid-song, wondering why I was depressed, and then my oldest son, Aaron, called. "Hey Dad! *Paint Your Wagon* is on again. Here it comes . . . there it is . . . your close-up . . . there it goes. Dad, is this ever weird for you?" Yes, it was.

Yes, missing my family, feeling like a music whore, wanting to be home, one more lonely hotel night—I hated what my life was that night—for about an hour. But then, I could make the house payment, I'd had good backstage food, a clean room, a free flight home. I had played my banjo, I was on TV twice in one night, and I would be back with my kids the next day. What's to complain about? I went to sleep thinking briefly of Steve the Newsman and shut myself up. I needed to make something new happen.

The same promoter called a few months later, asking me to open solo for the Doobies, in Provo, Utah, in front of twenty-two thousand people in the round at BYU. *Hmm.* This would be a challenge. At the venue a week later, I was warned by their road manager (the same mean one from the Indianapolis Doobies show) to not do over thirty-five minutes. As I was pacing the stage before sound check, in the middle of a mountain of equipment, the stage manager came up and said, "What do you need?"

I told him, "I need a four-foot-high, six-by-eight-foot riser with stairs in back right here, but I am sure that can't happen." He said, "Come back in twenty minutes." I did, and there it was. Astonished, I asked him, "Why did you do this? It's way more than an opener can ask for! Wow!"

Chuckling and smiling, he told me, "You must not remember me. I was running sound on a Louisiana festival about seven years ago—one with Willie on it—and I had run out to my truck to get something. Coming back in the festival I had to dig in my wallet for a stage pass. A joint fell out, and security arrested me and took me downtown. You came and bailed me out! What else do you need?" Ha. A good karma deed came back.

All was ready. I was no stranger to Mormons and knew how to reach those twenty-two thousand kids. My last bit was a duet with my tape recorder, with it challenging me to play "Dueling Banjos" and warning me I would lose. I started the song—*dun da dun dun dun dun dun dun dun*—and the tape responded by filling the coliseum with the Halleluiah chorus from Handel's *Messiah,* performed by the Mormon Tabernacle Choir. I threw my arms up, a loser to the tape machine, and left the stage. The crowd started stomping its forty-four thousand feet, causing the whole building to vibrate. Thirty-five minutes after I started, I ran to the dressing room and locked the door, as the din continued to build. It kept going, as I'd hoped it would. It was an encore that had to be taken, but I waited.

Someone knocked at my dressing room door, yelling, "Get out there and do another song!" I yelled back, "I can't! The road manager said only thirty-five minutes! He'll have to tell me it's OK." The feet were getting louder and the choir was still blaring—one of my instructions to the sound guy.

A long minute later, their road manager came back and said, "Would you please do one more?" I felt great that night, and went home to a house full of sleeping family. Teddy the dog was up, so I told him about the show.

———————

More changes were on the horizon.

Late one 1980 night, I came up with an idea for a show and called Chuck Morris in Denver. Chuck had become a major promoter there and liked my ideas, and a production show at Denver's Red Rocks Amphitheater was born: John McEuen's Rocky Mountain Opry. I will always remember when Steve Goodman (one of the performers I wanted), who was battling cancer, showed up a bit ragged, with his chemo-thin hairdo. The light still gleamed in his eyes as he said, "Well, four days of chemo almost knocks me out, but now I have the weekend and some shows to do. They'll have to do more than that to kill me!" He went out in front of eight thousand people and killed. He reminded me of the Newsman.

Soon after, I moved the family back to our Evergreen house in the mountains. We all felt more at home there, and the Rocky Mountain Opry shows ran for four more years. It was always great to drive home from work, which is something that rarely happens in this business. And again, more changes were on the horizon. The Dirt Band was working more, but I had hopes Jeff and Ibby would sing hits on country radio. To get there, we needed a new manager first. Oh, and Ibby wasn't in the band.

Steve Martin's career was so hot my brother wanted to focus all his attention on him, which meant bailing on NGDB management. Bill was making his million$ with Steve and had run out of patience dealing with the frustrating Dr. No and Fadden.

Fadden's acerbic comments to Bill killed his enthusiasm. Like the time Bill had laid out a dozen, great, eleven-by-fourteen blown up shots of us, and asked Fadden, "Jimmie, what do you think of some of these for the next cover?" Fadden said, "I think you should leave that up to the creative people." Bill was done. We talked about who could take over, and I said there was only one guy: Chuck Morris. Bill agreed.

When we called Chuck in Denver, he said, "John, if you are going to stay in the band, I'll do it. Otherwise no. It's funny how you're the only musician in a band better known than the lead singers!" I saw in this moment an opportunity to get certain things done, things that, if I had suggested them to Jeff and Fadden, would most likely have gotten mired in the usual endless discussion and would have never happened. I didn't want to argue, and I knew that Chuck's influence would get these things moving.

I gave him my five conditions:

1) Ibby is in the group.
2) We have a Nashville record deal.
3) We play NGDB country music, not music like on the *Jealousy* album (*Jealousy* was the most recent, not well received, "rock 'n' roll" album produced by Jeff.)
4) We record with a notable producer in Nashville.
5) The name changes back to Nitty Gritty Dirt Band.

He agreed.

———————

Around this time I met Toto's incredible guitarist—Steve Lukather— while we were both watching Steve Vai perform at the Anaheim Hard Rock. He told his name, and said, "I wanted to tell you what a big influence you've had on my music life." I had to ask, "Well, I play banjo, and—you're *the* Lukather who plays lead with Toto? How could I possibly have influenced you?" He responded, "You may not remember. In sixth grade in the Valley I'd been taking guitar lessons a couple of years but was not very fired up about it. You came to my school to demonstrate various instruments, around 1968. After watching you, I went home and started digging in, and have thought about your passion for music often. . . . I wanted to have as much fun as you were! I went to play on the *Jealousy* album because I thought I'd see you again so I could thank you."

13

Little Jean, Dancing, Brings Us Together

At some point, after Ibby's I-hate-us departure in the late 1970s, I had taken him on the road. I wanted to explore the mind of one of my favorite eclectics and to hear his singing and new music. He had been gone since 1976. To this day, he is one of the best singers I've known. I wanted to play new notes to accompany his voice again. I knew we weren't done together just yet. At our duo shows in late 1981, Ibby's new, never-recorded "Dance Little Jean" was going over like a hit. In Kansas City's Uptown Theater, audiences were singing along to a song they'd never heard before. In the music business, this is considered a very good sign! He needed another chance at reaching people and they needed him. I convinced Ibby that "Jean" was the first song we should record as soon as he was repatriated with the band, and that it would be a hit. The timing was right.

Ibby was reinstated around 1982, and some months later we were off on a Tennessee concert trip while our first Warner Brothers album was getting mixed by noted producer Norbert Putnam. "Dance Little Jean" was on it. I dreamt of one more musical part to add before the final mix. It literally came to me in a dream, in one of those rare times when I could sleep on the bus. I didn't know it would lead to one of my funnier road experiences.

We had a date in Cookeville, Tennessee, then a day off, and then a show in Knoxville. That day off gave me time to get to the studio—but the guys didn't want the bus to take me to Nashville for a one-hour session, and then have to backtrack to Knoxville. I hated days off on the road; if I wasn't home I wanted to work. I'd grown accustomed to the other guys' lack of support for my ideas, though. But then, I wouldn't want to add six hours to my bus trip either so I devised another plan: Continental Trailways.

After the Cookeville concert, around eleven forty-five at night, the band bus took us to a tiny Trailways station I'd found nearby. They were kind enough to wait for the midnight bus that would take me and my banjo to Music City for the overdub. As we pulled in, a young couple started embracing, right in front of our band bus. She started crying. They chatted, kissed deeply and for a long time, petted, stroked, caressed, and practically had sex with their clothes on. It became obvious we were watching the tearful goodbyes of the final scene of their movie through our bus window screen.

The young woman picked up her mismatched suitcases and tearfully headed for our bus door, ready to board her ride away from home and all she knew, leaving love behind. Through wet, puppy-dog eyes, she looked in our door's window. I hesitated to open it and break her spell. She glanced up at the door, over at her lover, and back through the door I was slowly opening. I understood the script and knew my line.

"I'm sorry, but this is not the Nashville bus." Both she and her hands lost their grip as suitcases dropped to the ground. She dashed back to her soon-to-be-ex lover's arms and broke down again, but not quite as far as previously. They said goodbye for another five minutes, until Trailways showed. I sat on her bus to Nashville rehearsing this banjo part in my head and never met her eyes again. At the studio the next morning, after a couple of hours' sleep, I laid down my part in about ten minutes. It's the little *tick-tock* background that goes through the song. Norbert Putnam liked it and added it to the final mix.

I flew to Knoxville to meet up with the band. I remember thinking on that flight about that girl's quiet grin, almost a smile, when she got off that bus in Nashville. She apparently was as eager for her new chapter to begin as I was for ours with Ibby. In 1983 "Jean" went to number nine, and to this day it's an audience favorite. I like to think that the banjo part did that, but of course it was the magic of Ibby's words and singing. For the record, both literally and figuratively, I played guitar, mandolin, and banjo on that cut, but Ibby's voice and words made it happen. Jeff sings Ibby's song now, but never gives him credit.

The Warner Bros. records would get us out there again, with other name acts we had played with before and better headlining shows. Being back in Colorado, I could drive my family of eight to a few shows, such as Cheyenne Frontier Days around 1984. NGDB was set to open for the Doobies again. The band flew in and I drove my family carload, but all of our equipment was on the band bus, which was stuck in Omaha. No gear for the show. My bandmates all said, "Too bad we have to cancel." I was having none of that. "We're not going to. I've made the calls and am renting stuff at two music stores here. John McFee [of the Doobies] will loan me his fiddle, and, of course, I have my banjo with me. The grandstands will be full—and we won't get paid unless we play." Jeff played through a simple guitar amp without trick pedals or fancy gear, and proved that night just how good of a guitar player he can be. I think it was because he was so nervous about no effects and the strange amp that he simply had to play his ass off, and he did. The show killed, and the Doobies were gracious hosts.

If my life were on videotape, I'd play back the part where Steve Goodman was asked by Chuck (a lifelong Goodman fan and supporter) to write us a Christmas song to be called "Colorado Christmas." Morris was Jewish, as was Goodman. Stevie said, "I have to get approval from my rabbi," and started fishing for the words for what was to become a perennial Colorado hit and one of my favorite songs in the fifty-year career of the Nitty Gritty Dirt Band. I say fishing, because that is how he seemed to approach the job. ("The words are out there somewhere! I just have to catch them," he said.) We left Myrtle Beach with the first verse ready to sing. I had to phone him (on a pay phone!) for new words as we headed from Virginia to Nashville to record. By the time the bus got to Roanoke, he said, "The second verse just came in. Waiting to catch some more words for the chorus." He said to call back from Knoxville or so. Steve was not obsessed with being the star songwriter that he was; he felt more like a conduit for the words. The chorus came in by Knoxville, and a few miles later, outside of Nashville, he "caught the other verse" and, voilà, we had the whole song and recorded it that evening. Ibby made it believable, and it became a Colorado favorite.

I never liked getting to a gig the night before. It always seemed like a wasted night, just sitting around, waiting. As Lightnin' Hopkins had advised, I spent some time looking around in E, and didn't find all of it, but with no one to jam with, I was done at about midnight. I was away from home, missing the family, and wasn't working, just waiting. I missed working closely with my brother and was questioning how I'd ended up in a cheap motel in the middle of Ohio farmland. At nine in the morning, after one of those almost wasted pre-cable, pre-Internet nights in a hotel, the promoter's van showed up—it was time to go to our afternoon show out in some pasture. With a two-hour drive ahead, we all expected we'd see more cows than people. The gig was called the Ohio Valley Jam, and it was billed as one of those big outdoor events; it sounded like another wannabe Woodstock that would probably have a much smaller turnout than the promoters hoped. Because we were going on early, I figured we'd play to about fifteen hundred people, and that the crowd would show up right after we'd finished.

We pulled in at about eleven and were amazed to see around forty thousand people sitting in a field, quietly waiting. No PA yet. Around eleven forty-five, the sound system finally turned on. A roadie went on stage and hit one giant, booming, bass guitar note and got a standing ovation—arguably the biggest response to a G-string on record. We knew now this would be a hot crowd, and the trip was already worth it.

The inadequate supply of audience porta-johns, combined with the Woodstock mentality that was pervading the crowd, led to hundreds of people answering nature's call au naturel. After making their own business space at the stage-left side of the audience, near the security fence that was out about ten yards from the too-few porta-johns, fifteen or so people at a time relieved themselves in a little trench, with guys waiting in a never-ending line for access to the yellow river. Guys stood with their legs spread, with a couple of squatting girls facing them, and as all chatted with the onlookers, they all did their business together. They were polite enough to target the trench, running their ex-beer stench directly under the security fence just far enough past the food catering area so one could still get a decent meal. I can still smell it.

Willie Nelson, Hank Williams Jr., Waylon Jennings, and a few other acts were on the bill, with NGDB scheduled at 2:30 PM. It looked like one of those shows you would want to write home about. We hit the stage and went into it, clueless that this would be memorable in other ways.

All was proceeding with the usual frenzy when Ibby pointed about 150 feet out from the stage at a space opening in the packed audience. It was as if a time-tunnel door into the '60s was opening, right in the midst of this countrified crowd. A completely naked woman was dancing as if it were a Woodstock Sunday, with her long, blonde, flowered hair flowing in the breeze. The crowd, more redneck than hippie, didn't quite know what to make of this flower-child apparition, and was just trying to give her some space.

"Something's happenin' here, but what it is, ain't exactly clear," came to mind, though that wasn't the song we were playing at the time. I was trying to keep track of as much as possible, so I'd have a good story to tell later. First one, then two, then three, then many people started pushing her around like a ball in a mad pinball game, apparently telling her to get dressed, move on, cool it, etc. But that only made her mad. This wasn't the attention she was after. She reached for the only defense weapon available to a naked woman at that time of her month.

Reaching between her legs, she grabbed a little string and pulled out her hidden weapon of mass revulsion. The crowd gasped. With our "Battle of New Orleans" blaring, she started swinging her red bomb-bursting-in-air in a circle over her head. The hole in the audience got immediately bigger, like an iris opening, giving her *lots* of room. "There weren't nigh as many as there were a while ago." Her ammo dried up as the space around her grew. Now the crowd was pretty mad, and slowly closed in around her. For a moment, she disappeared. Would this circle be unbroken?

The girl popped up like a cork from a bottle of fine red wine from a sunken ship; they hoisted her up on top of the crowd. Like leafcutter ants with a common mind, a wave of outstretched hands sent this naked, screaming fan, feet first, breasts pointing to the sky, snaking toward the stage over the heads of the audience. She was crowd surfing before anybody called it that, and she was now leaving. They placed her, now stomach side down, on top of the cyclone security fence, with feet pointed toward the stage. At least her legs were together. She was plucked to freedom by the security guards and vanished. I decided to not write home about that.

Next was the showdown between the crews for Willie Nelson and for Hank Williams Jr. I had just finished making a fun bus video for Willie, and as I brought the tape back to him, I couldn't help but notice some of his crew brandishing guns and knives. Their shifty eyes were jumping and they cast nervous glances and secretive nods of approval at each other. Their catlike movements seemed suspicious, to say the least. I had find out what was up.

During the previous night's concert with Willie, Hank Jr. had, against all instruction and requests, danced on the white grand piano on stage, which happened to belong to Willie's sister, Bobbie. Should Hank Jr. try it again, Willie said to throw Hank Jr. to his loving fans; they were armed and ready. Now this would be something to write home about! Like with *West Side Story*'s Sharks and Jets, there was going to be a rumble.

As Hank Jr.'s crew readied the stage, his southern mafia musclemen occupied it like the advance guard, acting like Hank Jr. was a superstar, when he was just a singing braggart. On the opposite side of the stage, Willie's mellow men sauntered into position, silently waiting for their cue. The two crews' eyes met across the stage as Hank Jr., arrogantly strutting like a prima donna, headed to the center of attention like he was constantly begging for. His band started.

I wish I could recount here that Hank Jr. mounted the piano, Willie's crew rushed the stage, shots were fired, two wounded roadies tossed Hank Jr. to the crowd for a well-deserved mauling, and his adoring biker fans ripped him to pieces for souvenirs to tie to their bikes. But I can't. Hank Jr. didn't dance on the piano, and his band was great. Willie's crew departed the stage with hung shoulders of disappointment. It was a beautiful day otherwise, except maybe for that river running right past the food tent.

A few months later, Willie made me the star for the night. I'd heard Willie needed someone to play chess with him, and he offered me a ride on his Lear Jet back to Denver from Casper, Wyoming, after our co-bill gig there. This would be something I could write home about. I couldn't face the eight-hour bus trip, and hopped on the jet. We arrived at the executive terminal in Denver around eleven thirty and realized we'd been so engrossed in the game that no one had called ahead for a cab. I trekked over to the main terminal to get one. The driver's eyes were fairly wide when this bedraggled hippie directed him to the Lear to pick up my even bushier friends. I'm sure it looked like a drug deal to him.

Heading up the I-70 hill out of Denver, the conversation was both expected and unexpected. The driver asked, "So, you guys in a band or what?" Expected.

Willie answered, "Yeah, he's the singer, I play bass, and my sister here plays piano. Just finished a gig in Wyoming and we're headed home." Unexpected. The driver nodded understandingly as we pulled up to my drop-off point in the middle of the forest, where my wife was waiting for me in our glamorous, rock star vehicle disguised as a beat-up Suburban. I wish I could have been able to see the cabbie's face when he delivered the "bass player" to Willie's Evergreen house, and pulled under the hand carved, two-foot-high letters over the entrance spelling out, "NELSON." I didn't need to write home about it. I was already home. And, I'd won the chess match.

I was glad to get back to the six kids early. The bus was still another six hours away, but I was home in time to get some sleep so we could go shopping early the next day. It was a shoe day, which now meant six kid pairs and two parent pairs. That was the most fun of life, being with my family. I wish I could remember more of it, but the kids all grew up so quick. When I *was* home, the constant prep work for the road, done at my home office, took a lot of time, even though I did that mostly while they were asleep. And, I rarely slept well.

Sometimes my memory is clogged with moments from the road, remembered in detail. For instance, the day we got revenge, which is also known as one thing I did that the group applauded. The guys were really hungry one night after a show, and the search for a little pile of food started as soon as we got in the car.

You don't know how good a southern Waffle House can be at one in the morning until you can't find one. Picture their windows steamed up by the frigid air-conditioning when it's eighty-five degrees with 95 percent humidity outside. Surprisingly, a Waffle House, with its simple, flat, American waffles, is great night food, but I never want to stop there in the daylight. That night, the drive was going by in dog-time (every minute seemed like seven), and there was no Waffle House in sight. Finally, up ahead in the low fog, we could see golden arches! That beautiful sign, just miles and minutes away, had everyone cheering, and soon enough, I pulled in for another fine road dinner. But of course, it wouldn't be a story unless just as we pulled in, the sign went dark. It did.

We begged the Mac-in-the-Box to answer our poor pilgrim's plea, and some teenager came on the speaker and said, "All we have left is one Big Mac. You can have it." Muffled cheers arose, and we rejoiced in this small victory, retrieved our little pile of food, and drove off to consume it.

Now, how do you split a Big Mac five ways at 1:00 AM without a knife? We speculated about how long ago this last burger of the day had been created. I asked the band to go along with me and just offer it up as a sacrifice to the Road God. I remember the episode as one of the finer moments in the life of the band, perhaps because it was one of the few very fleeting moments when we all agreed on something.

I got out of the car with our meal in hand. First, I put the Big Mac a few dozen feet ahead of the car, its foil wrapping glistened in the headlights. Still in Ronald's parking lot, right under the dark arches, a light mist that did not yet have the nerve to become rain floated in the air; I got back in the car. With adrenaline pumping, and eyes open wide, I gunned the engine. They all understood what had to be done, and I did it. It was only fair, as there was not enough to go around. I dropped the car into gear and told Mr. Big Mac to kiss its pickle goodbye.

I floored the gas pedal and drove over the hapless burger, then backed back over it, screeched forward again, then whipped back over it. Everyone was laughing as the poor Big Mac got bigger and bigger, and flatter and flatter. The arch lights appeared to blink. It now looked to be about the size of a pizza for a family of five, almost two feet in diameter. I got out, peeled it up from the pavement, held it in the headlights for the band's approval, which garnered more cheers, and then put it under the windshield wiper.

As we hauled down I-70, with windshield wipers slappin' time, that trapped burger was waving back and forth, spreading sauce and burger guts window-wide as we went. The laughs killed the hunger; it felt like we'd won. That's all I remember about that gig.

It was always a challenge to beat the boredom between shows on the road. It was more fun before people's drug use got heavy. We could be more creative about finding ways to break the monotony, like the day we decided to see how many times we could eat between Cleveland, Ohio, and Emporia, Kansas. The fourteen-hour trip became thirty-four. We ate *a lot*. I believe the count was twelve stops for food. It took an hour to eat at each stop, four stops for making room for more food, and one more for someone to throw up.

14

That "I-Became-Earl-Scruggs" Moment

Now, truth to tell, I actually felt Marty Stuart deserved to get pranked by me. I'd owed him one since he pulled a little something on me before he worked for Johnny Cash, back around late 1978. I had been happily asleep in my bed in the Hall of Fame—the infamous Nashville Hotel, not the famous museum of honor. I didn't have to fly that day, and I was really planning to sleep in until ten o'clock. When the room phone rang at four forty-five in the morning, it was Marty.

"McEuen, be in the lobby in fifteen minutes. I'm pickin' you up."

"What for?" I asked, having not expected his call.

"Be there, and bring your banjer." (That's what you call that instrument if you know Earl.) "Fifteen minutes." And he hung up.

He pulled up precisely fifteen minutes later, but I still didn't have a clue as to why.

"Where we going?"

"You'll get it when we get there. Say, 'Good mornin',' John!"

So I said, "Good morning, John. Where we going, Marty?"

"Nice out, isn't it? You'll see."

"Yeah, it's nice out. I think I'll leave it out. Where we going?"

As we crested a hill, the WSM radio tower came into view, and it became clear to me. We were headed to the iconic *Lester Flatt Martha*

183

White Morning Bluegrass show! I had read and fantasized about seeing this since I was a kid in Orange County. It felt like I was about to get into a time machine to go back to 1958. In the studio, Marty introduced me to Lester. It wasn't until the second commercial break was coming that I think I had my second anxiety attack, when Flatt led into the commercial with: "Mighty fine . . . Want y'all to know we have a special guest in the studio with us this mornin', and he's goin' to be joinin' us on a banjer tune right after this message." (He knew Earl, too.)

Lester and Earl Scruggs made the template for bluegrass music with their 1949 benchmark album, *The Original Sound*, on Mercury Records. Their high-voltage 1969 split was widely known to be less than amicable. (Their split was so harsh that Dobro-great Josh Graves had to call me just before the original *Circle* album to tell me, "John, I'm awful sorry . . . I cain't do the sessions . . . Lester says I'm on his payroll an' he don't want me pickin' with Earl.") I looked around trying to see who the guest was, and I realized it was me! I whipped my banjo out, started tuning it, crammed my picks on my stiff and morning-swollen fingers that felt like they'd never picked a banjo before, and hurried to get ready. The sun had come up, now I had to.

Just as I got in tune, I heard: "We're here with the Nitty Gritty Dirt Band's John McEuen, an' he's gonna pick us a tune. What do you have in mind, John?"

All I could think of in this icon's presence was my favorite and easiest tune, which I'd learned off one of his recordings years ago, when Lester was the lead singer of the Beatles of bluegrass.

"Earl's Breakdown!" I firmly stated, and Marty's wide-eyed look made me realize the choice was my host's ex-partner's famous tune. I felt as if I had just brought an evil ex-wife and an IRS auditor into the room.

Lester intoned, "That's a fine number—kick it off!" and I kicked it off. What a trip that was, having his famous, iconic G-run on guitar for this song, the same one I'd cut my teenage teeth on. This was a pure feeling of success to me: playing with *the man*.

Then, in the mid-1980s, I needed a backup picker for a few dates in the Northeast. I knew Marty was now out with Johnny Cash, and his tour was wrapping up in Poughkeepsie. He had the added benefit of being shorter than Cash, which was a little-known requirement for working for the Man in Black. Marty would be free. He toured with Cash for about six years before his own career kicked into gear. Always well-groomed, Marty was a great musician with a lot of road experience and he dressed like a star. Marty's great mane of flowing hair was a trademark, and he cared for it as carefully as the great female country stars looked after their own coiffures. Marty always told me, "You should look like a star if you want to be one." Marty was the first guy I knew who carried his own hair dryer on the road. Now I had a unique offer to make him.

"Marty, if you can get us the Cash penthouse in Manhattan for a few days, I can pay you a hundred dollars instead of fifty dollars a night." Well, Johnny was a big fan of the *Will the Circle Be Unbroken* album, and greatly appreciated that I had taken his mother-in-law, Maybelle Carter, her first gold record ever because of that album. He approved the deal, and I headed off to pick up Marty.

Backstage in Poughkeepsie, Mr. Cash asked me, "John, if you don't mind, come out with your banjer an' join June and me on the Carter Family songs, like on the *Circle* album." (That bad karma for Mr. Mancini's wayward daughter must have worn off by now.) I was on a higher plane than I had flown in on. It was a great honor to stand next to America's icon of real country music as an invited picker. I immediately called both my mom and brother Bill.

After the show, while driving toward our cash-free Cash crash pad on the edge of Central Park, atop a New York City high rise, Marty informed me dryly, "You *should* feel honored! But, don't get a big head. I gotta tell you, in six years with Cash I've only seen two other people sit in: one was a drunk, and the other was a ten-year-old girl." I decided, in spite of his comments, to retain this as a memorable, magical night. After arriving at the Cash condo, I used some of my Magic Shop experience to trick Marty on the coin toss, and got the bedroom, leaving Marty to get comfortable in the nice living room with the TV.

There I was, standing in the bedroom in front of The Closet, just staring. This was not just any closet—it was Johnny Cash's closet! I think many people would have succumbed to the temptation to peek inside the Man in Black's closet. I couldn't resist. As I opened it, an idea started to take shape in my brain as to how to pay Marty back for his previous mockery.

There were two of the Man's backup Blacks in dry-cleaner plastic, on standby, along with some great shirts and other accoutrements. I wondered if they'd fit me. Then I saw it: June Carter's nightgown—light pink chiffon, long and lacy, replete with a frilly collar. This was a real privilege and a special moment for me. I had recorded with her mother, played music with her, and now I was gazing at a beautiful representation of a very private part of her life.

I respectfully lifted the gown out of the closet on its cloth hanger to check it out. Holding it up against me, I realized she was tall, and it appeared new. I'm not sure what came over me just then, but I do remember thinking that this would make a great story someday. I did this for all of you who I reasoned would want me to, so I could tell you about it.

It fit like a glove, and except for being a bit short, it was perfect. It even occurred to me that my long hair went well with the outfit.

I snuck up behind Marty, who was sprawled sleepily on his living room floor bed, and focused on the TV. I softly sat down behind him, put a gentle hand on his shoulder and my chiffon-covered leg over his, and said, "Would the big boy like a back rub?"

Whipping around in surprise, he saw me in Mrs. Cash's hot pink bed dress, and shot up like a scared cat, shrieking like someone who had spilled hot coffee into his lap and bashing into the wall. He surprised me; I had never seen non-athlete Marty jump so high nor move as fast as at that moment. Having zinged Marty pretty good, I quickly put Mrs. Cash's beautiful pink gown carefully in its rightful place in The Closet.

In the 1980s, coming full circle, I went back to New York to promote my career on the *Robert Klein Radio Show* with Marty and coguest Gregg Allman. I'd not seen Gregg but once since the late 1960s. With Marty in tow we got to find out about Southern Rock Royalty.

Still feeling like I was being towed in the fast lane, the *Robert Klein Show* was a big deal, as was Gregg, and I wanted to impress Stuart since he was working so cheap for me. I saw an opportunity to catch up with Gregg. It felt great to have a talent such as Marty playing with me, as he was a conduit to the "real music" that I loved.

Gregg was promoting his career, now that the Allman Brothers Band seemed over. We greeted each other warmly, recalling the moments we shared in our early days, but then our conversation made me realize that this true rock legend and road renegade may have been too long on the hard road.

"Hey, John, good to see you. How's brother Bill?" (I doubted he would remember the help I gave him in 1969 when he stole Bill's car.) "I been out promotin' my new solo record. Hey, why don't you join us later after the show, you know, hang out?"

A nice invite from an old friend, I thought. "Sure, Gregg. Where are you staying?"

Gregg turned to his ever-present road manager and asked, "Hey, Paco, where are we staying?"

"Ramada Inn, New Jersey, by the tunnel," his life guide replied. Known as a great road manager, Paco's motto was "If you save a dollar a million times you've saved a million dollars." The Jersey Ramada cost about half as much as a Manhattan hotel.

"Oh, good," he said, turning back to me like he just remembered. "Ramada Inn. Uh, in New Jersey, by the tunnel."

He was warming up on a new guitar, and just to make conversation, I said, "Great sounding guitar, Gregg. Where'd you get it?"

Pondering the question as he looked at me, he slowly turned. "Hey, Paco, where'd I get my guitar?"

"Music store. Gainesville," aloof equipment manager Paco shot back.

Gregg turned back to me, as if it had just come to mind, and said, "Uh, I got it at a music store, in Gainesville."

I then asked where he was headed after the show. While facing me this time, he asked, "Hey, Paco, where are we goin' after this gig?"

"Leave day after tomorrow. We're heading back home," babysitter Paco replied.

Again, Gregg answered, slowly, like it was all coming back to him, "We're leavin' tomorrow. The day after, I mean. Headin' back home."

I shifted conversation back to what I thought might be easier territory. I had been admiring his unusual pair of custom boots, the kind you always wish you had when you see them on someone else. They must have cost $500 or more, and the interesting design fit Gregg perfectly. I assumed he had to have worked with the bootmaker himself. I asked one more question, "Hey, Gregg, really nice boots. Where'd they come from?"

He looked me straight in the eye for a moment, making me think, *OK, now we're getting somewhere.* He paused for a few more seconds, contemplating his boots, then without turning his gaze away from me, said to the room, "Hey Paco, where'd I get these boots?"

I wondered if Gregg could remember the words to "Tequila." I thought about how the long, rough years on the road can wear on one's brain. I don't remember the answer about the boots. I do remember Gregg proved again he was the real deal. Here he was, out passionately spreading the word of his new music, and when he sang, he was as great as ever, working it hard. If the NGDB had had an equal passion for music, we would have been more successful.

I parted company with Marty to head to Washington, DC, for a road day "off" on my way to Nashville. Jim and Jesse McReynolds, from Virginia, had had a strong bluegrass influence on my music, and had introduced me to the music of Vassar Clements. They were playing the famed Birchmere, just outside of DC in Alexandria, Virginia, and I was determined to meet them. I especially wanted to thank Jesse for his technique of "cross-picking" mandolin that I used on "Bojangles," which was the second song I learned on that instrument.

I showed up at their sound check. Jesse greeted me with, "Hey, John, good to see you!" I was shocked at how quickly he recognized me, like an old friend. He immediately invited me to play, saying, "You gonna pick with us?" Jesse talked about how the *Circle* album was a favorite of his, and how glad he was that it had given Vassar a new career.

I'd recorded one of their songs—my favorite banjo tune, "Dixie Hoedown"—on NGDB's *Stars and Stripes Forever* album. Jesse asked me to sit in with them and play it. To me, this was better than getting to play guitar on "Satisfaction" with the Stones. Although "Dixie Hoedown" always goes over great live, I could never get the Dirt Band to do it on stage.

After the show, Jesse said, "John, if you need to get to Nashville, hop on our bus. We'll be there by eight thirty in the mornin', and can drop you at your hotel."

"Wow," I said. "Be right back after I pack, check out of the hotel, turn in the rental car, cancel my flight, and get back here."

Jesse said, "We'll wait for you. How long will that take?" I told him thirty minutes, and pulled up with five minutes to spare, grateful for all the NGDB road-managing experience. The brothers switched off driving every two hours, and dropped me at my hotel in Nashville after my nine-hour, rolling, bluegrass history lesson.

Completely taken aback by their incredible hospitality, I let them know how appreciative I was of their treatment of a picker stranger. Jesse responded with, "Well, John. You're a good picker, and your band's *Stars and Stripes* album, where you put our 'Dixie Hoedown' on there with Vassar? Well, that was the biggest royalty check I'd ever seen!" I had forgotten that NGDB album had sold over four hundred thousand units.

Twenty years later, I leased that 1968, Hollywood living-room recording of Gregg's "Not My Cross to Bear" to PolyGram for a Gregg Allman anthology. In 2012, he'd invite me to sit in and record with ABB in New York. Like Jim and Jesse, he was a real southern gentleman.

15

The Candidate Didn't Make It to the White House— What the Pluck Happened?

Though the mid-1980s felt like something of a jumble, some band events stand out in my memory because of the strange crowds in which I found myself. I was spending a lot of time out on the road, where the band was establishing itself as a reliable country act and regularly producing country radio hits. We were, as they say, "living the dream." "Long Hard Road" was our first number-one single, right after "Dance Little Jean," but I missed my kids and home life greatly. The lure of the lights helped the road win that tug-of-war. Besides, I didn't make enough staying at home to keep the whole thing afloat.

I needed to make a solo album, and I had a lot of songs that NGDB did not want to do. Around 1984, when I was finally getting around to finishing those Aspen recordings, I asked the Oak Ridge Boys if they would sing on this record with me, and they said yes! The Oak Ridge Boys surely didn't need what little publicity they might get out of working on my solo project that didn't have a label yet, but I set a date. It felt great, and, even more surprising, their enthusiasm was equal to mine.

When I showed up at the Nashville studio an hour early to get ready with my tracks from Aspen, there was a band bus in the studio parking lot. *Well, surely they aren't here this early*, I thought. Wrong. The boys came strolling into Woodland Studios (the same studio we used to record *Circle* in 1971) around nine in the morning, ready to sing on two tracks I had ready. As it turned out, they had just played the Illinois State Fair the night before and had decided to drive to the studio, park the bus, sleep, and record the session before going home.

I could not have been happier with the result. My arrangement of the classic "Sleepwalk," with my fifteen dollar lap slide guitar, became one of my best recordings, made complete by great doo-wop vocals by the Oak Ridge Boys and excellent mixing by Bob Edwards. For once, I felt like I had made that slide sing. When my brother heard it, he told me, "You nailed it." I took pride in this personal accomplishment, but at the same time, I wished NGDB had recorded it with me.

Even though Jeff had let me know early on that "you shouldn't sing," one highlight of those sessions was the Boudleaux Bryant tune "Hey, Joe," which Carl Smith had made a country smash in 1953. I had been saving "Hey, Joe" for years, for an occasion like this. I was singing, playing fiddle, mandolin, guitar, and banjo, and making a real country record with hot Nashville pickers! But I was also about to learn a hard lesson in how important the "closed session" sign can be. The country duo Moe Bandy and Joe Stampley were recording in the next studio. One of them stuck their nose in to see what I was cutting. But then the next day Bandy and Stampley recorded their own version, "Hey, Joe (Hey, Moe)." Theirs came out only two weeks later and charted before I could get mine mixed. Ahhh, showbiz. I never used "Hey, Joe." Well, not yet—but some day I will use it. Darn, it's good.

The Oaks wouldn't let me pay them.

One of my personal goals when getting into showbiz was to be successful enough to make benefits happen, like the one for diabetes in Little Rock. Although I wasn't a big enough star on my own, I had access to several who were. With some of my kids in tow, I ran up to

Aspen to have lunch with John Denver and ask him if he would meet with Tom Campbell to discuss a benefit. Denver was laughing about the community service stint that he had just completed that day, which involved singing at the base of Aspen Mountain for an hour on eight different days. While telling me, "I guess they didn't know I love to sing!" a tourist approached us excitedly, asking him for an autograph. John very cordially said, "Well, I don't sign autographs in my hometown, but I would love to shake your hand and welcome you to Aspen." With everyone happy, and no crowd gathered, we went to lunch. He ended up doing many benefits with Tom.

Ten-year-old Andrew was scared of Denver's broad smile, saying, "He looks like the Cheshire cat."

I got a phone call right after that, which was another request for help. Colorado's Gary Hart must have been having a hard time when Chuck Morris called asking *me* to help Hart's 1984 presidential campaign in Tennessee. As a chiseled-faced man with unruly brown hair, Gary seemed to be one of us, and not "them," someone who was technically not part of the establishment, but whom we could trust. He was unlike the other politicos running, whose agendas were never completely clear, and he projected honesty and sincerity. I was intrigued to see what a presidential campaign trail might be like. I told Chuck I'd get Hart on the Grand Ole Opry, get a photo taken with Roy Acuff welcoming him, line up some Nashville interviews, and get him on TNN's *Nashville Now* (Ralph Emery's television show). Hart's team liked all that, asked me to get on it, and told me where to meet up with the candidate in Cincinnati the next week. Since politics is the mother of showbiz, I wanted to see how his show rolled, and got on the phone to Nashville.

Alone in my natty Cincinnati hotel, I couldn't raise anyone involved with the campaign. At 6:00 AM I decided to go downstairs to look around and wait for the 7:15 AM press conference. Being asked to participate had made me feel kind of important, as if I had something to contribute that might even justify those hours, months, and years away from family. I grabbed a bite, just to have something to do. It was too early to call my family, but in fact, that family was dissolving at the time. It had been during times on the road, like this, when my wife was home alone dealing with all six children, that the ties between us started to fray.

As I waited alone for Gary Hart and his entourage in that hotel, I wondered what I was really doing there: me, a banjo player, and him, running for president. He must be in trouble! Who wrote this script? At 7:00 AM the hotel lobby—which had been empty about twenty minutes earlier—was now crawling with people: three TV networks plus CNN, radio and newspaper reporters, and a growing crowd of supporters. A lot of guys in suits were prowling around, talking into their coat cuffs, and scanning the crowd.

Hart entered and talked, breaking for applause throughout his speech, which was followed by a lively Q & A. I liked what he said. As the candidate left and passed closely by me, a friendly guy came up to me and said, "How's it goin', buddy? Everything OK? Nice day?" A few seconds later, I realized this cuff-talker had patted down the new long-haired face in the crowd. Hart's people then turned their attention to the Presidential Ballroom, where they set up for a seven thirty breakfast of the University of Cincinnati Alumni; the news people swarmed in after them. Hart entered to applause and spoke. Seven minutes later, they were gone again.

I went back to my room for a few minutes, and the guy in DC who had set this all up called. "Can you play tomorrow in Chattanooga with a favorite local politician named Dalton? He'd love to meet you," he said. I agreed, and ten minutes later Dalton called, asking what tunes we could do. Like many who grew up in these states, he played guitar and sang "on the side." We scheduled rehearsal for two hours later, to occur in the airport motorcade while we drove to the Chattanooga rally. DC called again and said they needed to get thirty press people backstage at the Opry. *Hmmm.* Looked like I'd be getting busier than I thought.

I knew road travel, and had flown *a lot*, sometimes on three planes in a day. I'd played two cities in one day, even. I was ready for this. The phone rang. "Lobby call, leaving at 9:00 sharp."

I'd tried to get some kind of ID from the head press girl three times, but she said, "Don't worry about it. Get it on the plane." Hart had spoken twice this morning and now the motorcade was pulling out for the airport. I'd been talking with someone about country music, and when I asked what he did he told me he wrote for the *Los Angeles Times*. *Hmm.* I wondered if there might be a press opportunity for me in all of this, but that notion got stomped on pretty quickly.

On the way to the airport, we stopped at a factory where Hart talked to workers for a few minutes. As I got off the bus, a cuff-talker stopped me and firmly asked, "Who are you with?" Two other tough guys in suits immediately appeared to back him up.

"I'm with Hart?" I replied.

"*Who* are you with?" they shot back as they surrounded me. *I'm a dead guy soon,* I thought.

"Look, I'll just get back on the bus and not bother anyone."

"You'd better stay right here! Let's see your credentials. *Who are you with?*"

I spotted the press girl. "Cathy, I'm going to jail soon! Help!"

She signaled that I was OK and the first cuff-talker gave me a tiny tin badge that would let me go anywhere. *Badges, I don't need no stinking badges,* I thought. Hart continued getting applause and laughs, while I exhaled slowly to stop imagining a future in federal prison, and told some jokes to folks from the *Boston Globe*, the *L.A. Times*, and NBC.

I loved meeting the press corps; they were a bunch of road warriors like me. Owen, a photographer for the *L.A. Times*, had been "doing Sandinistas last month." His friend from *Newsweek* had recently been killed there. He told me Mondale's plane was really boring. At 10:15 AM we pulled away for the airport. Noticing a daredevil cameraman standing on the tailgate of the lead station wagon—now hitting fifty-five mph on the freeway—that was right behind the candidate, I commented to Owen that the guy seemed to know how to have a good time. Owen explained, "We've learned a lot since the Kennedys. We take turns for that closest access, so there's always a camera on the VIP or his car, with a bunch of lights ready to be turned on." The press corps agreed to share whatever footage might result. "It's called Deathwatch," he said.

With the freeways barricaded for us, we arrived at the 727 at 10:35 AM, and were wheels up at 10:45 AM. Everyone ignored the usual take-off rules, and people were writing or laughing while standing or walking around the plane. Someone even came sliding down the aisle on a tray as the plane lifted off the ground. Once airborne, I decided to warm up for Chattanooga, so I picked the ole banjo for about twenty minutes straight. When I finished, there was applause from the gathered crowd. A smiling Gary Hart was now standing in front of me and offered a welcoming, "Glad to have you aboard!" The general chaos and clowning went on until we landed, making me think, *Now, this is a strange gig.*

Dalton didn't make it to the airport. There was no motorcade rehearsal as we headed off in an advance car. A few minutes later, while standing at the side of a flatbed truck that was serving as a stage in downtown Chattanooga, I offered the Women's Glee Club an E note from my banjo. Dalton showed up while they sang, and we ran down a couple of tunes. We were on next and Dalton sang "Head Over Heels in Love" and we picked "Earl's Breakdown." Then, six solo minutes later, I introduced Hart. While sitting behind Hart with Dalton, I tried to listen to the speech, but Dalton kept whispering in my ear about his favorite bluegrass groups. At the end of the speech, Hart posed for photos, so I started playing "My Country 'Tis of Thee" on my banjo, with the Glee Club joining in.

With sirens blaring, it took us ten minutes to get back to the airport, and then we had another tarmac press conference on the way to the plane. The plane was wheels up at 12:50 PM with sandwich time on the BNA (the Nashville airport code) leg. The 12:25 PM touchdown (thanks to moving from Eastern to Central time) was followed by another press conference at the BNA hangar. My new friends in the press corps invited me to sit with them, so I took my Walkman and a pad of paper to look like I belonged. The reporters had spoken highly of Hart on the plane, but as he gave familiar answers to familiar questions, one of the journalists said sarcastically, "Oh, number 83—no MX—next will be number 105."

They were mostly on his side, so far. I got carried away listening to their commentary and missed the motorcade into town, so I had to grab a ride with a volunteer. I ended up with Hart's assistant, Cathy. We talked about the upcoming meeting that I'd arranged with Roy Acuff and Ralph Emery, and her unusual job.

Three interviews and one press conference later, I realized that I actually did like the guy. His ideas sounded good to me: stop MX, stop B-1, stop spending foolishly and rebuild the thousands of bridges and roads throughout the country; protect and don't abuse the environment; demand equal rights and pay for women; don't let our sons die protecting dictators' countries. He was responding to a lot of problems on people's minds with what sounded like very sensible solutions. But, in truth, by about six thirty that night, it all started to sound like, "Blah, blah, blah."

I saw what they meant when they had talked about Hart's being good on his feet when asked about Mondale returning the PAC money (which was fresh news he had not heard yet). He tossed off this quick response: "I don't think a president should go into office with any strings attached—or even ones that he has cut."

The week before, I had gone to see Mr. Roy Acuff and asked him if he would "welcome" Hart to the Opry stage. His first reaction was, "Well, John, you know he is a Democrat, and I am not. Now, how can I bring a man from the other party onto my stage?" I made my case: that music transcends politics, that the Opry is a great American institution, that Roy Acuff should welcome an out-of-town, fellow American to the show. To top it off, I argued that it would show everyone how confident Roy was about his Republican Party winning if he were to welcome the other party's candidate because it would make the opponent look weaker. Blah, blah, blah. Mr. Acuff listened, thought it over, squinted his eyes, and drawled, "Yes. That would be good. I look forward to meeting the young man." I felt like I, too, had been good on my feet.

On the way to Opryland, after the 7:00 PM fundraiser where more talk was accompanied by flesh-pressing at one hundred dollars per head (for about twenty-five heads), the Interstate was blocked again. Promptly at 7:45 PM, we left the fundraiser to head over to *Nashville Now.* I had him booked on that popular television show.

We walked on the Emery show for a nice, but non-political, fifteen-minute interview. With one more stop at the Opry to go, we walked toward the cars.

Hart asked, "How far is it to the Opry?"

"About a two-minute walk," I answered. He said OK, and turned to walk the way I pointed. Like a bird flock, forty-five people turned right and followed.

So there we went—three cuff-talkers in front, one on each side, and four in back. The bomb-sniffing dogs had preceded us as usual, and I began to notice that I couldn't see outside the unbroken circle that I was in. The Opry guard who usually hassled me on many backstage solo appearances gave a rather stunned look at "my" entourage. His expression alone was worth the trip. I'd seen entourages before, but this mass of people changed direction every thirty minutes like a school of fish, and was never more than five minutes off schedule. This was rock 'n' roll without the music

We got to Mr. Acuff's dressing room just in time for me to introduce them and let them chat for a few minutes before Roy left to start the Opry show. Alone again with Hart, in Acuff's dressing room, surrounded by historical Opry photos from earlier decades, it felt like 1948, when Flatt and Scruggs formed. It was a strange part of my overall journey to be in this dressing room, and then I saw a gold *Will the Circle Be Unbroken* album with my name on it on Acuff's wall. This was good for me, too. Even the presidential hopeful didn't have that, but I don't think he noticed it.

I said, "You know, you could be president, and here I am alone with you. I can ask you anything I want. What a privilege."

Hart smiled. "Go ahead."

I asked him how many socks he packed for a week, and if their colors matched, or if he went by thickness. As he laughed, I asked him if he liked doing this and he said, "Yes, I have to do this. I realized about 1980 that I had a chance. How could I turn it down? I have no money, my family has no money, my house is mortgaged to the hilt . . . Mondale has a lot of money . . . but it's going well . . . I think I can win. I think I have more than a chance. If Reagan can do it, anyone can." At this point, Hart had been "on" in front of audiences and the press for thirteen straight hours, but he still looked fresh. Like Dick Clark and Porter Wagoner, certain people just know how to keep the just-fixed-up-to-be-looked-at look.

Right then, someone stuck their head in and said, "Roy's ready." We went to stand in the wings and watch the Opry happen, which was always a magical trip into the past.

Right on cue, Roy told the fans that "the Opry attracts many different types, and has always been a favorite stop for candidates of various political offices." (He should know: he ran for governor in 1948.) He continued, "Although this boy from Colorado is not of the same party as I am, please help me make welcome a fellow American to the Grand Ole Opry stage, Mr. Gary Hart." They shook hands and posed for the photographers for a minute, then Hart walked off to the side, and, like Chevy Chase looking at the Grand Canyon in *National Lampoon's Vacation*, pretended to groove to the music for about a minute.

The Opry stopover was over, and so was my time on the campaign trail. As we parted ways at the motorcade, I remembered that my banjo was in the candidate's trunk.

"Hey wait!" I shouted. "SS guy, pop the trunk so I can get my stuff!" I unloaded my things as the guy on "Deathwatch" got in position behind Hart's car. The trip manager was yelling, "Get in! Everyone in! We're leaving! Now!" It dawned on me that I had been near a bullet's potential target for a couple of days, and was now glad to be out. Banjo players might get yelled at, but not shot at—not in my experience, anyway. Owen yelled, "Where can I write you?" I hollered back, "Anywhere along I-70!"

I tried to collect the five dollars I'd won off a guy named Frank from ABC who had bet me that Hank Williams had died at thirty-nine, not twenty-nine, but he just shouted, "Try and get it!" It was now 9:00 PM and they were twenty minutes from to the BNA airport, but scheduled to be wheels up at 9:20 PM. As the cars pulled out, I yelled to the "Deathwatch" guy, "Hit me with the floodlights one more time!" He let me bask in the star limelight blaze for a few seconds. As they pulled away, Cathy yelled, "Come to New Orleans with us!" I said "I can't," though I didn't really have any reason why not. With their sirens blaring, they pulled away, leaving me in the Opry parking lot alone with my suitcase and banjo, looking for a ride into town.

The Opry photo was in about 120 newspapers and the photos from *Nashville Now* were in about another twenty. Hart lost Tennessee, but I got a few free lunches the next week from those who thought I might be close to some future power. That was only before he got into too much *Monkey Business* on the love boat and lost his stature to affairs of the heart. The press was not on his side anymore. Never heard from him again, and the free lunches stopped. As Mark Twain said in 1848: "Politicians and diapers—you change them for the same reason." But, history does repeat itself, they say.

A few years down the road, I might have helped Al Gore a bit. In a Nashville bar, I'd rehearsed a band so he could sing "Rocky Top" with his dad. Al couldn't remember the words to his state's song, but his dad sang it great. I was in one of those smoky, sticky-floor bars my dad had warned me about, helping a future vice president get votes. That was only a senatorial race, but he won. Al wrote me a nice letter.

The Eagles had soared by then, as many had from our early years, such as John Denver. Now that we were in the midst of our own respectable and most consistent third run, it was fun running into them on the road. The Eagles had said in print more than once that NGDB had been an influence on them, which was a comment that led to backstage passes and other things. When Bernie and Meisner parted, I felt less connected, but it was still interesting when the bands crossed paths, particularly one time in a California hotel. (Not that one.)

At an Eagles concert after-party in Hollywood with the Dirt guys, I found myself sitting on a condo couch next to the guy we don't want knocking on our hotel room door late at night with an axe delivery— the "Heeeerrrrre's Johnny" guy himself. Jack Nicholson showing up at a Hollywood party in the mid-1980s was about as surprising as Chuck Berry breaking into a duck walk. I'd been watching him in the kitchen earlier, pontificating to Jeff, Bobby, and others, while they made sure to laugh at everything he said. But, now he was taking a break, and had headed for the free spot on "my" couch.

Jack has that special celebrity talent I've mentioned that always amuses me: the ability to walk around a crowded room, acting like they are looking for some important person who's also looking for them, while never once making eye contact with anyone in the room who they don't want to see. Nicholson was good at it.

But now, sitting next to this somewhat-imposing star, I wanted to make an impression of my own, at least so I could talk about my own time with Jack the way I knew Jeff would for the next six months. Obviously I wasn't on Jack's radar; he couldn't make his eyes meet mine as he approached the couch. I could see he wasn't going to address me, so after he settled into the couch, I dove in.

"Hi, my name is John." He made some kind of noise, but I wasn't sure what it signified. I pressed on. "What's yours?" Looking around the room, past me, he replied ever so slowly, "Jaaaaaacccckkk."

"Nice party. What do you do?" I asked

"I'm an aaactorrrrr," he growled, glancing back at the kitchen.

"I play banjo. It's a tough town for that. Great town for acting, I hear. Does it do well for you?"

"I've had a few parts . . . it's working out."

"Great. I wonder if I've seen you in anything?" As he got up with a loud silence, Jack parted the party.

About a week later in Aspen, we were having breakfast in one of those places that goes out of business every so often only to re-open with a different name but the same menu. In walked Mr. Nicholson. Jack was quietly scanning the room for a table, still unnoticed by the crowd, when Jeff spotted him and started chattering excitedly, "Hey! There's Jack! I've got to let him know we're here!" Jeff scrambled like an F-15 pilot on red alert and launched toward his target.

"Hey, Jack! Hey, Jack . . . Jack," Jeff stammered, while mumbling something back over his shoulder at us that sounded like, "haven't seen him since L.A."

Without actually looking at him, Nicholson saw Jeff heading toward him and turned to his companion. Even a blind lip reader could read him: "Ohhh, let's get out of here. Somebody's coming."

They were out the door before Jeff could strike. Our star-struck singer landed back at the booth a bit slower than when he took off, sitting down like a paint chip freshly fallen off the wall, otherwise known as a flake.

"Guess he didn't see me. Wish I'd caught his eye." To his credit, Jeff didn't know yet about the celebrity eye-radar trick, though he learned it later. Jack continued being the great actor he was destined to be, and when I cross paths again with him he just might ask me what I do—if I catch his eye.

So, things were going well, but there were still new fields to plow, one of them being in front of eighty thousand people at the first Farm Aid concert, in Champaign, Illinois, in September 1985. It was a huge event, with a cast of what seemed like thousands: workers, drivers, singers, food servers, musicians, "stars," reporters, and Willie. Some were skeptical, snidely wondering: *So what? Too little too late. Farmers created their problems. Why should we help solve them?* Whether or not the farmers created their own problems was not the question. Many were in trouble, and people were there to help. Everyone who didn't understand the situation at first agreed after learning more about the farmers' plight: it was good to help the backbone of America straighten out. John Denver had asked us to be his band, and we had our own set, too.

Excitement built as the start of the concert approached. Even the airport van driver, driving for free that day, reflected the mood of anticipation. "No one knows what this will accomplish, if it will help at all; today we'll all feel good for at least trying, and the music is going to be great!" And, people kept reminding us, it would be "good exposure."

In the Holiday Inn parking lot, I heard a familiar voice calling me from a balcony. Glen Campbell wanted me to know he'd be doing a five-song medley in a couple of hours. While we were talking, some hangers-on offered him a hit on a joint. "No," Glenn said. "I've got some important work to do. I don't need that." I saw this as a holdover from the days before Campbell's breakthrough as a star, when he was one of the studio professionals known as the Wrecking Crew, playing on countless major hits of the '60s. That was the only reference to drugs I heard around this event.

Hippies with their '60s hits, earthy country stars, heavy rockers, shiny Vegas types, country rockers, and folk legends had all gathered in a football stadium for a good cause, and everyone loved it! They believed in Willie. Those with notorious egos checked them at the door. Some critics had argued that the stars were only there for personal aggrandizement, but many were already plenty successful and rich. We all paid our own way. All gave a day of their lives to help, on the chance that their fans might tune into this cause. Like with Vietnam, a bunch of singers were trying to wake the country up about this major, national problem.

I'd retreated to a trailer dressing room with my banjo to warm up away from the band, thinking about the '60s Dylan photo in McCabe's with a sign in the background that read, "No bluegrass on Sunday." In walked Eddie Van Halen. Cordial, excited, friendly, and animated, Eddie listened to a few licks before picking up his guitar. Then Dylan himself entered, with a slower, more deliberate energy. The two of them went about preparing for their performances, with backs to each other, in their own worlds. Bob struggled with his harp rack, frenetic Eddie hammered at light speed on his guitar neck, and I started a very fast "Fireball Mail." After one time through, I stopped and faced them both.

"Hey, Bob, Eddie!" I began. "We could form a bluegrass band, use the initials from our first names, and call it JEB! I've heard bluegrass is going to be big this year. Whaddya think?" They paused from their preparations to give each other a *who-the-hell-is-he* glance, and went back to their disparate worlds within themselves. I made my exit and drifted to the stage. I should have thanked Bob for the banjo he bought for me in 1965.

Two hours later, I stood three feet from Van Halen witnessing some rock 'n' roll history up close: the reunion of Sammy Hagar with the Van Halen band. With their licks flashing hot, those two plowed some new ground that night, and quite a crop came in. They blew the clouds away with "Wild Thing," of all things.

Hagar came off stage and said, "Hey, John, how you doin'? Remember that gig in Omaha a few years back?" That he was so in touch seconds after burning in front of eighty thousand people impressed me. Seven years earlier, NGDB had played a show with him, opening in an Omaha stadium. Sammy and I had our oldest sons with us, who were both named Aaron and about nine years old. We let the boys run around and play together in the safe backstage area, as they obeyed the single rule: "Don't go out there!"

"Yeah, our sons played backstage for hours, and caught butterflies, and didn't remember we were performing. They both missed our sets! Hey, great to be here, eh?" I said.

We played the five songs with Denver. He had often sat in with us in Aspen for a few songs. Those impromptu moments paid off well, as our Farm Aid set went really well. Our own five songs were exciting, too.

All the performers that day felt they were needed, and they responded to that need. Rickie Lee Jones said, "I don't know what I can do besides sing, but if that helps, I'm here to do it." Outlaw singer David Allen Coe told me, "Willie asked me to come to be his bodyguard." For David, that was all he needed. He knew it would be worthwhile if Willie said so. Coe echoed the sentiments of many of the artists: "Our fellow countrymen are in trouble. Why not try and help?" It struck me that the current sound of patriotism was rather different than the previous decade's.

A couple of very good things came out of that show for me. I ended up playing on Coe's *Just Divorced* album the next year, and he returned the favor on my first solo album.

NGDB later played Farm Aid New Jersey, and other later iterations. By then Fadden had written "Workin' Man," which had become a number-one hit. Ibby sang it great—one of the best NGDB records.

The constant contrasts in my life are often so polar opposite of each other that I've felt like two or three lives are being lived by Walter McEuen (a.k.a., John McEuen to most). At birth, my father named me Walter (for his brother). Two months later, worried about me being nicknamed Wally, he renamed me John, but didn't change my birth certificate. Consequently, all my life I have been Walter for school, documents, driver's licenses, and elsewhere, but to those who knew me, I've been John, and of course Johnny, to some.

When my father laughed, he laughed loud and hard, but I can't remember him showing any sad emotions. I grew up learning that the manly thing to do was hold in any sadness. "You have to be strong," he said. I'd cried alone when the news about my sister came, but no one had seen me in that back room of McCabe's. That was the last time. It would be many years before I realized that it was wrong to worry about it. As the song says, "I'll cry if I want to."

Later, when my own kids were growing up, we had found a homeless puppy and named him Teddy. Teddy was the best damn dog you could have. He was always happy to serve and knew his position as the family dog: watch the kids, be nice to the cat, go outside when you need to, don't bark unless it means something.

When some of the kids were still little and needed a drink from the kitchen sink, Teddy would lay there, but not to get in the way. He had a purpose: the kids would stand on him to reach the water, and Teddy would sit rock still except for his flopping tail.

Sugar, the cat, would walk up on Teddy as he was laying down, gently fluff up a space in Teddy's fur with his claws, and take a nap on top of his friend. That was Teddy. But the time came when he could not get up anymore, could not drink out of his bowl, and would not eat. The night before his last day, I slept next to him in the living room. He was my pillow. I was strong. I kept my composure. I was not going to cry.

When I lifted Teddy into the car that next cloudy yet crisp Colorado morning, I sensed he somehow knew he was going to the vet. It was the only time in months he seemed excited, yet frightened. It was killing me, as I knew what I was going to have the vet do to him. I carried him in, and laid him on the vet's cold metal table as I petted his beautiful tan fur and his tail slowly flopped. He raised his weary head and his sad eyes looked at mine. Like my sister had so many years earlier, he was saying goodbye. Ten minutes later he was gone.

I got back in the car and sat there, as thoughts of my sister Maureen came to mind. I broke down and cried, and realized emotion was back in my life in a visible manner. Teddy deserved that. He was a great dog. It was hard to face the kids and tell them what I did. I still think about him thirty years later.

I needed to get on the mind-numbing road.

16

Can We Win This Crowd?
And Finally Waking Up

In spite of so many "differences of opinion" and "band things"—that is, the usual tensions and issues that arise between people who spend way too much time together for way too long—NGDB has been a unique group in American music. The highest of high points, for me, had been our Russia trip in 1977, but the tour of Europe we did in the year that I split with the band runs a very close second.

That seven-show 1988 tour, starting at London's Wembley Stadium, would hit eight European cities and put us on the bill with George Jones, Tammy Wynette, Bill Monroe, Cash and June, Johnny Russell, and a host of Grand Ole Opry greats. The always-in-turmoil promoter, Mervyn Conn, had scheduled us in the third slot in the first half of the eight-hour show, but after sitting in on our sound check, decided that we should close the first half. It was a little hard to follow the Dirt Band, even in a sound check. After the first night, he moved us again, to the show's second half, so we would go on just before the headliner, Johnny Cash. I don't know if we were really any better than other acts on the bill, but being different sometimes pays off. It certainly did in Europe.

When Cash came up behind me in the hotel lobby in London the week before Zurich, I knew it was him. The whole cast had that day off, but he had taken a date of his own. "Hey, McEuen, you wanna go pick with June and me and the band to Wales, and sit in? We could use you on the Carter Family songs. Hop on the bus with us?"

I blurted out, "Letmethinkaboutityes," and grabbed the banjo that was hidden behind a fake lobby tree. Cash laughed. He realized I was laying in wait for him. I couldn't turn down an invitation from the Man in Black. Neither could I share that it gave me a sense of redemption for my earlier escapades in Cash's apartment back in New York.

We did two shows in Wales. It was pretty heady stuff for a kid from Orange County. Cash always introduced himself from the stage, as if the audience wasn't sure who they'd come to see. "Hello, I'm Johnny Cash," he'd say, knowing they would clap again before he started. But Cash wasn't happy after the first show.

Back in the dressing room between shows he said, "You did great. But I need to give you a better build-up next show. These folks don't know Nitty Gritty and need to appreciate you more! Don't rush out . . . I think . . . I know . . . I can do better."

I wasn't sure what he meant, but for the second show, I waited in the wings for my cue. The Carter section came up, and Cash went into a dissertation about music. He talked about how the *Circle* album was his mother-in-law's first gold record, and about how it was put together with my brother Bill and "the *great* Nitty Gritty Dirt Band." Then he started describing a performer I had never met, "a combination of Earl Scruggs, Chet Atkins, Roy Clark, Vassar Clements, Roy Acuff, and Johnny Russell." I looked around, figuring we were about to be joined by someone else who just arrived from either Nashville or hillbilly heaven, while Cash continued.

"And tonight, coming to play with us because we love him, and we ask him whenever June and I get a chance to have him along, and because he did not want to leave the United Kingdom without playing for, in his words, the great people of Wales, his first time here . . . please make our good friend JOHN McEUEN feel welcome!"

Like a Pavlov dog, I was jolted on stage by hearing my name, arriving at the mic to a long, standing ovation from an audience who had never heard of me until then.

After the show, Cash walked up and in that signature voice, punched me in the shoulder, and simply said, "I told you . . . *I could do better.*"

———————

Knocking them out in Hitler's halls (one was where we were told he gave his last live speech, in Ludwigshafen) had never been part of my Orange County teenage dream, but we encountered hot crowds everywhere, winning every night, until we got to Zurich. That audience was a bit quiet, sedate, reserved, icy—OK, it was dead. Johnny Russell cornered me just before our set and told me why the whole cast was heading to the stage area. (Russell wrote "Act Naturally" among others.)

"*No one* is going over tonight. Dead audience . . . very little response. So, we figure if you guys don't get 'em, then it isn't us. But, we hope you do get 'em."

What a responsibility! We had to come through for all! I ran back to the dressing room for some insurance, and then headed up to the stage to join the band of brothers like we were facing the lions in the Colosseum. Fifteen minutes into it, the set was indeed going slow, but not horribly. We had seen horrible by then, and this wasn't it. But it wasn't hot yet. "Bojangles" got a respectful response, and bluegrass picked it up a bit, but it still wasn't killer. Other performers stood by the stage side, nodding to each other as we tried to wake up the crowd. But the Swiss had come for Cash only, and we were about to lose them.

Then came Cajun-style Dirt Band rock. Ibby introduced the next song with a little lecture about how we kicked British ass a long time ago and still sing about it as we broke into "The Battle of New Orleans." I kicked it off on the fiddle, then disappeared. When I jumped off the drum riser for the first fiddle solo, now wearing a British flag shirt, and got chased around by the American Ibby, the audience started waking up. I disappeared again, and showed up for the second solo, fiddle blaring, wearing an American flag shirt, and I heard the audience response kick up to another level as I chased Ibby back across the stage. Finally, as we got to the last solo, I ripped off the American flag shirt revealing a Swiss flag shirt and ran up on top of the PA speaker stacks, where I took off my silver shoes and threw them into the audience. Some of the crowd went nuts. Ibby chased me out into the middle of the front row and the whole audience roared.

I started the next tune, "Diggy Liggy Lo," fiddling barefoot from the audience, and we got them to their feet until the end. We had done ourselves proud, winning them over for the whole cast and crew. If we were ever great, that was the night.

I'd invited Bill Monroe to stop by at a club after that show, where I'd arranged a midnight jam. Sure enough, I was on stage, about an hour into it, when in walks the Father of Bluegrass with a sweet Swiss Miss on each arm. I invited him up and watched that white hat come trotting through the crowd with Bill under it.

Monroe hopped up on stage and turned to me. "You know 'Uncle Pen' on that fiddle? Pick it, an' we'll get some music played."

So there I was, playing behind the grand ole man of bluegrass, twenty years after the Ash Grove, digging every bar in this bar, which was one of "those bars" my father had warned me about. (He always said, "You'll end up in bars playing for people who are drinking and not listening." I'd had different plans.) We did about four tunes with Monroe that night, and when Jeff Hanna's harmony with Carlene Carter filled in, the moment was cemented in my mind and has stayed with me ever since. I felt like I'd lived up to Johnny Cash's grandiose introduction in Wales earlier in the week.

Europe was good to me, especially from a financial perspective; it took a lot of money to raise a six-kid family at eighty-five hundred feet in the Rockies. But money would not keep the family together.

Earlier that year, while home after a ten-city run in Canada, their mom was "out of the house" for a couple of days and I found myself home tending kids alone again. I didn't know what was going on; she was just gone when I got there. Trying to juggle breakfast, getting kids off to school, carpooling, school play rehearsal, housecleaning, laundry, grocery shopping, and getting dinner on the table felt as if a 747 captain woke me out of a nap and said, "Bring this thing in for me."

Figuring familiar would work, I decided to try a lasagna dinner—for seven. The kids might eat it. The kids were skeptical. My abilities as a cook were as limited as my sports abilities; I could make a great breakfast, but that was it. They knew it. After a couple hours of gathering ingredients and reading most of the instructions, I put the beautiful lasagna assembly in the oven. Watching like a baby hawk patiently waiting for food, six-year-old Nathan chirped, in a matter-of-fact tone, "You didn't cook the noodles first?"

I replied, "I'm cooking them now, right in there," with the same confidence I'd had ripping into my fiddle in front of a hot, screaming audience, knowing I could get them on their feet. I knew what I was doing; the lasagna *looked* picture perfect, just like the photo.

"Well, Mom boils noodles about seventeen minutes until they're soft first, *then* puts them together with the stuff." Skeptical of his understanding of the intricacies of cooking, I checked the noodles with a fork about twenty minutes later and found them as hard as the dish they were in. After another five minutes, but still no change, I ripped it out of the oven, pulled the noodles out (and, for some reason, washed them), boiled them for seventeen minutes, reassembled it, then put it back in the oven, and waited. *This is harder than I thought*, I thought. The bell finally said it was ready.

Six hungry kids, from six to sixteen years old, gathered for a now-late dinner, staring suspiciously at this steaming, bubbling concoction that looked like a dish of placenta in the middle of the table. It was not a pretty sight, nor a familiar one. No one moved. It was the meal most dreaded by kids: *something new.*

"What's that?" one skeptically queried, speaking for all who sat silently staring with curled lips. One even went into a full-body quiver. It was easier to do an interview for the *Washington Post* than to figure out what to say to those six doubting faces.

Grasping for a lifeline, I declared, "It's Mexican pizza. Saw it on the road in Texas last week." Frankly, it looked like something scraped off the road. Their exchanged glances were encouraging. "Who's first? There's barely enough," I said. The limited supply trick helped, too.

It went over great. Maybe they were just being kind, or just hungry. They ate it all.

I reached their mom by phone at her gym-instructor boyfriend's house the next morning.

"How did you find me here!" she demanded, and I detected an unusual but unmistakable rhythm in her voice, which was something I'd heard before.

I said, "You're pregnant!"

We met up on a mountain road to talk. After many tears from both, I told her, to assuage her guilt of an affair of the heart, that she wasn't alone in how she dealt with being alone. I, too, had gotten sidetracked, but it was long over.

She blew up, saying, loudly, "I'm done. Done. How horrible," and a bunch of other things I can't remember. Of course, she was hurt and mad, but she was the one who was pregnant! I found that I really didn't mind that much. Must have been my California raisin'. She made beautiful children, as she proved again when she'd delivered her number seven, named Jade, and confirmed he wasn't mine. I couldn't fault the father's taste in women, but his timing was off. I couldn't hate her.

Not long after I got home from that European trip the "agreed on" separation day arrived, and I left the family to go live somewhere else. My offer to stay and adopt Jade was turned down, so I drove away on an early December morning in the oldest of the two cars we had, and could not believe the fog in my head. I couldn't make myself think about anything except *I am out*. By that time I was out of the band; I had no agent, manager, record company, or accountant, no kids, and no family. I felt worthless, but at least I wasn't pregnant. But I was hungry.

I read somewhere, "After a mother gets done raising four kids, she should do something easy, like run General Motors." I had six. I had to figure out how I was going to do this—live, work, raise kids—without a home.

I remember walking into the Safeway in Idaho Springs, minutes before their midnight closing. Just as I went through the door "Bojangles" came on the store's loudspeakers, plunging me even deeper into a funk. I lost my appetite and left, with Johnny Cash's "I could do better" echoing in my head.

Gary Regester (my photographer friend) had decided I should stay with his family a while. It made sense. After our Russia trip, he'd moved from L.A. to Colorado and found Silver Plume, an old 130-acre mining town at ninety-five hundred feet with fewer than two hundred people, where he had started a family. It was wonderful for me.

This is a perfect example of the strange contradictions of my life: on the one hand, I was a single father with no money and a lousy rusty car, living in a friend's tiny basement, waiting for the weekends to see my kids; on the other, when I went to work, there were nice hotels, shiny new rental cars, and people who wanted to see me.

I got to play with Gary and Joanie's friendly and happy kids when I couldn't see mine. My kids would spend weekends with dad, sprawled around the Regesters' home. It was a great time for me, in a warm home with such great people. Gary's wife, Joanie, could make real lasagna really well, was always happy, and it spread.

One fine, summer day months later, Aaron—the same kid who, when he was five, asked if he could go to the airport with me to see which plane I "worked" on—was ready for that great, American male rite of passage. I offered him the chance to try out his new license—that ticket to American manhood—by going for "a drive," and he jumped at the chance. I had something more in mind than a slow crawl around the neighborhood, though. I was going to see if he could go the distance on his maiden voyage.

One morning before dawn, Aaron and I left Denver for my Illinois State Fair job, which we could reach in a single day of nonstop driving. In the same way that one might best learn Spanish by moving to Spain, a great way to learn about driving—and to start to develop some road knowledge—is to head out on I-70 across middle America.

Aaron's excitement started waning as the daytime moon rose over central Kansas. Then the wind started. Wyoming invented wind, and Kansas shows us how to use it. You could almost see us being sucked up into the sky like Dorothy and Toto as the Kansas wind tossed the van about. If you haven't driven across Kansas before, put your nose on a ping-pong table, a little to the right of the centerline, and stare at the other end for about eight hours. Put a little train set's Motel 6 sign facing you at the other end of the table for lifelike detail. This might sound like a string of one-liners, but that is it in Kansas. It can lull you into a stupor, unless the wind is up. Every minute was a great experience with Aaron. He was becoming a young man, and with stars in his eyes for planetary things, he loved that Kansas clear night sky.

I had driven I-70 so many times with NGDB, I knew we'd have long patches of monotony. To relieve some of the boredom, I bought an air pistol at a truck stop that looked exactly like a long-barreled German Luger. It was a deadly looking thing, but it only fired BBs, and it would become the star of its own road story before this trip was done.

By the time we reached Missouri, the wind had passed with the sun, and my rapidly ripening young man was asking for his relief driver. I wasn't ready yet, and fired up the CB radio. Aaron woke up when sex-education class suddenly came on the air. Truckers didn't need Dr. Laura in the days of CB radio; the CB airwaves were constantly full of advice and dissent. Their commentaries kept him interested as he waited for each new, crazy, bragging, good buddy to roll into range. Halfway across Missouri, even the CB banter began to wear thin, until chatter of a "pickle park" came up. Not all the motor homes housed Branson-bound blue-hairs or beer-bellied bubbas going out to kill deer or fish. At a certain rest area about sixty miles ahead waited an RV whose red lights were actually "tail" lights. I explained to Aaron what it all meant.

This motorized madame's publicity was all "word of mouth" on radio free CB. She was pulling down a good piece of business, according to the drivers' reviews. The Walmarts and Safeways and others along I-70 were going to wait an hour or two extra for their deliveries. Listening to the hilarious dares and tales of conquest of these interstate Don Juans kept us awake for our three-hour stretch across the Show-Me State, which was better even than caffeine at this point in Aaron's inauguration to road life.

We laughed all the way to the St. Louis airport, where we picked up the great drummer Merel Bregante. He had spent some time with NGDB in the late 1970s. Merel and I had worked together so much that our deal went something like this: "Merel, meet me at baggage sidewalk of Delta in St. Louis on the twelfth, first morning flight, week-long gig." Aaron got to tell all his newly minted crazy road stories, but Merel had already lived most of them. After all, Merel had even met Little Rock Connie years ago. After a while he simply asked, "Where we playing and how much am I making?"

I had my Denver buddies Jim and Salli Ratts and their Runaway Express band to back me (with Merel) for that week-long, three-set-a-day run. We had been friends since I first met him in Colorado, and Jim had been a fan since "Buy for Me the Rain." They were two of the nicest people I've ever met, and they saved me more times than I can count.

I delivered Aaron to the Springfield airport a few days later for a quicker trip home, so he wouldn't miss his first marching band practice. As wonderful as it had been for him and me, it also made me feel how much I missed time with all my family. I ached often for my kids to be close, and now I had to send this one off, after too few days and so much fun. I didn't want him to go. Although one last bit of road craziness made me thankful that we're still free men.

The vice president of the free world, George Bush, was scheduled to honor the Springfield fair on Aaron's departure day. That his appearance was eminent was evident as we approached the airport. Air Force Two was landing, and even then, years before 9/11, security seemed excessive. The airport was crawling with cops.

I bade Aaron adieu at the security check, winking and saying, "I'll bring that BB thing back with me." I was careful not to say "gun" in any airport, especially that day.

"Don't worry about it, Dad," Aaron said cheerfully, "I got it already." My eyes widened. *Uh-oh.* "Where is it?" I asked nervously.

"Oh, it's in my carry-on bag. I just threw it in there with my shorts and stuff." Aaron smiled at me with a look of pure innocence, while I turned pale watching his bag being sucked in to the X-ray machine, on its way to deliver us into a lifetime of taxpayer-sponsored room and board.

"Well, you may not get home today, or even this year," I said. "We might be doing a lot of quality time together soon." He looked at me, wondering what I was talking about. I had always imagined a future of us making things together, but I didn't want it to be license plates.

"Aaron, my son, watch the security people at the bag X-ray machine, and do not move. Don't run, don't make any loud noises."

Looking puzzled, he said, "Dad, look! There's the vice president's plane, by my gate! Where's my camera? I can get a good shot of him."

Just then, I overheard a security girl say, "Hey, Bob! Come over here a minute! Look at this," pointing at her X-ray screen, which was zeroed in on Aaron's bag.

Bob stared at the screen, put his hand on his radio, and, before calling in the sergeant, said quietly and firmly to the officer by the other machine, "Jack, come over here right now," and then into the radio, "Chief, come on down to Gate Three." His free hand unsnapped his holster.

Aaron was whipping out his camera, and blurting out, "Maybe we'll get a clear shot at the vice president!"

"Son. Do not speak any more. And, tell the absolute truth when you do," I said grimly. He didn't get it, but he was going to soon. Five uniformed officers were staring at the X-ray of Aaron's carry-on cannon. I could feel the blood draining out of my body.

"Who owns this bag?" the sergeant said loudly, his eyes swinging over to us like a prison yard searchlight, looking directly at me. I knew it would be good to show a bit of fatherly wisdom so I said, pointing at Aaron, "He does!" I figured honesty might keep us out of jail, and my son needed to learn a lesson about guns and responsibility, but it's possible I was more worried about missing the gig that afternoon.

"Would you both slowly take a few steps over here, please?" one of them said, as another walked around behind us. Despite my long hair and shaggy beard, I was obviously the adult, and was asked to explain ourselves to the six officers.

"My sixteen-year-old scatterbrained son is so insensitive—as we all know all teenagers can be—to goings on around him in the world and this airport in particular today. He didn't leave our toy, target, BB air pistol—which, by the way, barely has enough power to shoot through paper—in the van like I'd told him. 'Don't even think of taking it out at the airport with the great vice president of America here, as everyone will be doing the security job they are so well qualified for, and they would sense its presence . . .'" I said again that he was sixteen, had hardly been out of the house, was heading to Salt Lake City, and had to get back for school marching band practice at his new high school. Aaron stood there grinning, exuding innocence, and asked what was going on.

The sergeant turned to Aaron, "Get on your plane, boy, you're goin' home," as he wrapped the pistol in a newspaper. Turning to me, he ordered, "Now, you take this out to that van and put it away and don't bring it out till you're in a different state."

I always have preferred memorably exciting days to the ones that just go by unnoticed, but I think I could have passed on this one. Still, somehow, this shared adventure erased my guilt over not being there for Aaron's birth, while I was working in Aspen. As his was the only birth I missed, I had regretted it until that day, which Aaron and I still laugh about. It was a big day—and the night ahead would hold its own surprises. I was about to become Stanley Jordan.

The fair's booker, the renowned Tony Conway, came to me late in that afternoon after the airport debacle. "John, I have a problem. The great jazz guitar man, Stanley Jordan, was going to open tonight for Kenny G. on the main stage, but can't make it. Can you and your band do it? I'll warn you, there are eight thousand jazz fans and it might not be easy."

Well, playing a banjo for a living is fun, so I said, "Sure." It had to be better than opening for Foreigner, and I survived that. Celtic-sounding music with flute and hot bluegrass might do it. And, if I could get them on my side, they might listen. Tony said many were there to see Jordan, the incredible, tall, black guitarist. Walking to center stage alone, I reached the mic and firmly announced to sixteen thousand jazz ears: "Hi! I'm Stanley Jordan. . . . It's been a rough year."

That got a huge laugh, and tricked them in to listening. "Let me take you to the 1800s and the beginnings of jazz!" Starting with my instrumental "Miner's Night Out," the band came out one by one (flute first, which surprised them), with one more player joining us on stage every sixteen bars. We did great, and after thirty-five minutes, we got an encore we didn't take. We had the night off, and picked up a bonus of $1,000.

I missed my kids more than ever, but my oldest son had made it safely to the new home of Salt Lake City just before this set. And, his Utah marching band later took first in the national competition.

A most important event that year came just before my move out of Colorado, when my mother sent me a newspaper article about sleep apnea, with her trademark scribbling in the paper's margins. I followed her advice to get myself examined. My ever-snoring father had severe apnea and had died in his sleep, before people understood the condition. My sleep study in Denver that week revealed that I had not really slept through the night in twenty years. No wonder I could fall asleep at a stop sign, in the middle of a loud concert, on the phone, or in a road case; I'd even been known to sometimes pass out at a party. As a teenager, I always had trouble waking up but figured that was normal, since I stayed up late. As it turns out, I was up late because I finally felt good and alert at that time of day. I knew that when I woke up in the morning, I would not feel nearly as good. I got my CPAP machine to regulate my breathing at night. I would realize my teenage dream of wanting to be an astronaut every night when I put on that mask and closed my eyes. I was in my space capsule.

Still, I would give in to moments of darkness and depression. Thoughts of a perfect suicide—an easy out that would allow the kids to get insurance money—flitted through my mind for a week: wait for a black ice night on I-70, head down to Georgetown from my home in the mountains driving too fast, go over the railing off the fifteen-hundred-foot cliff at the big turn for one last ride, and crash into the

Georgetown train bridge. Thankfully, I shook that off with a renewed commitment to get back to work, watch the kids grow up, and see what I could make of myself. After all, I still had new rental cars, nice hotels, and people who wanted to hear me play. Napoleon Hill's words were starting to make more sense.

Up late one night talking with Joanie, I mused, "I can't believe it's been a year that I've been here already." She looked at me and said, "Johnny, it's been two years."

So much for staying "a while" with Gary's family. Leaving my halfway house to single parenthood, I moved to Utah the next month, where my soon-to-be ex had taken her new baby Jade, her boyfriend, and my six children to live. I found a house in Murray, just south of Salt Lake City, about three miles from theirs. Or, as she screamed on the phone, "ISN'T THAT CONVENIENT!" It was.

Colorado stayed in all our hearts, and even though that desert town of Deseret numbed my mind, I got down to work those ten years in Salt Lake City. I could think again, thanks to CPAP. There was a lot to do to raise six kids and support myself without a band income. If I made $12,000 a month, my road expenses, commissions, alimony, child support, car payment, house payment, and taxes would leave me with zero. I had to make more. And now, with sleep, I did. I started life as a single father and loved it.

I would stay in Utah until my youngest, Nathan, graduated.

17

Party of Seven—
Single Father to the Max

It was never quite the same, but it did get easier and better, and life would still be very fulfilling. My mother had looked after me very well for my first twenty years, doing laundry and ironing, keeping a well-stocked pantry from which she produced regular meals, and so on. I never learned the basic skills of living alone, and then I got married very young to a woman who also took great care of me. The daily-life things had been well administered for me since birth, until around age forty-four. Twelve years of school won't prepare you for all of life's little realities. Take, for example, the dishwasher soap incident that occurred a bit after moving to Utah in 1990.

A few weeks into what would turn out to be ten years solo in Salt Lake, the dishes needed washing before I headed out on the road. After a four-day weekend looking after five boys, I'd let the dirty dishes stack up because we had no dishwasher soap. As an alternative to going out to buy more at two in the morning, I went ahead and used the pink liquid, sink stuff. Soap is soap, right? I was just being an arrogant guy, thinking, *I know how to do this*, like when I tried to make lasagna without knowing how. After guessing at what the right amount of soap should be, and adding a little extra, I started the machine, and went to pack for a 6:30 AM flight.

At 2:45 AM, once I was all packed, I went to the kitchen for a quick snack, and was met by a three-foot-high wall of suds, advancing slowly down the hall like the Blob. The entire kitchen and hall leading out of it had become like a Disney attraction, a slow-moving pulsating wave of pretty bubbles that were still pouring out of the dishwasher. I waded through the foam in search of the OFF switch.

I felt very stupid and cried without shame for the hour it took to clean up the suds; the tears helped keep my eyes clear. I was piling suds on the lawn or stuffing them in the bathtub and sinks. It was like putting toothpaste back in a tube. But then, when I saw how clean the kitchen floor was, I went to bed happy, laughing like an idiot. It was the best, cleanest hour of ZZZs I'd ever had. I was really glad to get on the road.

The day after I got home from that trip to a beautifully clean kitchen, I was tired but with enough money from three gigs to cover the month, when the phone rang. It was NGDB's manager Chuck, asking if I would record with the guys on *Will the Circle Be Unbroken, Volume II*, which they were putting together. My brother Bill and I had turned down offers in earlier years for a *Circle II* with the comment, "There wasn't a *Circle I.*" A *Circle II* would not have been possible if I had not asked Earl and Doc. There would not have been a *Circle* album if it were not for NGDB, but—it had to start somewhere. I will say right here it started with me and my banjo, and my questions to Earl and Doc following my teenage dream to record with them.

I told Chuck that would be great, and jumped in with some ideas and names that would be good to include, and mentioned one of my songs that I thought would be perfect. The answer was that they wanted me only on banjo for one song.

Chuck said, "We'll fly you out here in a couple of weeks, cover all expenses, and pay you for a session. We have the rest of the music covered."

It would take two and a half days of my life to make the $280 that he offered, which would come out to about $190 after taxes. I was incensed and insulted—yet I still wanted to record. Thinking of the next month's bills and that I would have to postpone a show, I said, "I'll do it for $1,500 and expenses."

"OK," Chuck said. I had just sold out.

Now, Bernie Leadon and Bela Fleck were picking in place of me. It was like someone you knew and liked taking your wife and children, even after a divorce.

The Dirt Band recognized that Nashville understood the real history of the *Circle* album and would not have looked kindly on leaving me out of it. Right after recording "Lost River" with Michael Martin Murphey, I asked if I could overdub frailing banjo on the title song, but was told, "Oh, we're not doing any overdubs on the record . . . it's all live." I could hear Earl through the studio door, overdubbing a solo on "Will the Circle Be Unbroken." Earl's son Gary told me his dad said to him one night, "That John McEuen is the best banjer frailer I've heard," but I wasn't good enough for NGDB.

After the session, I had a show coming up with Jim and Salli to get ready for that was in a new town: Deadwood, South Dakota. I headed home feeling excited about exploring some new territory. I had always wanted to see Saloon #10 where Wild Bill Hickok was killed, and to see what would happen in what I heard was a crazy casino town.

Oh. I almost forgot.

This is such a painful memory that I've successfully repressed until this part of the story, about how much NGDB disliked my presence, which was not apparent until later. The next fall, agent Tony Conway called me with exciting news, saying, "John, I'm in charge of lining up people for this year's Country Music Awards show, and I want you to be part of a special *Will the Circle Be Unbroken* segment with the Dirt Band and a lot of others. Everyone on the committee agrees you should be a part of it! Now, it will be just maybe ten seconds of face-time, part of a solo, or such . . . but you belong there!" I was *very* excited about being included in this major network television event. It had been a little over a year since doing a TV show, and I thought it sounded great. I thanked Tony and told all my kids about it, as well as my mother and Bill, and anyone who would listen.

He had not yet talked to NGDB.

After I wrote a press release that I intended to use, two days later a hesitantly speaking Tony called again. He was very embarrassed, not quite knowing how to deliver bad news. I told him I wouldn't shoot the messenger, saying, "Tony, what's up? What are you trying to tell me?"

He said, "Well, I guess I was too excited about getting you on the CMA show, and when I told Chuck Morris about it he said he had to call me back in a few minutes. He called back to let me know if you were on the show he would pull the Dirt Band off, and that if you were on there with them it would be, as Chuck said, 'over my dead body.'" Tony continued, "So I hate to say this, but I have to cancel you. Sorry."

I thanked him for the day off, hung up, went and stared at the gold *Circle* LP for a few minutes, and felt fine. Jeff and Fadden were showing their true colors. I wish I hadn't thrown away that press release! I didn't watch the show. I would like to believe that Chuck was doing what he had to do as their manager.

The next year, the Dirt Band came to Salt Lake. The kids went nuts with questions.

"Dad! Are you going to sit in with the band?"

"Are they coming by the house?"

"You going to the show?"

"Have they called?"

"You gonna play?"

I was sure the twin ex-wives would go. But not this ex.

We had first played Salt Lake in 1967 at the University of Utah ballroom when I met my kids' mom and her sister. Many NGDB memories went through my thoughts that night. Once, in 1971, NGDB and our opening act Steve Martin were trying to get to Pocatello in a 737, and the fog was too thick to see the ground. On the third pass, the ground showed up, as it eventually always will with a plane, appearing suddenly through the fog. The runway was about a hundred yards off to the right! The pilot came close to plowing a new potato patch, slamming the throttle hard enough to pin us back in our seats as he climbed practically straight up out of trouble. After aborting, he calmly informed us there would be a bus waiting in Salt Lake to deliver us safely. As we deplaned I asked the captain if that had scared him. Steve says he'll never forget that answer: "Sheeyit-yes!"

Then there was the time after the Monica Mancini incident when I (and a roadie) drove the equipment van from Walla Walla to Denver, through a winter snowstorm, sliding most of the way over snowy roads on bald tires, finally stopping in Salt Lake for new tires. Jeff was there visiting as I passed through. He was sleeping in a bed; I was sleeping on top of the equipment in the Econoline van, with my nose about four inches from the freezing, snow-covered roof. I really don't know why I did that, other than it had to be done.

I'd been with these guys for twenty-one and a half years, with eleven as our road manager, too, initiating the *Circle* album, kiting checks to make payroll, driving the band, working thirty to forty hours a week at home between road trips, doing more than eighty-five hundred interviews, loaning the band's bank account money, hiring/firing employees, clearing dates with agents, serving as president of the corporation, signing all gig contracts, getting Ibby back in the band, blah, blah, blah. None of it meant anything to them.

Years prior to this Dirt Band show, Jeff's ex-wife (my wife's twin) had lived with my family twice during her hard times. It was great for my kids to have their cousins around and I loved the crowed and helping her. But, I had housed, fed, and clothed Jeff's kids for over a year after their divorce, something he never mentioned. My kids later told me they'd had some great times. It was difficult for me, as those were also the heaviest coke years for the band entourage, and that made road work not as mentally rewarding for me. Home was where I wanted to be.

As expected, no one called, and no invite appeared.

My present was very different, and I wasn't complaining. I had recently finished my first film score, for *Man Outside*, an indie film starring Levon Helm, and spent a bit of time with Helm after that. I had Vince Gill sing the title track, "Lowlands," with the Nashville Symphony. I'd sat in with the Band, as well as with Leon Russell, Earl

Scruggs, Doc Watson, America, Marshall Tucker, Lyle Lovett, and a host of other people. I didn't care if NGDB called or not.

I had been doing about sixty road shows a year since leaving NGDB, many folky solo shows, some festivals, casinos, and sometimes I picked up various musicians along the way, including great singers/players. I was making more money performing as "a former founding member of NGDB" and I was not missing the Dirt Band. And, I played about three dozen grade schools and high schools—a great secondary education! You learn that if you can't keep their attention in the first few minutes, you will lose the room. Thankfully, that Magic Shop experience with crowds came in handy, as always. It was, to say the least, humbling. Thinking of all I had going on, I believed there were greater things ahead.

No one called. I went somewhere else that night, and I don't remember where. It was a good lesson for my kids about human nature. I guess I did care.

18

Surfing in Kansas

As I settled into the 1990s and found it easier to adjust to "formerly of," I read again Napoleon Hill's *Think and Grow Rich*, hoping to find more inspiration for kick-starting my career. Hill's solid advice kicked me in to overdrive. Over the next few years I'd record two solo albums, write and produce film scores, be gigging regularly with a great assortment of artists, and, after playing Deadwood, South Dakota, that first time, I'd create and produce the Deadwood Jam, booking a dozen acts each year. Things were purty good, and new marker events were coming into my life.

I was a single father with an occasional houseful of boys. Noel was already out of the house and mothering a child of her own, Morgan—my first grandkid! Noel was so much like my own sister that my mother often called her Maureen; young Noel was reluctant to answer a phone, saying, "What will I tell them? What if I don't know what to say? Will I get in trouble?" She cried when Marty Robbins died, and when Roger Waters left Pink Floyd. All she wanted for her sixteenth birthday was the *Imagine* album. And, she likes *my* music! Noel's single motherhood of three beautiful girls—Morgan, Hannah, and Jessica—made me even more proud of her; it was her kids who dubbed me Grandpa Banjo. She soon developed many people skills out of necessity as a single mom.

Aaron called excitedly in June 1992 to ask me to charter a jet so we could go to Mexico to see a solar eclipse. My response: "You want me to what?" He finally calmed down enough to tell me the full story: "There's a young astronomy group that's going to charter a 737 to take people to the best spot on earth to see a coming eclipse in its totality—we can go for only $500 . . . each."

"Sure," I said, "sounds good to me." I hung up, wondering where I would get the money. Aaron was a stubborn kid, but justifiably so since he was usually right. Inquisitive to the point of almost being exhausting, he showed early signs of brilliance. One morning, I was trying to get Aaron, who was at the time not quite two, to say "milk" instead of the sound he was making, which was something like, "guh."

"Aaron," I said, "say *mmmmilllk*."

He responded, "Mmm *guh*."

"No, Aaron, *mmiiillllK*. Milk!"

"*Guh*!" he said, and chortled.

"AARON! Milk! Milk! It is not *guh*, it is *milk*!"

Aaron looked up at me with an angelic smile and said, "You call it milk... I call it *guh*."

Around his seventh year, I had shown him how a star map worked on the deck of our Colorado house. The clear night and eighty-five-hundred-foot altitude made the stars seem close enough to touch. He came in crying at sunup as the stars were gone, then slept all day, and went out again the next night.

I was grateful for the chance to make Aaron happy and do something exciting together, but the idea also appealed to me on another level: it didn't involve his mother. Aaron, now nineteen, was on his own, and for the first time I realized that, yes, I would have a life of my own to live with my kids. I did not need to ask permission for whether or not I could do something with my own son. The "or not" had shown up enough. I dipped into my secret emergency fund (called next month's house payment), and booked it.

We took off a couple weeks later from Salt Lake, with a chattering gaggle of teenage space geeks laden with telescopes, cameras, film, and pocket protectors. You would have thought *they* were actually traveling into space. For most of them, the plane ride alone was a novelty. We arrived in a small, hot Mexican airstrip in mid–Baja Peninsula, where no one bothered to check passports. The science crew spilled out like ants knowing where honey was and started unloading their gear in a scrubby field of dead grass, setting up as if the eclipse were ten minutes away, instead of five hours. The airstrip people told them to move off "the lawn," so they went to an even more barren patch of dust. When Aaron dropped a lens it sent up a little puff cloud as it disappeared into the hot, fine desert dust. The gangly gringos all chickened around, chattering, debating, drinking from their water bottles, swatting gnats, eating Salt Lake sandwiches, and waiting.

My own road instincts told me this could be improved. "Hey, Aaron, let's go to that little town and watch from there. We have about five hours until dark." He declined, insisting that he needed to stay with the geek gang. I grabbed the only cab and headed to old town paradise. It was a clean town, quiet except for a mariachi band playing on the corner, not too many people, but with shade under the palm trees, bars overlooking the bay and beach—and real tacos! It was just what you might expect in a small town south of the border, a Jack Kerouac–novel town "with real sweaty, beautiful-eyed people." I took the cab back to the airport to get my Neal Cassady and told grumbling Aaron, "Trust me! Better view. Free beer, ten minutes away. Shade. Food, beach, trees. No dust. Get in."

Somewhere around "free beer," he was swayed. He stopped grumbling when he saw the cute little town, and we sat down to order lunch. As we waited for our food to arrive and the blazing Baja July sun to go dark, the people of the town went about their slow day, now and then eyeing us curiously. We realized that they might not have known an eclipse was imminent. I wanted to say to the waiter, "If we not get food free we make sun go dark!" But I resisted the temptation. We ate. And waited.

Like a sci-fi dream, the dark disc of the moon moved across the sun's fire face, with a little black bite at first, like the Apple logo. Then it moved a quarter of the way, then half, as the sky got darker and darker. We will never forget what happened next: the moon's shadow, like a shade being drawn, came silently rushing at a thousand mph from faraway mountains, across the flat, dry Mexican desert toward our dusty town to cover us in its blanket of dark.

Darkness. We spent seven minutes in the shadow of the moon, with Aaron shooting, everyone smiling, pointing, and chattering in the eerie near-night, as time stood still. It was perfect. Our time together etched lifelong memories that were captured by fine photos taken by my starstruck son. I'm eternally proud of Aaron's continuing passionate pursuit of the sky. This experience seemed to make up for seemingly endless days away from him and his siblings, days spent pursuing my own brand of starstruck dreams. I did not miss NGDB that day. Aaron is now one of the top planetarium program designers in the world, with shows running in twenty-three countries. His license plate? I C STARS. Aaron's two bright daughters, Sydney and Audrey, continue to amaze Grandpa Banjo.

Neither Aaron nor any of the kids expressed resentment at my being away. Nathan told me, years later, while having his seventeenth birthday in some town on the road, "Dad, quit worrying about that stuff. Most of my friends haven't been out of the state, and I've been in twenty-two state capitols." I quit worrying about it. It is what it was. Noel would remind me of the dollhouse and backyard ice rink I built her, as well as other things.

Soon I had to get ready for a work trek that would take me again through Kansas City and beyond, which required renting a motor home. I'd be taking four boys with me on the summer road. First, there would be ten days in Branson, with shows on five of those days; then one Kansas City show. That would pay for the trip. Then, we'd head back through Denver to earn some money that I could actually take home.

We had to drive all night from KC's North Town Opry to get back to Denver for a television show to promote the gig there. For years, I had sung my kids to sleep with the words, "Somewhere outside of Kansas City, on a highway that leads to Cheyenne." (These lyrics are to a song called "Reno and Me" that was written by Kevin Welch and is also on my first solo album.) That night, the song became reality.

I couldn't drive it all myself. Managing the boys on the road, while trying to do my jobs, wore me down. Around 1:55 AM, in the middle of Kansas I asked Jonathan—who was not quite sixteen—if he was awake enough to drive.

He sat up, nodded his head, and said, "Yup."

The relief driver came to life. Laying on the couch, waiting for sweet slumber to come over me as Jonathan continued down I-70 at seventy mph, I drifted off thinking how fortunate I was to have these unusual trips to share with my boys, one of whom was old enough to be a relief driver. Memories took me off into dreamland . . . but now I was not on a jet, but getting to Denver in a motor home . . . on a bumpy, swishy road . . .

To Denver in a motor home . . . to Denver, *John* . . . wake up! I was jolted out of that dreamy jet memory, trying to make sense of the feeling that we were surfing on a giant marshmallow, across Jello waves. There was something wrong. Clearly, there was no I-70 under us. I scream-whispered softly, "Jonathan, are you awake?"

"I thought I was," he muttered, as we sailed across amber waves of grain, mid-prairie, in the belly of this bobbing beast, now down to about forty-five mph and slowing, with no freeway in sight. Then I saw the lights of the road!

"Turn a little bit left and keep your foot lightly on the gas, head back toward the lights, you're doing fine." I'm not sure how much control Jonathan actually had over that vehicle, but I'm pretty sure it wasn't the driver alone that guided us to safety. The front half of the beast came to rest on solid ground and the back half was elevated on the brush that was about twenty feet short of I-70. We were, luckily, alive and safe, all of us. Had Jonathan dozed seconds earlier or seconds later, we would have hit one of those concrete poles, or bridge abutments, or the metal mileage poles, and been in a heap of burning trouble.

Hoping luck had not quite run out, I sat there reassuring my now wide-awake boys, "Everything's fine, just a little glitch, I can fix it." The back wheels weren't touching the ground, so we couldn't move. Two minutes later, a guy in a pickup with one of "them thar newfangled cell phone things" pulled up, and called a tow truck. The tow arrived, and by 2:30 AM we were back on the road. I was driving.

I downplayed the incident for the boys' sake, but it scared me. A lot. We finally crossed the Colorado border around five in the morning, as the strips of white lines were starting to dance in front of my eyes and I realized I was asleep with my eyes open. Not good. I couldn't go any further. I had to get some ZZZs. I parked at a truck stop, bought a ten-dollar wind-up alarm clock, set it for sixty-two minutes, and put it on the dashboard. I closed my eyes, put the seat back, and wondered if sleep would come. I was at the same truck stop that Gary and I had first hit while going to Colorado in 1970. The alarm went off about a minute later, but the clock hands said it had been the full sixty-two. I made it to the TV show on time, but I'm still not sure it was worth it in the long run. One main accomplishment of the Branson trip is that I convinced Rodney Dillard to let me make a live music documentary on the Dillards. So now I had to get home and raise money for that.

I would not be in music if it had not been for Rodney and the Dillards showing me the way out of Orange County. I produced and directed *A Night in the Ozarks with the Dillards* to honor their contribution to my life. It's one of the coolest things I've made; we shot it with four film cameras and the live music was recorded by Mike Denecke. I had known Mike since the time he engineered "Mr. Bojangles," and he knew of things like this. Humble and mild-mannered Denecke seemed to know everything about sound and he made my mandolin sound better than it was. A sound engineering expert, and his name was Mike. That's like being a plumber named Pipe. But he was also a film location sound man, engineer, classical guitarist, genius, inventor, and lifelong friend, with the nickname Dr. Time. He had invented the time code slate that bears his name, the Denecke Slate, and is now a standard tool in the film business. It enables sprocketed film to synch with audio and video tape, and it won him an Oscar. Mike worked on many projects with me over the years. The film was financed by a fan from the Golden Bear days, executive producer Scott Flanagan. I raised just enough to shoot each song one and a half times! But we got a lot of first takes. Saving money at every corner, I hired Jon Mark Fletcher, a banjoist who was also a longtime fan and friend, for fifty dollars for a week to be a cameraman. It was a great time for all.

Scriptwriter Ray Herbeck called me in Salt Lake, telling me, "I'm working on a ten-hour mini-series for Warner Bros. called *The Wild West*. I want you to do the music for the two hours I'm producing, and I think if you come down here to Burbank you could get all ten hours to score."

After renting another motor home a week later, I drove my boys to L.A. and parked us at a hotel to wait for the next day's meeting with the head producer, John Copeland, to try to get the whole ten-hour series. It was to be another summer week with dad.

After the eleven-hour drive and five hours of nervous sleep, I was grateful to have my boys and my CPAP, and I woke up ready to attack that meeting. I told them, "If I come back and say we are going to Universal today, I got the job. Otherwise, we go to the beach." Two hours later, I returned and triumphantly announced, "We're heading to Universal!" They all cheered. The job would pay over $120,000, and I had about five months to finish it.

I dropped them off at their mom's the next week and threw myself into the work. I needed to produce six and a half hours of unique music, which was equivalent to making seven albums from scratch, in just a few months.

I wrote, arranged, and produced the music, recording eighty-eight people in seven cities, using five different formats, all to be mixed at the Carpinteria studios. I didn't have this freedom with my former bandmates. This *Wild West* made me forget all that. I worked seventy-two twelve-hour days, delivered the first mixes, felt great, and took three days off to go to Nashville. It was a small vacation for a few days as I was heading there for a television show, some media interviews, and to see a few people. A perfect few days off!

The final mixing the night before leaving ran up to 1:00 AM. I had to head to LAX at about 5:00 AM for the early flight. While almost starting to whine as I loaded my guitar and banjo into the rental car, Steve the Newsman came to mind and again I felt fortunate.

It was sometimes briefly difficult dealing with being away from NGDB even five years later, as there is a certain power of a group that is intoxicating to all those who drink from that fountain. My drive to LAX was one of those times. I turned on Ventura's KHAY radio station to get away from those thoughts, but the instant it came on my guitar in the backseat was coming through the airwaves into my car. Then Ibby started singing, "Way back in my memory there's a scene I recall," and my banjo in the back joined in. My mind was racing and my eyes were getting wet as this NGDB recording from ten long years earlier described part of my current life, ending with "don'tcha know, it's a long hard road." Yes, I knew. I boarded my 8:00 AM Nashville flight to where those "city lights that ain't all that bright" and kept "dreamin' that a song I'd be singin'" would take me to where my name was known." It went well there, and afterward I went back to the studio to spend another four weeks putting music together with picture, which was called "layback."

Back at home, a phone conversation I had with J. R. Cash right after that inspired me. I'd called him in his St. Louis hotel room to ask about the rights to one of his songs for the film *Johnny Got His Gun*, which was a Dalton Trumbo script produced by a friend, Bruce

Campbell. After he granted permission, the conversation drifted to his current state of mind.

On his Sunday afternoon road day off, Cash was grumbling. "It's OK to be called 'legendary' sometimes [as the current ads for his shows were saying]. I guess it helps sell tickets. But . . . it seems negative. Doesn't 'legend' sound like you're done? I have new songs and ideas! I'm not done!" Cash just wanted to reach people, to create and produce and be relevant. That's what I wanted to do. His record label had just dropped him, and none of the other labels wanted him. Nashville had "thrown him out"—but he was never done. Mr. Cash proved right up until the end he could still knock it out and knock you out. You can always do more.

The album I produced from the score won the prestigious Western Heritage Award, and was presented to me the next year by Hugh O'Brian, with fellow banjoist Ernest Borgnine in the front row. While staring at that award and album late one night, my thoughts wandered back to Cash wanting to do more and doing it. I decided to make a film called *The Music of the Wild West* with Nashville Network (TNN). A few months later, I met with Paul Corbin, the man who ran TNN, to present to him my fourth pitch for a project (he had turned down the previous three). I said, "Paul, I think you will want to do this." I slid a one-page treatment across his desk.

Paul read it slowly and looked up and said, "How much?" I said, "$200,000 and I can deliver the one-hour special in nine weeks." To which he said, "Well, you're right. I do want it. Get started." I called my waiting line producer, Billy Paul Jones, and said, "Billy Paul! We have a problem!" He said, "What happened? He turn it down?" I told him, "No! He said yes! The problem is I don't have a script!" I started writing that night and kept writing for the next five nights at the back table at South Street, my favorite Mexican restaurant in Nashville. A month later, we shot in Old Tuscon for five days. I hired my kids as extras. It was a great time, and we delivered on time.

As that year began, my life underwent another unexpected change. In those days, I would occasionally get invited to celebrity fundraisers.

Some of these were golf tournaments, where they'd offer airfare and a few days of room and board. I'd do a show and play a round of golf partnered with one of the donors, eat free, and be in showbiz. I didn't understand how I qualified as a celebrity, but I'd go anyway.

My good fortune struck when I was invited to a celebrity golf tournament near Tampa, Florida, for the fourth time. The night before golfing, at the end of the party at which the celebrities were all paired with their donor/partners, I was leaving for the hotel when I looked across the darkened conference room. I had started to believe that I would not have another woman in my life for a long time, or ever. Then I saw her, standing alone next to an ice sculpture of a swan, under a cone of light from a ceiling fixture: a beautiful, pert woman, standing practically motionless, scanning the room. I stood staring for a good two minutes before the guy next to me, who knew her, offered to introduce us, saying, "That's Marilyn. She's in charge of the PR for the event, and does a great job." She was gorgeous with fine features, the kind of girl you were afraid to ask for a date in high school, but now I couldn't miss the chance. Her pensive eyes, confident stance, and perky smile reached across the room. She seemed to be waiting to leave. I took the opportunity to meet her, wondering why it seemed my heart was beating faster.

As we talked, I learned that she had never heard of NGDB, or "Mr. Bojangles," or anything that I had done. I could finally get to know someone who was talking to *me*, not someone on an album cover nor a "formerly of." The NGDB grew more distant than ever. All these years later, we're still talking—as husband and wife.

Her experience and expertise was in PR and advertising. She was one of the top five businesswomen in Tampa. She could magically glance at a page of copy and see the wrong word in an instant. I would also learn the difference between Puerto Rican high-energy talking and my laid-back California upbringing. Hers was louder and I liked it. My 1990s were going well, and would include an Emmy nomination for a film score, a Grammy nomination for my third solo album, *String Wizards II*, the Western Heritage Award for the music of *The Wild*

West, and, most importantly, the woman I was falling in love with, with whom I could share all those wonderful celebrations. Taking her to these events made me feel like a star and the luckiest man in the room. Things were looking up, even before a new film score opportunity landed on my doorstep.

19

Tommy Lee Jones, Sissy Spacek, and Four Ex-Wives

L et me backtrack for a moment. At the Troubadour in Hollywood in 1967, I was sitting with the band in the dressing room, waiting for showtime. We were opening for blues legends Brownie McGhee and Sonny Terry for a week, and had been working up a 1930s song ("Collegiana") that afternoon, and having trouble with it.

While rocking back and forth rhythmically, blind Sonny chunked on his harmonica and offered advice I have followed my whole career. "Boys, 'bout that 'rangement of that music, know this: They's gotta know when it starts, so they listen; and you gotta let 'em know when it's over, so they know to clap. In between, mess with it however you want." It always seemed to me that black people had secrets about what made music work best, and I was just given one of them.

Eventually, little bits of wisdom picked up along the way will come in handy if you let them. I'll come back to this shave-and-a-haircut advice. I also learned a lesson that would come into play thirty years later, along with one other that week.

While waiting for the Dirt Band's 11:00 AM rehearsal to start that next day, a phone call informed me they had called it off. Alone in the club with nothing to keep me occupied, I took apart the club's upright piano to see how it worked. After about an hour, I stood back to admire

239

the accomplishment: keys, hammers, and rods were laid neatly across the stage, looking like a Christmas-present kit that daddy had to assemble while the kids slept. Troubadour owner Doug Weston strode in and, with a shocked look at the display across his stage, screamed, "What have you done to my piano?"

I said, "I do this all the time. It needed cleaning. Some keys were sticking. It'll be together by showtime." I went back to work as he went about his business. These two lessons would eventually converge.

I had just returned from taking the boys to see our favorite movie, *The Fugitive*, for the third time, when an unexpected, hard-to-believe phone call came. The noise made by four boys had a way of getting louder anytime the phone would ring.

"Is this John McEuen?" a gruff voice inquired. Straining to hear against the background din of the boys' happy camaraderie, I answered yes.

The caller got right to the point. "This is Tommy Lee Jones. I understand you want to do the music for my movie," he said in his dry Texas drawl. He then filled the space left by my shocked silence with, "Is that right?" Excited, but also wary, I answered over the background noise, "Who is this again? Is this Merle? Bob?" thinking it couldn't really be Jones. I motioned to the kids for silence, but my plea was unheeded.

"This is Tommy Lee Jones." A bit impatient, and more emphatically, he said, "I hear you want to do the music score for my little movie." Now I recognized that marshal's voice and felt like I was about to be hauled off to jail. In a moment of clarity, I remembered that a friend had given my *String Wizards* and *Wild West* music to TLJ. My mind was racing about this opportunity.

Turning to the assembled group staring shamelessly at me as they disobeyed my request for silence, I covered the phone and asked them with thin lips, "Would you behave like this at your mom's?"

"Well, no, of course not," came the answer from one, emphasized with nods of agreement from all.

"Well, why not?" I demanded. "What would she do if you didn't mind?" *Tommy Lee is waiting*, I thought.

"Uhhh, well, if we don't mind her, she *looks* at us," the spokesman said, as all the kids' eyes rolled back in remembered fear of a determined mother's cold stare. This is when I learned about "mother's eyes."

Covering the receiver as best I could, calmly holding it by my side, and focusing my stare somehow in all their faces at once, like one of those paintings with eyes that follow you around the room, I whisper-yelled at the boys, "This is *Tommy-Lee-Jones* on the phone, calling me to do music for his next movie! Quiet!" All went silent. For once, I'd managed "mother's eyes."

Back to the phone, I said, "Well, let me get over the fact that I am talking with *the* Tommy Lee Jones, and I—"

"OK, you're over it," he said. "Now what music do you think would work?"

The rap about his film, to be set in 1906, went well. A Hollywood appointment was made for two days later; a script and plane ticket showed up the next day. At our private Beverly Hills lunch he decided that starting in a week I should live with him on a ranch in Marfa, Texas, to learn about the film and talk about music. It was a few tumbleweeds away from Alpine, where the sets and production office were being built. Alpine is where Jones assumes the true identity he has chosen for himself: a Texas cattleman. The acting is just to pay for the ranch, he told me. I moved in the next week.

At 2:30 AM on a mid-May Marfa night a week later, after looking for the mysterious Marfa lights, I watched my Texas host nursing his last beer of ten for the night, guessing this was how he worked his way into the Hewey Calloway character for his film, *The Good Old Boys*. Hunched over a bowl of five-hour-old, no-alarm, cold chili, he went into a dark spiel about the Vietnam War. His slow, low-voiced growling and tight-faced commentary about napalm, bombs, burning villages, rockets, VC, and blood went on for five long minutes. Then he paused in thought, staring at imaginary incoming, seeming to grasp for another recollection.

Breaking the silence, I said, "I was unaware you served in the military."

His voice and countenance changed suddenly and completely, from derelict cowboy Vietnam vet to sober judge as he said, "Oh, that was from *Heaven and Earth*. One of my favorite scenes." I had been privy to the acting equivalent of a great singer singing one of his favorite songs to himself, and hadn't realized it until he was done. I was learning every day with him.

TLJ showed me around part of his beloved Texas, and talked about life, film, and this film in particular. I had to see if it was possible to get behind the façade of this great actor, and occasionally highly drunk cowboy, and catch him off guard. Very late another night, when he was visibly tired and not possibly thinking clearly, I broke through his haze and asked him if he ever played chess. His immediate answer amazed me. He had been up about twenty-three hours and had knocked off yet another six-pack since dark.

"Never had time . . . to look for the ball . . . to play . . . golf, either," he drawled to the ceiling, and dragged himself off to go to sleep. Since we were to head for *The Good Old Boys'* farmhouse set early the next day, I turned in, too.

Setting out to the set as dawn broke, he took me first to an overlook down ten miles of bumpy dirt road to see the beautiful, desolate expanse of the west Texas country. You could see a hundred miles down into Mexico without any sign of human encroachment on the landscape. Gesturing at the grandeur with a sweep of his arm, TLJ said, "I want you to capture that on your guitar in that open tuning for Hewey Calloway [his character in the film], and make me feel with your music that we are out here in his thoughts." My month of living with this burnt out, good-hearted, old cowboy at night, and daytime Rhodes scholar, was a privilege. (I sometimes wondered if the nighttime version I was getting to know was him assuming the film's character or the real Tommy Lee.) I learned a lot in those weeks in Texas with Tommy Lee, but, like I mentioned earlier, I would have the opportunity to call up some lessons from earlier Troubadour days.

A month later, I was again living in Alpine. As it was my summer time with my sons, they rode down with me in my old motor home.

After we moved into the local motel, work on the film got underway. One assignment from TLJ was to write a song for Spring Renfro (Sissy Spacek) to sing and play on the living room piano after dinner. Part of the assignment included my teaching her how to play. I suggested to TLJ that the dinner host/rancher could play along (on autoharp) with his "wife" on mandolin, as Hewey looked on and fell in love with Spring. There was a one-hundred-year-old upright piano with great sound that she could use in the set's parlor, and I set out to write her song. I would have three weeks to teach them all how to play and I planned to record the music live while filming. Or so I thought.

A few days before this scene was to be shot, the unit production manager (UPM) told me it was time to pre-record them, so they could lip-synch with the recorded music while filming the scene. I protested, "They can do the song, they've almost got it learned, but it's never the same way twice. They won't be able to synch with a pre-record. I was planning on them doing it live." I knew these non-musicians would not be able to match the recorded version with any believability. He snidely objected, "It's not done that way in the movies. Get them ready to pre-record." I did some homework and called my best friend in L.A., mild-mannered Mike Denecke.

Mike said it would work.

Well, I went over the UPM's head, straight to director TLJ, getting his "permission" first to talk about a directing idea, as one does not usually tell a director how to do his job. I told him, "It won't be possible to have non-musicians pre-record then synch to playback. I wrote the piece so you can start tight on her hands at the keyboard, then pull back to reveal Sissy as she starts singing, eight seconds in. Then, keep pulling back to reveal each of the others in turn as they come in, eight seconds apart. The forty-eight-second shot could be done in forty-eight seconds. They can play it live, and you can get the shot in one take. And, I had my friend Mike Denecke, who invented the slate, talk to your location sound guy and they agreed it should work great." He knew who Mike was.

Like Earl Scruggs, Tommy Lee was not a man to use more words than needed, and he responded, "Have 'em ready." I had to ask him why he took a direction idea from "the music guy," and he said, "I listen to everyone's ideas. If they're good, I use them, and I get the credit."

To prepare for this scene, Sissy would come in from the set at the end of every twelve-hour shooting day (working in 105-degree heat sometimes) for three straight weeks prior to the scene, take a fifteen-minute rest, and then come to me for a piano lesson. One evening, it seemed she was going to pass out at the piano as we rehearsed, after the long hours on a running wagon shot in that heat. I offered to quit for the night. She countered, "Let me do it a few more times. I almost have it! I'll wake up." She was right. She kept at it, beaming as she improved with each pass, becoming more alert and intent until she got it. She was ready. I rehearsed her with the other two, and they nailed it. "For the Love of a True Woman's Heart" was ready, perfect for the next day's shoot—right when I had to leave town.

I had started to feel like one of the locals after a month in Alpine, but I was booked solo at Michael Martin Murphey's West Fest in Santa Fe on that shooting day. Then, I had to get us to Denver to catch a flight to Seattle to meet up with my wife-to-be Marilyn and her son, Richi, to head to Anchorage that night—all on the day scheduled to shoot this most important scene. It was just another day for most of the crew, but hugely important for me. I wouldn't be there when cameras rolled on my idea. I was nervous. Knowing they had only one shot at this, I went to check out the piano on the set the night before to assuage my fears. Good thing I did.

Alone in the 1906 Texas farmhouse parlor, I stumbled up to the piano by flashlight and hit middle C, the key of the song. It was the note Sissy would start the song on, the note on which I based all the rest of her fingering, the most important note in the whole piece. The middle C (and E above it) were sticking and rattling in a way that would ruin the scene, not to mention my song, the recording, and whatever reputation I had fabricated. It would start and finish on a note that sounded like a broken speaker or kazoo. Like Sonny Terry had advised me in 1967, it was written so everyone would know the start and finish, each of which involved that worst note on the instrument. Deal killer; I was dead. A saying in the film business rang in my ears: "One 'Oh, shit!' erases fifty 'attaboys.'"

Recalling that earlier Troubadour piano, I went about tearing this relic apart, and fixed the offending keys. By two in the morning, the piano didn't rattle. I left town at three in the morning with my sons alseep in the motor home, as I was sweating bullets and wondering if this scoring job was about to end prematurely. I planned to place a call to the set sound man just before going on stage in Santa Fe, 460 miles away, to see if the shooting was on schedule. If it wasn't, it would mean the piano had fallen apart, and I would be on the "oh, shit" list. The musicians had it down. I worried that I'd have to make up an excuse that wouldn't work, but then I got the news before my set: "We finished shooting the scene three hours ahead of schedule. They got it in one take. The director was happy." I then reached Jones and heard his enthusiasm: "Worked just like you said it would. We got it." And he hung up. All my worries vanished. With one more "attaboy," I headed for that Santa Fe stage and my two o'clock stage call.

I played solo, a couple of acts before the Dirt Band went on. After the show, parked and packed up behind the stage, I waited patiently in our motor home to see if my old "partners, brothers, and friends" would ask their old "friend" to sit in on some tunes. It was like wondering if ex-wives (the ex-bandmates) would have the old husband over for dessert. My sons were again constantly asking, "Dad, are you going to play with them or not?" My fleeting depression about not getting an invitation to play the Dirt party got just a little deeper when only Ibby could barely muster a "Hey" when he accidentally saw me. I had gotten him back in the band and he'd made thousands of dollars since with his songs recorded by NGDB. It was just like before in Salt Lake, only this time I was forty feet away.

There was no invitation. We drove away as the band went on. The boys watched the stage through the open motor-home windows. The band started playing "Partners, Brothers, and Friends," but when they got to the lyric about "as long as Johnny's got his fiddle," they'd changed it to "as long as we got the Nitty Gritty." I thought that was kind of clever, but my boys said all at once, "That sucks! What jerks! Why'd they do that?" and closed the windows as the stage and song receded into the distance. They grew up to our music.

"It's called the music business," I told the boys, trying to sound unfazed. Even though I thought it was clever, I felt sad, mad, and glad all at once, and started down a depressing train of thought for about a minute. Then I thought about the phone call to Jones before my set and his great, happy comments on Sissy's song. I counted the money I picked up that day for playing the show, realizing it was more than twice what the band guys made, and I felt fine.

In that month in Alpine, Nathan had worked in the production office making call sheets and such, Andrew ran some errands and fished, Ryan held the boom mic on a young Matt Damon and Tommy Lee, and Jonathan played the local bar sometimes and practiced guitar. That alone made this trip a priceless experience. I had more pressing matters to worry about: we had to get to Denver and fly to Anchorage, and the motor home was acting up.

Once again, the poor paradise pig of a rig motor home died, this time just before the crest of the last mountain pass into Colorado, and I sat there on the side of the road, a few minutes past sundown, wondering how to get us the next 280 miles. If we could just have gotten about a mile further, we could practically have coasted down the gentle sloping landscape to Denver. To doubtful, watching kids' eyes I said, "The engine needs a break and so do I. Everything's fine." It was high-altitude vapor lock it seemed, which will often resolve on its own if you let it sit. We sat.

Twenty minutes later, on the first try, the motor started! We crept up the hill, made it to the top, started coasting down the long descent, and got to Denver. Stapleton Airport soon came into sight, ahead of schedule. The earlier Dirt Band frosty embargo now felt long in the past, and seemed foolish, and I felt foolish for letting it get to me. We were heading to unknown Cordova and Alaskan thrills for ten days, with a quick five-hour stopover I'd booked in Seattle to take everyone to Pike's Market where they threw fish around. They'd love that. I thought of what a great life I had been allowed to lead, and how privileged I was to take my boys along to see it. But, I had a plane to catch, and hadn't bought the net yet.

———————————

I'd asked my Anchorage promoter to find a "back up" for an Anchorage gig, but *one that I could not get to by car.* It had been a longtime fantasy of mine to find my way to a little frontier town that you actually "can't get there from here." An offer came from Cordova, reachable only by a couple of daily flights or a semi-weekly ferry. I jumped at the chance for a foray to a new land with a banjo on my knee.

Libbie and Gary Graham, our Cordova hosts and two of the finest people one could meet, met us at the rainy Cordova airstrip. I had Marilyn, her son Richi, and four of my boys on this trip (Jonathan, Ryan, Nathan, and Andrew). Gary handed me his Suburban keys and said, "Meet you at the house, the only brown one a couple of streets up on the right side when you get to town."

I knew I was in a different part of the world when I asked where the house key was. He turned my question over to Libbie, who replied, "Well, let's see. Gary gave it to me when we moved in. When was that? Um, eighteen years ago. I haven't seen it since." Libbie and Gary were full of energy and welcomed us with great warmth. It reminded me of stories my mom had told me about the Depression. The way she told it, one of the good things then was that nobody locked up. Besides being restaurateurs, Gary and Libbie both were fishermen, dependent on their boats to catch the fishing season's money flow. Gary also doubled, or tripled, as a charter bush pilot. Later in the week we'd hear about how there were "no drive-by shootings, nothing to drive by," and how at the grocery store in the winter, everyone would leave their engines running while they were inside shopping, to keep cars warm. Who'd steal a car in a place with only fifty miles of road anyway?

The call of this wild area had brought us to the Powderhouse, a place lost in a time that fell out of a Jack London novel. Crammed full of fishermen, bush pilots, schoolteachers, canning factory workers, mechanics, and others who had gotten fed up with the lower forty-eight, it was like the old days in good ways: Libbie taking ticket money and cooking shrimp, Gary tending bar and taking tickets, Marilyn shucking shrimp in the kitchen and selling tapes and CDs between sets to a filled room of folks ranging in age from eight to eighty, and those in between. I was their king of "showbiz," the biggest act to hit town!

After a couple of nights playing, we prepared for unforgettable adventures: overnights on their two fory-five-foot fishing boats, and two motorized rubber Zodiaks. The boys ate it all up. During the first hour away from the dock, we counted twenty-eight orcas visible in the water, described by Libbie as a complete family, including grandchildren. *She knew them.* With two boats and about seven kids and four adults, it was an Alaskan version of a motor home trip up to the wilderness, only this wilderness began about six feet from the little town's dock, and seemed infinite. Glaciers and blue skies, dozens of bald eagles, otters, moose, salmon, whales and ninety-pound halibut catches—Alaska is a wonderful wilderness in which to run around, and the water everywhere was so clear it hurt to look into it.

When we got back to town, we were intrigued by an invitation to head out to Belle's and search out even more wilderness adventure. Older, schoolmarm-ish Belle was enthusiastic about all things musical, and she found purpose igniting that same passion in the youngsters of Cordova, which she did so well. I felt grateful that my career had put me here, in a world I would not have known with NGDB.

One crisp morning, our two small motorboats took a thirty-minute full-throttle run, following Belle's lead to her corner of the wilds. The motors droned on in harmony, breaking the hoarfrost's silence, with no signs of human life on the shore for miles. Belle's cove finally showed up like it was dropped out of a fairy tale. We docked our boats for two nights in their wilderness to stay at a home that looked like it had been built by the Swiss Family Robinson: a combination of lumber, Lincoln

Logs, plywood, and giant Legos. It was the kind of place I would have built, except that I can't hang a pre-hung door.

At the next morning's woodstove breakfast, it sunk in just how different things really were out there. Belle's husband, Pete, lazily chatted away the dawn fog, recounting their home's past over his steaming coffee. Pete reminded me of Paul Bunyan. He loved holding court for an audience, with his pipe stuck in his bearded face as its cherry tobacco smoke filled the kitchen, mingling with the smell of bacon and eggs on the stove.

The big black phone, with a toggle switch on its side, began to ring. His narrative droned pleasantly on, accompanied by the phone's pealing punctuations, and it seemed like I was the only one hearing its demand for attention. *Ring ring*, chat chat, *ring ring*. The noise persisted from the big toaster-sized radio-phone (no lines could run out this far).

Finally, I cut in, "Pete, I don't mind if you get that phone. Go ahead and answer. I'll wait." (My job insecurity as a musician demanded that I answer *every* call because it might be someone wanting to hire you.) He turned and looked at it with an Oliver Hardy, slow burn stare. It rang again. Then he reached as quickly as Zorro and threw the side switch, killing it midring.

"That damn thing does that every time I turn it on," he said, and then picked up his place in the story about all the bird watchers that stay with them every summer.

After breakfast, needing to answer nature's call, I discovered another feature of Belle's home I'd never forget. The outhouse, conveniently located inside the house, had a surprise under the commode lid: it was full of leaves, almost to the brim. I thought one of my kids had made a mistake and inexplicably stuffed it with leaves. And, without a visible handle to flush it, I went to ask Belle what to do.

"Well, it's a compost gathering 'machine,' you just do your business, and then cover it up with the leaves from the basket next to it. Lay a few over everything. That's all, nothing to flush."

That's great, I thought. "But then what? How long does that pile, pile up?" I had to ask.

"In the winter," she explained, "after those leaves and all have dried out, we burn it, use it like little logs for firewood. Burns great."

That just froze everything up. I was locked up tight and couldn't get out of my mind the idea that some snowy, midwinter, cold evening, Belle's husband would say, "Hey, Belle, throw a few more turds on the fire. Grab some from that pile from when John and the boys were here. They burn good." I did what business I could that night but didn't leave anything that could burn.

We got back from Alaska in time for layback of the final *Good Old Boys* music in SoCal. TLJ was reviewing the final cues while he was off filming *Men in Black*, and he called me to share some thoughts.

"John, that piece with Hewey at the rodeo grounds is perfect . . . and when he's in the store, that cue works great," he said. Then his happy tone grew somber, "But, when he's riding out of town, what the hell is that? Sounds like a bunch of goddamned Nashville elevator music. What can we do about that?"

I quickly answered, "I'm just starting to work on that. Glad you feel the same way I do about it. I'll have a new one to you tomorrow."

"You do that. Look forward to hearing it," TLJ intoned, speaking with that memorable federal-marshall-caught-the-fugitive timbre, and hung up. I informed my engineer Jim the twelve-hour shift that we had just finished had merely been a warm up, and we got back to work until sunup.

TLJ loved the new music and, when I heard it matched with the picture, I realized how right he was about the bad cue. All was right. The musical score turned out fine, but since he had already moved on to *Men in Black* before finishing the post-production work on his own film, time with him had become scarce.

Ahead of me was the very successful Nashville premiere of *The Good Old Boys* at which, thanks to help from my longtime publicist, Vernell Hackett, the entire Belcourt Theatre was packed with Music City's finest. I later sat between Jones and Gary Busey at the Hollywood premiere in the Directors Guild of America Theatre. I felt great about how well things had turned out after all the ups and downs. I had not seen Busey since having him play drums on that NGDB recording at Leon Russell's in 1975. I felt like I was one of the boys that night.

That season generated a months' worth of great what-I-did-last-summer stories, except for that low moment driving away from that Murphey festival, but even that makes a better story as various threads of my life began to weave together in ways I could not predict. I thought maybe in a few years I might start playing with NGDB again, and wondered if it would be this much fun. I shook that off and, well, the beat goes on. And there was too much to do.

20

The Fog of Wall
and Phishing for Notes

At one point in the mid-1990s I got to appear on NPR's *Prairie Home Companion* to strut my stuff for Garrison Keillor. It was the end of a three-year quest to reach his several million listeners. I greatly admired Garrison, and I wanted to impress his audience with a classical tune on banjo. For thirty or so years, I'd been performing Muzio Clementi's "Opus 36" to the amazement of audiences—even for Rolling Stone Bill Wyman—and it had always gone well. For Keillor's show, I worked it out so it would come at the end of one of his special monologues, drifting out of the applause with tinklings of my classical pièce de résistance, to leave an indelible impression. It was indelible, all right. Advice: *always* check beforehand to see if what you are sitting on during a performance is right.

It wasn't until I had already started in on this spotlight performance that I discovered the rung on my stool was about two inches two low. My leg started getting nervous and jumping, right in the middle. I started focusing on that, instead of the music. *It's OK*, I thought, *not as good as the dressing room, but OK. Ignore that cramp heading up your calf! Listen to the music or you'll hit a big clam.*

And sure enough, there was a big clunk. My left hand practically froze. I thought, *Anyone could have heard that . . . if I keep thinking about it, it'll happen again.* And it did. It wasn't one of those bad notes you only hear if you play music; it sounded like I had only been playing the banjo for about three days. I suffered my second most embarrassing moment in showbiz. It felt like I was somebody else trying to impersonate me. I shuffled off to the dressing room with echoes of Dan Rowan's director in my brain. *They flew him out here for this?* Thankfully, Jonathan was on that show too, and we did fine on the songs we played together.

The next day, I phoned my brother Bill and told him, "The show went OK, well, except for one thing—"

Bill interrupted. "What do you mean OK? Why did you have to pick the hardest song you know to play live? It would have been OK *if* you'd played it right, but those were more than just mistakes. It sounded like someone threw a rock at the banjo." Bill never pulled his punches and was one more person who told me I should get out of Salt Lake.

Salt Lake was a show-business dead zone. The only deal I made there was for a car I didn't really like. In response to my whining one day about not getting calls returned, an L.A. agent said, "Look at your area code! Who wants to call Utah! Even the Osmonds all moved." It was true. They'd all moved to Branson by then. I missed having close connections to the music business. Then an invitation came from Nashville to join a new "super group" of players, all from known groups, all of whom wanted to hit it big again with a new band. The idea of getting out of Salt Lake was tempting, but my solo career let me spend more time raising my growing kids. After a few days thinking about it, and remembering not that fondly what band life could be, I told them I'd already had the band I wanted and was not interested in another. After all, I had made my mark on music by playing music behind Jeff's and Ibby's voices. They were great together, and I had been part of it. I soon took a gig in New York instead.

I had gotten completely comfortable with how to take care of myself and get around the Big Apple, having traveled there for so many years. By that time, I had almost spent a year of my life in the Apple's hotels. And, I learned something on every trip since NGDB's first 1967 gig at the Bitter End.

A few blocks from the site of that long-ago Village debut stood the now-shuttered Bottom Line (where Raitt, Ronstadt, and others had played with us years before). Another view of the Apple would open there, when John Sebastian called me to sit in at my own show there in 1998.

After a midtown interview stop, I'd hurried through the afternoon rush hour to sound check and ran in from the cab to do another pre-show interview at the venue with Roger Dietz from *Sing Out!* magazine. Sebastian was already there, having just left an all-day session with Paul Simon. Everything was going fine until the interviewer asked to see my 1927 Gibson Florentine banjo. I realized then that, in my haste, I had left the $125,000 relic in the trunk of the cab! I thanked the interviewer, told him we were done, and began my search. It's interesting to note that everyone from New York City assured me I'd get my banjo back. All the New York transplants and out-of-towners said something to the effect of, "Too bad . . . that one is gone." Checking the cab number on the receipt, I called the cab company and got connected to a nice Greek lady who said my driver would be told about it, and it would come back. I waited.

Meanwhile, Sebastian had called Simon and told him of my plight, and Paul sent one of his roadies out to find a banjo for me. We had about four hours until showtime, and the situation looked bleak. Eating helped, but I was done in a New York minute. I distinctly remember thinking if my banjo did come back, a press release about this could get a lot of coverage. Simon called and said they'd found something. I started writing the release.

Right then, the local police precinct called the club asking for me by name. The cabbie had dropped off a banjo with them, and since all the cassettes in the case were mine, they looked up my name in the *Village Voice* and called the club. The locals cheered. Sebastian let Simon know New York's finest had saved the day. He knew the precinct and went to retrieve my banjo. John came back, the audience showed up, and we played. With banjo on my knee, I was livin' the dream; all was well with the world, except that I was missing my kids and wished they had seen how great New York can be.

After the show I finished the press release. It got a lot of coverage, thanks to Vernell. Roger's article was the cover story!

I never got a chance to meet Simon and thank him, but there was a strange circle-like interconnectedness about all the little things in my world that year. I've had a lifelong memory of working Disneyland's Magic Shop where the Wurlitzer store's jukebox next door often played Simon's "Homeward Bound." I'd listened to his lyrics coming through the open door—"sittin' in a railroad station, got a ticket for my destination, on a tour of one-night stands, suitcase and guitar in hand"—and it sounded like a great life to me.

In between road trips and home stands as a single father, I mused about life and wrote some album liner notes and proposals for things like Mayberry in Branson, a development deal with Rodney Dillard that never happened. Rodney and I had spent about a year making plans for a re-creation of Mayberry in Branson, which was a great idea until we found out Andy Griffith did not want his ex-wife to make any more money and killed it.

It took me from January to August to book the Deadwood Jam for the September shows. I read more Napoleon Hill, hoping to understand the things that could better drive me along. I got closer to figuring out what makes me tick. If someone said to me, "I know who you are," I could only respond, "You know what I do; I am still trying to figure out who I am." I still am. Someone did tell me, "You put the tic in eclectic."

I'd studied philosophy and religion, reading Dalai Lama, Mahatma Gandhi, Deepak Chopra, Joel Osteen, *The Secret*, Napoleon Hill, Paulo Coelho, and even some Scientology. I added Suze Orman and other financial books, and some political books and other thinkers, seeking opinions and answers about the world and life. I wondered what it is all about and kept looking for a place and a direction that worked for me. I had done this for years in my travels, trying to figure it all out. I found one simple formula, an easy-to-remember phrase that would encapsulate everything that was important and that I could carry with me as a guide through my lifetime. Seriously, it was from Popeye, the sailor man: "I yams what I yam, and that's all that I yam."

I had many great moments raising sons on the road, creating memories for them while making new ones for myself. (I never forgot the *one* road trip my father took me on, to Reno and Oakland, when I was eleven.) In 1995, to get four affordable airfares for three East Coast weekend dates, we had to fly in and out of Baltimore (BWI). This weekend-with-dad gig then required a three-hour drive from the last show in Norfolk, Virgina, at midnight to make the early flight home, unless the boys agreed to an alternative.

"Guys, for our 7:30 AM flight home, we have to leave right after the show, drive to BWI, get there about 3:00 AM, get a room for about two hours, then get up to turn in the car, and catch the plane home." They listened attentively as I delivered this lousy news before our Father's Day show in Norfolk. "Or, we go to downtown DC in the middle of the night, spend a few hours at the monuments, see the Vietnam Wall, and visit Vietnam vets."

They all excitedly agreed, "The monuments! Then the plane!" I was proud to have great kids—and saved about $300 on rooms.

Before 9/11, you could park right next to the Lincoln Memorial at two thirty in the morning, close to the Vietnam Wall. With a chilly night fog rolling in, I told the boys, "The statues by the wall represent guys not much older than you, and they'd met death in this terrible mistaken venture. Go talk to the vets here. They survived. Meet me at the wall in thirty minutes." It was amazing to see my sons, on the verge of manhood themselves, respectfully talking with the vets, studying them intently and learning about a different kind of life, as the men maintained their overnight vigil in their various booths. I don't know what they took away from this, but the experience led to one of my life's strangest realizations.

"War is a terrible thing," I started telling them at the wall. "Government and 'things' of the world and what people are doing should be kept track of; there's always an 'over there' over there somewhere and someone makes a *lot* of money from it. Those who vote for war have rarely ever been, and young people that get sent to fight the old men's wars often come back in boxes, or hurt." I was pointing at the names as I spoke, and randomly placed my finger on the wall, saying, "A lot of these guys were eighteen to twenty-one years old, and fought for their lives and lost. My name could have been up here. And I—"

One son interrupted, "Hey, Dad, look at the name your finger is on."

My finger was on the name McEuen. I recognized the first name. I was shaken, and stopped talking. The surprised brood watched their father silently look up the man's information in the name register book.

"Guys, this guy was two years older than me, lived two blocks away in Garden Grove. One day I ripped open my mail frantically because my draft notice had come. At seventeen, I hadn't even had a physical yet! But, like his mail did often, his draft notice came to my house by mistake. It was his! What a relief that was! I took it over to his house. He wasn't home, so I gave it to his mother. She thanked me. Now . . . he's here. I don't think she would thank me now." The point was made.

I wanted to thank him for helping me—after that misdirected letter had showed up, I realized my own physical wasn't too far away. I started working on my 1-Y medical deferment. McEuen had helped me dodge a literal bullet. The realization came over my boys that this could have been their dad, and that they wouldn't have existed. Jonathan said, "Dad, is this ever weird for you?" Yes, it was.

Around then, my younger sons introduced to me to the music of a new band, swearing, "They're going to be big." After listening to their first album, I believed Phish *could* be big. While "doing time" in Salt Lake I kept hearing they were getting bigger, taking on the mantle of the Grateful Dead in their own way, gathering new and old hippie fans, though not appearing on the record charts. In 1996, I asked my drummer son Ryan for his birthday wish.

"I want to meet Phish, and [their drummer, Jon] Fishman."

"OK, pick a city. We'll meet there."

Ryan responded, "How about Sacramento? But how can I meet Fishman?"

I figured an underground band should be easy to get to. "Meet me at their venue's load-in door at four o'clock. We'll catch them going to sound check."

"I hope this works, Dad. They have gotten bigger. . . . See you in Sacramento."

Serious and brilliant from the start, Ryan could sometimes be acerbic and abusive in a brotherly way. His siblings often tolerated his critical nature while always welcoming his help. At about fourteen years old, he had an old VW engine completely disassembled in my driveway one day. Knowing that Ryan had difficulty reading because of mild dyslexia, I praised him on understanding the manual to take the engine apart. He said, "It's all easy. I didn't need the manual." He had it back together by nightfall. I was reminded of an old piano at the Troubadour.

On the drive to Sacramento with Nathan from his grandma's (my mom) Visalia house, I picked up a Sacramento newspaper. I couldn't find anything about the concert on the page with all the club ads, but then flipped to a full-page ad: "PHISH—SOLD OUT!" The "club" was the fourteen-thousand-seat ARCO Arena. This seemed an awful lot like the big time to me. Anyway, we headed to the parking lot and spotted Ryan hanging with some phriends.

"Hi, Ry, they're doing well—it's sold out!"

"I told you they're big, Dad! Now what?"

"Let's get to the load-in ramp. It's almost four o'clock. They'll still do sound check, no matter how big they are."

At about ten minutes before four, Ryan was getting antsy. "Dad, how do you know?"

I didn't know, other than so many years' worth of road intuition—and a call I made to a promoter friend who confirmed, "Yes. They love sound checks." Five minutes later, I heard the familiar low-end diesel rumble far in the distance. Ryan said, "They're probably inside. How long do we wait?" *Tick, tick, tick.*

"It's almost four o'clock," I said. "Hear that? Look—"

A bus was plying its way toward us, rumbling louder and louder, now visible. "Hey, Dad! It's the band's bus! I know it from the other shows. It's the one they're on! Cool. What are we going to do?"

"Wait," I said. *Tick, tick, tick.* After another minute or two, the bus pulled up and stopped right where we were standing, at the top of the sloping load-in ramp.

"Dad, that's Trey, by the door!" The door popped open, and guitar man Trey Anastasio hopped off.

"John McEuen! Always wanted to meet you! Cool! You want to sit-in with us tonight?"

"Well, sure. This is my son, Ryan. If we can get dinner . . . I'll go get my stuff."

"Hey, Ryan, hop on the bus. We got a sound check to do at four o'clock." Ryan gave me a look that to this day can bring tears to my eyes when I think about it. It was better than an award, and made up for some of that lost parenting time.

My more doubtful son Nathan had gone around the front to score a ticket, but I found him inside later. The food was great. The band was better. I played seven songs with them, including a couple of Dillards songs, so I called Rodney Dillard to tell him. Before the show, I was fiddling around with my lap slide trying to learn "Amazing Grace" with harmonics. About halfway through, Trey said, "We'll start the second set with that, just you solo." I noticed Trey writing a set list for the second half of the four-hour concert and said, "Looks like you're making sure you don't repeat anything from the first set." He responded, "Well, trying to make sure we don't repeat anything from the previous five shows, actually." That made twenty hours of music without repeating anything. Whew!

After this show, Trey invited me to play a couple nights later in Las Vegas with them, which was to be recorded. Ryan hitched a ride with me, and on the way to Vegas we dropped Nathan at some airport that neither of us can remember. While pulled over later in a rest area somewhere by the Zzyzx exit, under the glare of a mercury vapor yellow light with bugs zapped and dying around it, we saw a flowered VW bus, surrounded by young hippies who could have come straight out of 1968.

"They're Phish phans heading to the Vegas show," Ryan commented. I wasn't ready for what I was about to hear. A lithe, young hippie chick bedecked with beads wandered over to us. She surprised me with her toe-stabbing-the-ground bashful question.

"Say, uhh, aren't you the old folk dude that sat in with Phish in Sacramento?"

I said, "No duh, uh huh," or something equally wise.

"Ohhhh. I thought so. Cool."

Old folk dude. I felt like Bojangles's dog. A few more zapped bugs up and died, Ryan laughed hard, and we got back on the road.

From the Vegas dressing room I called Andrew (he named his first kid Trey). "Some guy named Les Claypool is playing too," I said. "Do you know him?"

I thought the phone went dead. His wife, Alyson, picked up and said, "What did you say to Andrew? He just did a back flip off the couch and hit his head on the wall! I think he's OK . . ."

I hadn't heard of Primus before. After playing behind Claypool, I wished I had. What a great player! I remain impressed by Phish as both people and as musicians. I admired the risks they enjoyed taking, and couldn't get over how well their audience knew their music. I was grateful I'd had that Sacramento "rehearsal" before the Las Vegas show—it ended up on their DVD and CD years later.

The later 1990s would barrel along with small victories. Once, in the spring of 1997, Ibby called me when the Dirt Band was re-recording Steve Goodman's "Colorado Christmas" for their Christmas album. Ibby told me they were having trouble making it sound like the version I played on—getting the "real nitty-gritty sound"—without my mandolin and banjo. It was good to see Ibby again and play on that song as well as on a bluegrass rendition of "We Three Kings." Although I'd missed working with them, the good feeling was fleeting, lasting only until those songs were done. Other than Ibby, nobody in the band seemed at all excited about recording other music, and they paid little attention to my few suggestions. They didn't seem to love recording, but it is a good album.

Around this time, still loving his voice and his enthusiasm, I started booking some duo shows with Ibby again. Most of those went great, and the next year I set up an album called *Stories and Songs*, to be recorded live in a Richmond, Virginia, studio. The first half went great, but someone kept setting up a glass of tequila for Ibby, which he would wolf down every time. After a break, the second half went a little "left." It did capture the separate realities of playing both sober and not on one recording. I have known few singers whom I wanted to play behind, and even though he is one of them, the drugs and alcohol made it too difficult at some shows. I had to give that a rest for a while, and returned to solo pursuits.

The Deadwood Jam was in its eighth year and humming along perfectly. I booked a dozen acts over a two-day period to rock the town and, well, have a job on a big stage where I could play solo. I had produced the first Chief Jim Billie album, *Alligator Tales*, for the chief of the Florida Seminoles. Singer-songwriter Chief Jim, a successful alligator wrestler (meaning he was still alive), was like a Native American version of Hoyt Axton in both voice and stature. The Seminoles never surrendered nor lost to the United States, and Jim Billie was the man who brought gaming to the reservations. They won in that regard. He came up in his jet to see the show. The Jam concerts I produced always ran smoothly, thanks to my perfect partner in production, Melody Dennis. Having done about two hundred acts by this time, the Deadwood Jam made me feel successful for a few days every year. I had left NGDB for many reasons, but now, ironically, I hired them for a Jam concert.

I spent a lot of time that year mentally pacing back and forth, contemplating the major life change that would start off what was to be a most important and great year, 1998.

Soon that day arrived: I married Marilyn in a postcard perfect little church in Silver Plume, Colorado. The Regesters (Gary married us) and my kids and Richi were there, as well as a few other friends, including Chief Jim Billie. It had been four years since I met Marilyn by the ice sculpture. We'd maintained a sometimes difficult long-distance relationship until my kids were grown and out of the house, when I could save up enough money to be married again. Now I gladly added one more kid to the lineup. I'd been getting to know Richi, an energetic achiever, from the day I met him. Our regular debates about whether or not Tupac was bigger than Paul McCartney would always end with laughs. Friendly and excitable, he was a welcome addition to this strange combination of individuals I was raising. He openly welcomed them all, as they did him. His passion for the film industry would ignite when he was about nineteen. He has been working ever since graduating from Full Sail University in Orlando, being dubbed "Mercury" by other crew members. As one of the youngest members of the Directors Guild of America, and having won some awards for his work, he has the adventurousness to explore things he does not know, which I greatly admire.

Neither Marilyn nor I wanted to live in Salt Lake nor Tampa. The day after Nathan graduated from high school I watched Utah recede in the twelve-foot Ryder truck's rearview mirror and headed to L.A. with everything I owned. We stayed for the next eleven years. Marilyn, a Bronx girl, knew New York but not L.A. She impressed me by bravely getting to know L.A., in the space of just one year, better than many natives. Nothing intimidated her, which I loved. Marilyn would teach me so much over the years and be a big help in my pursuits.

With the new millennium ahead, it seemed the potential was unlimited. There was a lot to do. I was trying to figure out just where life was headed. What was old will become new again.

21

Closing the Decade and Opening the New Century

The 1990s had been a great decade for me. I had produced projects with many stars, including Vince Gill, Crystal Gayle, Marty Stuart, Steve Martin, Jennifer Warnes, Earl Scruggs, Vassar Clements, Leon Russell, Jose Feliciano, and many others. I'd performed with dozens of music icons, like Willie, Dolly, and America, either sitting in or as an opener, and I'd done hundreds of shows of my own. I'd worked with Sissy Spacek, Alan Arkin, Arlo Guthrie, and Tommy Lee Jones. Deadwood Jam was up to its tenth great year, with no end in sight. My sons performed with me occasionally as well, and I did shows with Jonathan, or with Jonathan and Nathan together.

Combined with a lot of television exposure (including appearing on Ralph Emery's *Nashville Now* about forty times), I was really getting out there. It's hard for anyone to be a "formerly of," but I was making it work. I took in some awards and recognitions like the Uncle Dave Macon award, Grammy nominations, and an Emmy nomination for a film score. The old millennium was ending well, but change was in the air. The NGDB years were behind me, but I found myself missing that effect our music had on people when we played together. I suppose it was the old "whole being greater than the sum of its parts" thing.

Chief Jim Billie of the Florida Seminoles called me and asked, "You ever heard of a group called Fishes, or Fishies or such?" I had produced two cool albums for Jim Billie (with Jennifer Warnes on one) and done some concert productions for him over the last five years. He often came to me with showbiz questions. Phish was trying to find a venue for their New Year's Eve show, The Millennium Show, and the historic Big Cypress Swamp in the Everglades, on Seminole sovereign land, was perfect.

I wanted to help make it happen. I set up meetings the next week between the Chief and Phish's management to start the deal. I told Phish how to talk to Chief, and told Chief when to be reserved but to know the tribe would make a *lot* of money. I flew from Hollywood, California, to Hollywood, Florida, to coordinate the meeting. After a couple of days it was underway.

The Phish show—more than eighty thousand people for three days—brought in $12,000,000, the second largest one-act gross in showbiz history at the time. I was the only one who didn't make any money, but I got some good photos, two plane tickets, stage passes for a couple of my kids, and a backstage motor home for a few days. The new millennium appeared to be starting as well as the old one had ended.

It was looking to be a great year. I was living with Marilyn in a Hollywood Hills house with a fantastic view, my home studio was coming together, I had a couple of film scores to work on, good road gigs on the solo front were coming in, and we were heading into another great Deadwood Jam year. I got Jennifer Warnes to join me and Ibby, and produced the DVD *Nitty Gritty Surround* for AIX Records. The cast included my son Jonathan and the always-affable Matt Cartsonis. While touring solo in the 1980s, I went to sit in with Matt's band at a club called Cave Creek in the mountains outside of Phoenix. We got along instantly, having similar attitudes toward life and music, and would cross paths more often in the coming years. In the late 1990s, I enlisted him as my music partner for projects outside of NGDB, much to my benefit. Matt can play just about anything with strings and his high, acrobatic voice always makes audiences yell. I'm lucky to have found Matt, a friend, confidante, collaborator, and often, my unofficial therapist. We have worked together since.

Ibby did great, as did all on this very fun five-camera shoot.

When *Nitty Gritty Surround* got great reviews, Jeff complained to a *Billboard* writer, grumbling, "It's not right they used the phrase 'Nitty Gritty.'" That prompted her to call me and comment, "That guy's got too much time on his hands!" Ever since Les Thompson had called to have me play in "his band," I had been called a "nitty gritty guy," as we all often are. The DVD won four Surround Sound awards, even beating out Graham Nash for Best of Show. At the Beverly Hilton on awards night, the emcee announced, "And the award goes to John McEuen, whoever that is." Despite previous accomplishments and winning, it was a sharp reminder I hadn't really made it yet.

Back in 1987, my first year away from NGDB, countless people told me, "They're done without you." But my response was always, "Just wait. They'll hit it again." And when the Dirt Band caught "Fishin' in the Dark" without me, which was a huge song, I felt like my alma mater had just won the finals, and I cheered for them. It jumpstarted the Dirt Band's career, seeming to prove I wasn't needed. Ten years later, things were different.

Chuck Morris had written to all of the NGDB in April of 2000 suggesting we play together again. It was under consideration, and he said it was the best thing to do. His number one request that "John must be in the band" felt good, and it reminded me of when I called him twenty years earlier. He stated it would increase the band's price by about 50 percent. He had many great plans and ideas, many of which would not get done due to recalcitrance of the current members, but he opened the door to that starting. I thought heavily about past differences.

I always tried to be a team player with NGDB, and wanted to do what was best for the whole group. In interviews, I constantly promoted the others—their songs, talents, and our recordings. It's not something I like to ponder, but it is a fact: Jimmie Fadden, Jeff Hanna, and I have slept next to each other more than with any women in our lives. Although our bus bunks have always been three feet apart, we'd grown further apart artistically than ever. That drift started back in the 1980s when the bandmates informed me that my instrumental songs were no longer needed—nor wanted—on the albums. My pieces always received great notices in reviews. It was emotionally devastating, and a loss of exposure and publishing income. They wanted more of that territory for their songs. Some bands are like that.

Then, in 1984 Jeff's keeping me off a song hit me *very* hard. When I got to the studio to do my part Jeff told me "we needed a different approach for banjo than yours." He had recorded someone else playing banjo before I got there! The banjo, my main voice in NGDB, had now been taken away. I felt like I was in the Monkees. I didn't understand why then, nor now, and it hurt. There were dozens of other slights and grievances besides my divorce that drove my decision to part. It was the only band I'd wanted to be a part of. I got over it, and was later grateful their attitude drove me to do more on my own. Solo projects and performances had been more rewarding, and I finally concluded it just wasn't worth arguing about.

Ibby was never a part of that contention, as he was always ready to try anything. He loved playing music and taking chances, and was always willing to go for it when we didn't know for sure where we were headed. The duo shows with Ibby in the late 1990s were part of what drew me back into NGDB then. I wanted to be in a band with him again, too, to play behind his voice and songs, to be the jockey on that winning horse. And, as Ibby said, "It's great to be part of something so good that's lasted so long."

Unknown to all of them, I had plans for remastering the original *Circle* album, which would lumber along as the company was being bought by another company, creating problems inherent in the music business of who owns what. There were big plans being made for 2001, not by just us, that could greatly affect all of our lives. Some were not music business plans. I was home alone on an unusually clear L.A. day in September when the phone rang at precisely 6:14 AM.

Marilyn was frantically calling from her business trip in Florida, shouting, "Turn on the TV! Turn on the TV!" Groggy at first, I turned it on. The first tower was hit.

I hated more than ever that we were apart although we spent as much time on the phone as much as we could, talking back and forth about what was going on. Marilyn had become the calm in my storms, my confidant and companion, and we knew we had a great future ahead. People now felt like the future wasn't what it used to be. Everyone was numb. No one could travel by air, but I had to get to Deadwood for Jam week. What mattered first was that she and the kids were all safe—but no one knew what "safe" was anymore.

With Jam shows scheduled that Friday and Saturday, I rented a car and drove twenty-three hours straight to South Dakota, arriving on Wednesday morning. The world was in tremendous turmoil that week, but the drive I took was beautiful and peaceful. I told myself that the show must go on. Or should it? All my friends in New York City insisted that we go ahead with the show. Once in Deadwood, I hashed it over with the committee for two hours. It was my opinion that if we did not do the show, "those people" would win even more. We voted. The consensus was to go ahead.

Then the governor of South Dakota called to inform us we had to cancel Friday. Melody and the staff decided that we would offer people a choice: they could get a refund, or we'd send their money to a Manhattan firehouse. There were four refunds. On Friday night, Melody stuffed Delbert McClinton in Saloon #10, where Wild Bill Hickok was shot, and he played for a long time. Other groups found places around town, and we got ready for Saturday with Big Head Todd and others.

The Saturday Jam stage was jammed. I'd arranged for about twenty singers and musicians to be on stage at 9:30 PM to sing, "This Land Is Your Land." Everyone with a cell phone was asked to call someone and hold their phones up; many connected to New York. With about thirty verses, it must have gone on for twenty-five minutes, and the packed-out audience got louder and more inspiring with each chorus. I thought about that night in Latvia with Pete Anderson. It was one of the most exhilarating feelings I ever had in front of an audience. I had orchestrated something good, and it made it better for a while for many. I flew home on Sunday, after US airlines began flying again. That Sunday, after flying to Boston from various places around the United States over the previous few days (when we Americans could not fly), over 150 Saudis flew back to their homeland. By executive order, the FBI was only allowed to match names to passports. Thirty-five of the last names were Bin Laden. No questions were allowed. That bothers me to this day.

Next year's 9/11 would be interesting for us in its own way.

Earlier in 2001, the several months' worth of discussions with Capitol Records president Mike Dungan about remastering the *Circle* album for its thirtieth anniversary had progressed well. I had sequestered—stolen—the master tapes from the record company twenty-five years earlier for safekeeping. With Dungan's blessing, I got to work. By year's end, I'd transferred the analog tapes to digital, added photos, added four cuts that were not on the original, and wrote liner notes. Digging in to those masters was great fun!

With Mark Waldrep, the genius owner of AIX Records, we captured them on two different machines at once for digital transfers. We held our breath, not knowing if they'd crumble, as many old tapes do, or shed, meaning the playback heads actually scrape the music off the tape. But they played smooth as butter. I delivered CD masters for replication and started writing the liner notes. The first draft drew critical comments from Jeff. He complained to Capitol art director Fletcher Foster about a quote from Earl Scruggs: "When I asked Earl Scruggs why he came to see us, Earl said to me, 'I wanted to meet the boy who played "Randy Lynn Rag" the way I intended to.'" Earl had been referring to me. Fletcher told me that Jeff was insisting it be changed to "the *boys* who played 'Randy Lynn Rag.'" I didn't think someone would go to see Babe Ruth's team and say "I want to meet the *boys* who hit that home run last night." I had hit a home run and was proud of it.

"What's wrong with that guy?" Fletcher wanted to know.

"Nothing," I said, "that's Jeff." I wouldn't change it. Fletcher told me it should stay as written. True to form, Jeff successfully pressured

Capitol to exclude my writing credit for the liner notes. I listed the credit to Alan Smithee. Jeff's attitude was disappointing, as it had been countless times. Neither he nor Fadden would ever mention that I had asked Earl and Doc to record with us. Ibby and Les always did, but maybe that's why they got kicked out. Years later at the Bonaroo radio station the interviewer said, "John, I understand you were the one who asked Earl Scruggs and Doc Watson to record with the band . . . tell me about that." As I was answering his question, Fadden and Jeff got up, without a word, and walked out of the live radio interview.

Yes, it might be pride or ego. But it was simply true. I knew that without Jeff's talents and quirks meeting up with mine years before, there might not have been a *Circle* album. But I would have recorded with Earl and Doc.

Chuck Morris had written the NGDB members a letter earlier that year saying I should be back in the group, and that when that happened their price would increase by 50 percent so that extra cost would be covered. With the *Circle* remaster pushing us back together even more, I'd been considering the possibility of rejoining the band. It brought up memories of all the reasons for leaving in the first place.

Things were looking good—the Dirt band of my past, thanks to *Circle* and Chuck, was now again in the future in a good way. Although Jeff was already hard to work with again, I liked his voice and most of the songs he and Ibby sang, and I was again a member of the only band I wanted to be in. We were moving ahead. It was fine. People saw it as the partners, brothers, and friends being reunited—a good marketing angle. Events of the previous 9/11 year made that potential financial security more appealing, and I needed the health insurance.

With the *Circle* reissue moving along, I got to work on my next film score project, *Manassas: End of Innocence*, which came my way through my *Wild West* contact and writer, Ray Herbeck. (In 1965, Ray was my first guitar student.) Directed by *Star Wars* sound design genius and editor, Ben Burtt, it was great fun to record. I enlisted Jennifer to sing again, and we shot at the actual Manassas battlefield in Virginia. Ray had Ibby and me appear as 1861 musicians around a campfire. Ibby was impressed and grateful.

I recorded the score at home but did layback at the Skywalker Ranch with engineer Bob Edwards, who had hopped on my Oakland charter jet. I spent three days at the pinnacle of the film industry. The second day, in an empty studio editing room for a phone interview about the *Circle* reissue, scenes from *Star Wars* that were being mixed somewhere else in the complex kept running on the screens in my editing room. I was watching C-3PO and R2-D2 running around silently while focused on music circa 1930s to 1950s from the *Circle* album, and yet with thoughts of the *Manassas* mixes covering 1845 to 1868 . . . it almost cracked my brain! This film is now running at the Manassas Battlefield Park.

As the *Circle* reissue release approached, Jeff and I went out to do some promotional interviews. Together we were always the best in front of media mics. It became obvious that I should play with the band again. Although this was genuinely exciting, there was also the lingering doubt and uncertainty. I would quickly confront the same old lack of support for most suggestions or comments or set ideas, and the same reluctance to include my music in the show or to not to hear me out on matters of business. I hoped that would all have changed, but at least I was back in a band, which did feel great. According to Jeff, I was often still the guy who had replaced Jackson Browne.

I believed that the years I'd spent outside the Dirt Band gave me experience that would benefit the band, and I hoped they'd be willing to listen. If I'd known NGDB would make only two albums between 2002 and 2016—and that each one would be a struggle in its way—I don't think I would have come back. But I had high hopes, and now, medical coverage.

On September 11, 2002, though, they went along with me. It seemed most people in showbiz were afraid to work on that first anniversary of that terrible event, afraid of somehow dishonoring those who had died. My contention was if we did not do what Americans do—live free, work, party, play—and be the capitalists that we are, that would dishonor the victims. "We must play a show!" I said to blank stares. I said, "If we don't do a show because of that then those Saudis will have won."

"Give me that day, and I will find a place to do a benefit to raise money for a good cause," I said to the group.

"How do you know you can do that?" they all wanted to know.

By then I'd promoted and bought over 250 acts from Dylan to Doc Watson to Leon Russell. I knew the drill. I was adamant, and firmly said to their snide question, "This is part of what I do, and I do it very well." In rare agreement to go along with an idea of mine, they acquiesced, and I got started.

I called our William Morris agent and said, "Find me a town between our September 10 and September 12 shows, a town to do a benefit and raise some money for." He found Bemidji, Minnesota, home of Paul Bunyan. Perfect. American Heartland. I got to work.

I arranged for the two competing radio stations in town to partner and be copresentors; the PA company to work for half price; hotel rooms to be donated; the venue to charge for only expenses; paper ads to run for free; and for posters, sound, and lights to cost half the usual rate. Thirty-two sponsors got on board. Everyone jumped in and, with less than three weeks' notice, the town's biggest gym sold out and was packed. I had two fire trucks cross their ladders over the entry doors and a color guard open the show, with DJs from both stations offering welcome remarks. The show killed. At the end of the night I handed the EMT/Fire Department a check for over $30,000. The band took no money. It was a great night off.

Backstage the guys quietly said, "Good job." Ibby said it first, but the others followed: "Yeah, good job." That was one of three times in fifty years I remember comments of congratulations from those guys, and I relished it. I couldn't have done it without them. As we had been that night in Zurich, we were a team. It was a great team, but . . .

Soon *Circle III* started coming together in Nashville. I was excited to call Rodney Dillard and Josh Graves (the dobro player who had missed out on the first *Circle* record) and invite them to be a part of it. Rodney deserved to be part of *Circle III* and in front of our audience. And it was time for his song, "There Is a Time." He killed it.

Johnny Cash was not in the best physical shape when he came to record *Circle III*. He was having difficulty walking, but he came to life when he sat in front of that mic, shedding twenty years. June was finishing her *Circle III* song about the Carter Family in the studio after him, and Johnny hit the talk-back and said, "June Carter! Aren't you ever going to get this song done? We got a lot to do today!" Then, with his mischievous Cash grin, Johnny turned to Marilyn and said, "I just love to needle that woman. You know what we like to do when we have a day off on the road? We just love to go to the nearest Wal-Mart, get us a coupla those little 'lectric carts, an' go up and down the aisles, buyin' stuff. Yesterday that woman bought *three* birdcages. What's she goin' to do with three birdcages? We don't even own a bird!"

I couldn't get the image out of my brain of the Man in Black, rolling up and down Wal-Mart aisles as he hummed, "Shot a man in Reno, just to watch him diiiiiiiiiie" while June hollered, "Hey, Johnny, look up there, a special on those bird cages."

As great as Mr. and Mrs. Cash were as stars, the impression they made on most people was as fundamentally nice folks. I'm told that is how they wanted it. Cash inspired me to keep going, to keep creating and trying new things, to do better. It was the same year he made the indelible video for the song "Hurt" by Nine Inch Nails that is just riveting and chilling. It is considered the best video ever by *New Musical Express*. We were indeed privileged to know them.

June Carter's death later that year put the important things of life into perspective for me. June was always friendly, nice, and welcoming, just like her husband. I got to see their wonderful life firsthand. The fact that I had brought her mother, Maybelle, that *Circle* Gold Record endeared me to her and family. I was always amazed that I, a kid from Orange County, had become friends with the actual Carter family. Johnny passed away four months later, crushed that the light of his life had been extinguished. Mr. Cash was meant to be together with June, and now they were. In his death, I realized once more my good fortune of knowing him. It was probably a good thing that I never told them I had worn that nightgown, but I think they would have laughed. I now do a lot of projects with their son, John Carter Cash. The circle continues.

When we recorded Willie Nelson at Ocean Way Studios in L.A. for *Circle III*, I was able to get great L.A. bass man and friend David Jackson to play. I was excited about recording again with Mr. Nelson, and I wanted to see if I could bring in one more notable musician to this mix by knocking on a door of opportunity. It's sometimes good to open a door just to see what the other side has in store. Tom Petty was mixing in the studio down the hall. *Hmm. That would be a good name*, I thought. I stood outside Petty's studio, waiting for playback to stop, wondering what to say to convince him to contribute to our album. His playback stopped, and without knocking, in I went to see if opportunity was waiting.

"Hi, Mr. Petty. I'm here recording with my band, Nitty Gritty Dirt Band, and wondered, would you like to sing with Willie Nelson someday?"

Caught off guard, but curious, he said, "I love Willie Nelson! Sure I would. But how?"

I explained, "We're getting ready to cut 'Goodnight Irene' with Willie right now. We'd like you to sing the 'sometimes I live in the country . . .' verse and do harmony with him."

"Take me there. Let's do it. Be glad to."

It was fun to bring him into the studio. Everyone lit up for that "celebrity recognition moment" when you first meet someone you have long admired. Tom showed no signs of celebrity eyesight, giving attention to everyone. Tom's respectful glow of awe meeting Willie, and the mutual admiration expressed by both, was nice to see. Everybody knew a new voice had been found for the track, and he was *pretty good*. Within a few minutes, they got down to figuring out who would sing which verse where, as Jeff, Ibby, and Bob worked out parts. It went great, and we got it in one take, just like Acuff had preached. I played banjo with Tom Petty, and Willie played my Martin guitar.

Overall, *Circle III* became a great collection of wonderful players and well recorded good songs, and an example of one of the worst album covers in the history of NGDB. It was Jeff's concept; he made sure no one could see it until it was too late to change. I showed it to my brother Bill, who was responsible for all our great 1970s covers, including the Grammy nominated *Circle* cover. Bill asked, "What out-of-work guy from Pep Boys did that?" Later, I hid it behind my back while preparing Rodney with the explanation that it was to represent "folk art." When I turned it around so he could see it, he said, "What country? Peru? It looks like Freddy Krueger's mother."

After *Circle III*, I settled back into the old puzzling relationship with the band. I was probably an equal aggravation to them, always harping on things to do or not do. A couple times they asked me for advice or an opinion on something, but only about business or travel, never music. Once, the road manager Leonard asked me about a promoter who hoped we would take less than the fee he had committed to. I had dealt with that promoter many times in the past, and he was good at what he did. This time he'd overpaid and was looking at a substantial loss. For twenty-one years I had handled these things alone, and often renegotiated when logical. This time it was justified, as his ad placements, radio time buys, and posters all were perfect. But things were different after rejoining. Acting as a go-between, I suggested to the band that we take a little less, reduce the guy's losses, and we'd most likely work with him again. But their consensus was, "He signed a contract? Fuck him." I had no influence anymore, and I quit asking. I repeated to him what they agreed on. We never did work with that promoter again.

Typically, late at night is my time for scheming. That's when I wrack my brain trying to figure out what to do next, and usually to find it's waiting right there in front of me. One night's aha moment was: put together Willie Nelson, Paul Williams, Gonzo the Muppet, and AIX Records. I thought it could make a great DVD! Emboldened by the four awards won with my other AIX DVD, I called Paul the next day, met at a restaurant, did the pitch, and he bit. Paul suggested Melissa Manchester—she had recorded some of his songs and they knew each other well. This was a perfect example of something Napoleon Hill says: "If you start making something it can become more than you envisioned." The Mastermind Group, if allowed, will create more than any one person would.

I'd known Paul since the late 1960s, when I hung out and jammed at a pub on Sunset Boulevard called the Hock Shop, where all the music played there was from before 1950. Paul and his brother, Mentor, also to become a hit songwriter, hung out there as well, just before Paul's "We've Only Just Begun" went from a bank commercial to a mega-hit.

Next I went to AIX, and Waldrep jumped in too, so I called Gonzo's office. The Henson company loved Paul (he wrote a lot of Muppets music) and by the second day, everyone had said yes! Paul thanked me later for "the best thing I've made in my career." *I'm Going Back There Someday* was great fun to make. We recorded it in two days, mixed for two weeks, and I started learning Final Cut Pro for video editing, with an eye toward applying this experience to an NGDB project for our stage show someday.

Although things were going all right enough with the Dirt Band shows, I still didn't really feel like part of a team. Jeff wanted control, and I only had input into arrangements or anything musical, with Ibby. Recalling our early years together, I realized nothing had really changed. Rather than impede me, though, that realization spurred me to keep trying new things of my own. The one thing all did agree on was that Billy Hoyt was the best stage manager a band could have. He came to us from the Allman Brothers and does a perfect job every night, making sure everything always works. (He has, as of this writing, been with NGDB for thirty-three years.) Even tempered and nice, we all could have learned a lot from him.

There was one trip when I got complete cooperation from the Dirt Band guys on one thing. This time, the group followed my lead. Sleep is sacred on the bus. As we motored to Winnipeg from Edmonton with everyone in their bunks around two thirty in the morning, I was up front watching the endless highway of the north country roll under us. I had the bus pull over and got everyone up to see something. I went through the bus urging, "Everyone—up! Please get up and see something outside that very few people in the world have experienced! Give me five minutes and you won't regret it! Come on now!" They all got up somewhat grumpy, but once they got off the bus and saw what the cold night sky held, they saw magic. The aurora borealis was so active that the entire sky was various shades of red, with streaks swarming like swirling paint. It seemed you could hear it. It was fantastic and the five minutes lasted ten, and all were thankful to see this unusual display. When we arrived in Winnipeg the next morning, the paper's front page was dedicated to the "unusually active northern lights last night." This was one of the reasons I love the road: we see so many things others don't get a chance to see.

It was on that Canada trip, several years after rejoining, that I realized that "Fishin'" had built an invisible fence between me and the others. I wasn't on that record, which they never quite let me forget.

There were plenty of nice people in this business and I loved finding them. While waiting to present someone an award at a Hollywood showbiz function for agents, managers, and buyers (the Pollstar convention), I met the comedian who was acting as emcee. I hadn't heard of him before, but he played banjo and was a fan, and we formed an instant, amicable relationship. I gave him my freeway joke; he used it five minutes later, and it went over great! ("Know why they call it the 405? You go four or five miles an hour.") I told him I'd be glad to teach him a few banjo licks, and we set a time. It was fun to find out the next day from Noel that Kevin Nealon did "Weekend Update" on *Saturday Night Live* for ten years and that she was a huge fan! She was more excited about that than hearing from me.

Later that month, on Sunset Boulevard at the Nickelodeon Theater (which was the Hullabaloo theater after it was the Aquarius, where the Allman brothers, in their Hour Glass days, had opened for us in 1967), while waiting for Kevin to finish his *Conspiracy Theory* TV show so we could get a bite somewhere, Kevin said, "Can you give me another lesson? I'm running up to Salt Lake City tomorrow for a private corporate show. They supplied a jet. Bring your banjo and show me stuff?" After our airborne banjo lesson at 28,000 feet as we passed over Vegas, I got to see some of my kids for few of hours in Salt Lake! The jet took us back after the show. I was home by ten thirty. Rock 'n' roll on a banjo budget.

Things like that are always fun and make me feel more accomplished. Kevin later used my "Miner's Night Out" as a music score for his DVD special. I get along with most comedians, maybe because they're insecure, too. We all want to get approval via applause to validate ourselves.

Arnold Schwarzenegger was personable from day one, and would prove to have a great memory for a long-ago encounter. He had come to see the NGDB in the mid-1970s at a UCLA concert, wanting to meet me for advice on fiddle playing for a film part. I will never forget the shock of Arnold walking in to the dressing room at the height of his body-building career.

I couldn't help asking, "Do people ever try to get you to fight to prove they are macho?" When he said yes, I wondered, "Well, what do you do?"

"I never fought," Arnold answered. "I just took off my shirt," and apparently, that was that. You would not have imagined him as the next big worldwide star, let alone governor of California. Thirty years later, Marilyn and I were having dinner at Spago's in Hollywood with neighbor/actor Bill Duke when Arnold walked in. Passing our table, he paid his regards to Duke, with whom he had worked in the film, *Commando*, then turned to me and said, "Hi, John. Remember when you showed me how to play 'Soldier's Joy' years ago?"

Many of the biggest stars I've met are basically nice people and, if they let you into their space, can be sincere when they talk to you, especially if it is about them. I have actually heard, "Enough talk about *me*, have *you* heard my new album?" Many whom I have been fortunate to get to know better are genuinely nice across the board; I don't think that is just because I got close enough to see their private selves. I never thought I would meet Eric Idle, for instance, but when I did, he turned out to be just a decent guy in spite of the fact that I couldn't beat him at Ping Pong.

22

You Never Know Who You Know until You Meet Them

The experience of meeting Kevin Nealon and others like him reinforced how gratifying it is to know my work has made a positive impression on others who try to reach the world in the same way, with their art and their desire to entertain. Their respect is the icing on my showbiz cake.

Whether they make music or write books or tell jokes or paint or make movies, I know that if they've achieved success, it means they, too, have spent their lives in airports and hotels, grinding out a living, and most of all waiting—for flights, cabs, rides, a room to check into, in traffic, in courtesy vans, for jobs—in mud, dust, extreme heat, freezing cold, rain, snow, hail, wind, most likely with very little sleep, all to perform, just as I have. Most of the previous things have the underlying quest for a little pile of food, a quest that leads one to saying things like "Hey, vending machine food isn't all that bad."

As far back as 1964, a few years before NGDB—and after we started—I made many friends who were extremely gifted and had the potential to achieve the greatest heights. Various reasons, most notably drugs, would keep some from making it. But a lot of those early acquaintances—Linda Ronstadt, Karen Carpenter (she and Richard opened for us as Spectrum), Steve Martin, Kenny Loggins, Gregg Allman, Pat

Paulsen (when he was still a house painter), Poco, Vince Gill, Robin Williams, John Denver, Jimmy Buffett, Jose Feliciano, and many others—who opened for us would go on to be major stars. Billy Bob Thornton had even been a sound company roadie in Texas for several of our shows in the 1970s. Rejoining NGDB reminded me that being in the band would create so many opportunities to see more great artists and entertainers up close.

We were all going through our own changes of life. Leon Russell went from backup musician to star to mysterious mega-star, and then became an early legend, showcasing the roots of rock, and remained a friend throughout, just as Levon Helm and others did.

My backstage pass had opened the door to some pretty unusual situations, many bringing to mind that one 1960s hit song that expressed more about the mystery of life than any other: "What's it all about, Alfie?"

If not for NGDB, I probably wouldn't have been at the Troubadour that night in August 1970, to catch the first American performance of one obvious up-and-comer. I watched from the sound booth as Elton John sang "I hope you don't mind . . ." and it was obvious that audiences were going to go for this guy. Dressed simply in a suit and tie, and accompanied by Dee Murray and Nigel Olsson, he knocked out the packed Hollywood club. *Rolling Stone* declared it among the twenty most important concerts in the history of rock 'n' roll. The same thing happened a week later, downstairs in the "small room" at San Francisco's Troubadour club. NGDB headlined upstairs, but you could feel the audience hanging on every note that Elton sang. You knew the word was spreading.

As friend's careers grew, I enjoyed seeing them move up the radio charts, get on TV, or show up in movies or magazines. Many became famous at various levels through the years, which gave me a unique look at celebrity, beyond my own life somewhat in the public eye.

At first, the music biz seemed a good idea—I could both stay up late, then sleep late. Peter, Paul and Mary's "Leavin' on a Jet Plane" (written by John Denver), which I heard in 1969, started coming true for me after NGDB started on the road.

But what came with being towed in the fast lane was usually needing to be up by five or six in the morning to start driving to a gig, or to get the first plane out, or to be ready for an interview (for instance, a 9:00 AM East Coast interview means you have to be up by 5:30 AM if you're on the West Coast). After a few years, I learned that the first plane out is always at the airport the night before, and that subsequent flights might not come in. Solid sleep would come on the plane, sometimes even better than at home, with spacey dreams and thoughts as part of the ride; I'd drift in and out between announcements. At twenty-one years old, I couldn't really imagine a moment fifty years and three million miles later. But it became obvious this was not going to be a life where you get much sleep!

Early on, I'd developed a talent for falling asleep on a plane, usually before takeoff. It was probably the only benefit derived from sleep apnea. At 30,000 feet, you are safe and at peace with the world—no phone calls, yard work, bills to pay, or worries about mugging, just nice ladies bringing free stuff when you push a button. When we first started our road life, some flights were stressful. I'd worry, then panic, about arrival or departure times, or whether they'd allow our equipment on the flight. I'd have scary visions of sliding off an icy runway, aborted landings and takeoffs, trucks on snowy roads, and other mishaps. But I got good at it by the second year and began to find it exciting and quit worrying about dangers. In the early 1970s, I even helped load planes directly from the Ryder truck, right on the tarmac. I quit that after "the P-13 incident." In 1975, inside a 737 luggage bay, while shoving amplifiers, drums, band gear, and instruments across the top of a large long metallic air freight box, I heard a ground-crew guy outside yelling, "Where's that other guy?" His coworker's answer was, "He's on top of that P-13, loading band gear."

From on top of that P-13, I yelled, "What's a P-13?"

He yelled up, "Human remains! A coffin." I got out of the hold really quick, thanked them, and never did that again.

One tour covered eighteen cities in seventeen days, and I was responsible for getting us to where we had to go, keeping us on schedule, settling up the money, and other typical details of the road. It made me feel good, and kind of important. For instance, I set up two small charter planes to take us from an Iowa festival at two o'clock to get us on stage at Milwaukee Fest by seven o'clock. Never missing a show required a lot of meticulous planning. Though good at it, road managing took so much extra time—on the road I was up an hour earlier and to bed an hour later than the other guys, and I often worked another thirty to forty hours a week when at home—and did not make a penny extra. I'd get an occasional hint that it was all too much for me, like catching myself dialing 8 for a long-distance call—when I was at home. I don't miss that.

At one point in the mid-1970s, I asked the guys for five dollars an hour for the road managing prep work I was doing at home. They acted surprised, and even a little outraged, at the suggestion. "You love doing that! That wouldn't be fair to get 'extra' money! We work when we're home." So I dropped the subject and kept on pushing forward. Whenever I started to whine about feeling overburdened, my mind always sent me back to Steve the Newsman, selling newspapers in Hollywood, day in and day out, against impossible odds. The thought of that guy reminded me how fortunate I was.

I do miss some things that used to happen. I haven't experienced this one in a while, but I've always wondered if it has happened to others: I'd wake up foggy-headed on an airplane at cruising altitude, not knowing where I was headed nor where I had just been. Looking out the window didn't always help, especially if there was cloud cover. It was really embarrassing to ask anyone where we were going, and besides, I liked that happy netherland. I would just stay quiet, sitting there and waiting. Then, after a few minutes, it would hit me. *Ahhh, I'm going to Spokane—from Denver!*

On one particularly shocking episode, after groggily waking, I gazed out the window to determine where we were. When the sky is your highway, various geography becomes easily identifiable from high up: the Rocky Mountains, the deserts of Arizona, the green of Alabama and Mississippi, the Great Lakes. It's easy to spot major cities, as if you were looking down at a giant Rand-McNally atlas, as I did with Lubbock when I met Lynn Anderson. Geography was one of the classes I loved in high school.

I was headed to Phoenix from St. Louis. *Hey,* I thought smugly to myself, *I've had so much experience; it's easy to tell what flyover state we are flying over.* This must be Kansas. The circular-irrigated Kansas farms were obvious. They were pretty much unique to that state. There are thousands, giving away the state's identity from high above. I saw nice even rows this time, even on this very gray day, with other perpendicular parallel rows perfectly bisecting them. That was unusual. They are usually not that parallel for such a distance. Then it dawned on me that I couldn't see any roads, but even more strangely, I could see mysterious symbols carved into a farmer's precious crop—crop circles! We must be going over North Kansas along the Nebraska line, in the hinterlands, I thought.

But there was more. I wondered why a farmer would carve "NO STEP" with what appeared to be huge letters about one hundred yards long, into his field. And, it seemed like they were following us.

I started waking up for real, and my mind became clear: the irrigation circles were rivets; the words were a warning to mechanics and ground crew. I was staring down at the plane's gray wing. I closed the shade and went back to safe netherland. I had to drive the band to the next town that night after the gig.

———

From Linda to Jackson Browne, and Steve to Eagles to Buffett, we were all at one point trying make it as unknowns. Many blew by the Dirt Band in a whirl, reaching the highest levels of stardom. I was trying to reach a lot of people, the way Johnny Cash did. Exactly who that audience was, for me or the band, was always something of a question. But what always mattered to me was being in the game, playing it, and I began enjoying it more. It was just like the big time, only smaller.

Gratifying moments when I'd briefly felt on a par with some of those big names began to happen more often. One was at Kevin Nealon's fiftieth birthday party, with Marilyn in Hollywood, where I hoped to get to finally thank someone I'd never met on behalf of my daughter.

Sitting with Kevin, Steve Martin and I were chatting about how long we had known each other—at that time, it was forty-two years. Once, on *The Tonight Show*, Johnny Carson said, "Well, Steve, now with all this success, and money, you must really be happy." Steve replied, "Johnny, one thing I have learned is that money doesn't buy happiness," to which Carson approvingly nodded. Steve continued with, "It buys the things that make you happy." I wasn't sure he had found those happy things yet. With Marilyn and the kids, I felt I had.

I looked up from my chat with Steve and saw Brooke Shields walk in the front, looking for Kevin to give him her birthday good wishes. Before Nealon got up to go greet her, he said he would introduce me to her. About six years younger than Brooke, Noel admired Brooke greatly. I wanted to thank her for having been such a good role model and to get her autograph for Noel.

I waited for about fifteen minutes while Kevin chatted to "the most beautiful woman in the world," and then he motioned me over. I got up and walked over to them, anxious to not look anxious, hoping the fan glaze in my eyes had dissipated a bit.

Kevin said, "Brooke, I'd like to introduce you to—" when she cut him off.

"Oh, Kevin, you don't have to introduce me to *this* man! I know who *he* is." Then, looking right at me, she shocked me further. "And it's not because of the Nitty Gritty Dirt Band, John." It was like a movie scene, in which all the chatter and party noise just disappeared, and the only sound I heard was her voice. "Going to college and modeling at the same time, living in Manhattan, about age seventeen through nineteen, I spent a lot of time alone, and had very little time away from things," she said. Though it was lot for a teenager to deal with, she did it with grace, never supplying any fodder for paparazzi and tabloids.

"So little free time, homework with twenty-two units at school . . . only one thing helped me get away. Someone had given me a copy of 'The Mountain Whippoorwill' with you and your banjo. I'd listen to it almost every night, sometimes twice a night. It would take me away from everything. I don't want to embarrass you, but can I have your autograph?"

As I picked my jaw up off the floor, and put all my energy in to not asking, "*Why* didn't you *call*!" I said, "Well, sure, Brooke." We traded signatures. The other beautiful woman in the room, Marilyn, took a great picture of us. I still have Brooke's autograph, and Marilyn. Sorry Noel, you're old enough to get your own now.

I felt a successful part of Hollywood showbiz that night. Two blocks from where I first heard "Buy for Me the Rain" on KRLA, three blocks from where NGDB played in a music store parking lot in 1967, one block from where we went to the Cinerama Dome for the 1969 *Paint Your Wagon* premiere, three blocks from the Hullabaloo where the Allmans opened for us, three blocks from the Merv Griffin Theater where I did his show solo, and so on, and so on. You never knew who you might run into at a Hollywood party, or when one of the stars would turn out to be an admirer like Brooke. It would happen from time to time, and was always a shock·to me.

I'd cross paths with Steve again next summer. Flying to "Hollywood North" (Toronto's Cinespace film studio area) to meet up with Steve on the way to a Dirt Band show, he was shooting *Cheaper by the Dozen 2*. I was thinking about how far we had come since the high-school lunchtime chess matches. My mission was to hang out, watch him work, deliver a gift from an admirer, have dinner, and maybe play a game of chess.

I was pleasantly surprised he called a couple times to make sure his driver found me and was heading to the set. When I arrived between shots, Steve was sitting outside his dressing room trailer, petting his beloved dog, Roger. They both looked up, both visibly excited at seeing me. Though he is definitely way ahead at the showbiz game, you wouldn't know it from his humility. Always the cordial host, Steve introduced me to his wardrobe man, Don Vargas. Don said, "I did your costuming on *Paint Your Wagon!*"

"Don Vargas! I saw you every day! I remember you!" I said. We chatted about those months spent in Oregon making that singing Western; it made me feel like an old showbiz guy.

Steve immediately asked, "What's that?" pointing at the box I was carrying.

I said, "Janet Deering [of the Deering Banjo company] wanted to give you one of their Goodtime banjos as a gift of appreciation for spreading banjo music. No strings attached, except to the neck."

This multimillionaire movie star's eyes opened wide, along with a genuine, big, old Steve Martin grin of surprise and pleasure. He ripped open the box like a kid opening his hoped-for toy train under the Christmas tree. Even Roger's tail and panting got faster.

"I played one somewhere, and loved it. My driver asked me today what kind of banjo he should get [Steve played banjo in the car on the way to the set every day]. I told him a Deering Goodtime would be the best. I want to play it! Roger, go get my picks—never mind. You don't know where they are—I'll get them."

He crammed his picks on while bubbling over, saying, "What great action! I wish we'd had something this good when we started." He lit into my favorite tune of his, "Pitkin County Turnaround." Roger watched, wagging approval at his master's song choice. "What a perfect instrument for a beginner. Don, can you get the camera? Let's get a shot to send to Deering."

I wanted to show him a few licks I had figured out, but someone shouted, "Picture's up!" right after the photo-op. I watched him work on the set a while, then they wrapped and we headed to his tenth floor, studio supplied, two-bedroom downtown residence with full kitchen, chef, and a great view of Toronto. Happy Roger carried in the paper, and Steve was full of questions and stories.

Steve was thrilled that Roger was alive, as earlier in the year he almost "up and died" with liver problems. "He wasn't eating, wouldn't drink water," Steve shared. His worry about losing Roger showed a rarely seen side of Steve Martin as he talked. "I had to force feed him by hand, carry him to the doctor, walk him around in the lake." I felt privileged to be an audience of two (Roger was intently listening and wagging), as he continued, "One day, he took a bite of something I offered him! Then another day, he walked to his bowl and took a drink! It was close. It's great to have him back." I was enjoying Steve's unusually chatty queries about my family, music, Bill, business, banjos, and the band. This is where our lives were at that point: my kids are grown, Steve's kid was not here yet. There we were, in a town we don't live in, doing what we dreamed of doing in 1960s Orange County, hoping somehow we'd be plucked out of there, and we were.

As the night drew to a close, the driver took me to my twelve-foot by fifteen-foot, ground floor, airport Super 8 room to wait for the next day's Dirt Band festival show somewhere in a rainy Canadian field. We went on at 4:30 PM, grateful to play to five thousand people. But they were spread around an area that by 8:00 PM would have forty thousand. Our set was like being in Carnegie Hall—with two hundred people. It was, in its way, fun. The fourteen-hour bus trip after was not so much fun.

I still wish we had played chess that night before.

23

McNamara Fog—
Speed of Life—to NYC

It was interesting to me that in a room with luminaries like Garry Shandling, Kevin Nealon, Steve Martin, Peter Asher, and Martin Short, everyone was willing to give up the attention when Tom Hanks walked in. I felt at ease around all the others, but when Hanks showed up, I got as nervous as the first time I met Earl Scruggs. The scene was a party celebrating Eric Idle's birthday, in his 1930s Spanish-style Hollywood Hills home. I watched from a distance as Tom came in and greeted people. He seemed to be the same affable guy in real life that he always was on screen. He did one thing that was rare among many of his ilk: he listened, with interest and reaction, to what others were telling him, while looking them in the eye. Shaking off my nervousness, I ventured forth. I wanted to meet Forrest.

Eric pointed my direction and said, "Tom, I'd like to introduce you to a friend of mine." One could not have asked for a better introduction. "This is—"

Hanks interrupted politely, reminiscent of Brooke Shields' comment. "Oh, I know you! John, from Nitty Gritty Dirt Band! Yes! What is it you say that sounds like Japanese on that banjo instrumental on the *Dream* album? I listened to that album over and over, driving from New York to Aspen the first time, all the way, late 1970s. 'Ripplin'

Waters'—one of my favorites. Only tape I had! 'Daddy Was a Sailor' . . . love those songs."

Astonished by how quickly Tom could call up from memory so many aspects of that 1976 album, and happy my instrumental had caught his ear, I told him, "It was Japanese for 'that really cracks me up . . . are you ready? Yes, please.'" We chatted about our trips to Japan and other things Dirt Band.

Tom knew our stuff. "That *Circle* album! Roy Acuff's 'philosophy in the studio' speech ['Get it right the first time, and t' hell with the rest of them'] was great! Everyone listened to the Dirt Band in the seventies." Once again I was thankful I'd asked Earl and Doc to pick with NGDB—and also that I was back in the band, even with all its incessant infernal internal difficulties. It was a good night.

Eric invited Marilyn and me that year to his English Music Hall show in Las Vegas, supplying a big charter jet from Burbank for about 130 friends. The show was killer. Like Willie, Eric made sure the last autograph got signed, and all hands got shaken—further proof one can be a star and still be personable. He even mentioned both of us when talking about his travels in his *Greedy Bastards* book. Marilyn was happily shocked to see her name in a book in a bookstore. (Now she's in another one.)

Months later, I asked Eric if I could get something signed for a huge fan, my agent. He answered, "Well I'll be driving down your road. I'll just bring something by. See you in a few minutes." He stopped by with a photo and two CDs. When I asked what he was working on, he talked excitedly about making a Monty Python musical. He signed the swag to the guy's name and went on his way. The musical sounded interesting, but it seemed he might have run out of ideas. That night, he reminded me of Johnny Cash on that 1994 phone call. He did not want to just live off legendary iconic status. He wasn't done. Of course, I couldn't have been more wrong about doubting Eric's good ideas. So far, *Spamalot* has grossed over $200 million. I loved it both times I saw it.

I wish the Dirt Band had that kind of creative drive rather than just playing it as it is. But ironically, their lack of desire to make anything new made me put my energy into other work. That was part of how Eric inspired me to continue on my own path. He was known for Monty Python but was now working outside of the group with more success. The lesson I took from Cash, Steve, Hanks, Idle, and others who keep producing work that makes people happy, is that one should *never* give up making things. Always never. I felt there might be hope for my endeavors.

Sometimes my kids made me feel the most successful, like the time when Noel called me from Cupertino, California, before an interview for an Apple Store manager position in Salt Lake.

She whimpered, "Dad, there are like seven hundred other people here interviewing who all have college degrees! I don't think I have a chance." I didn't share her pessimism. I told her, "You have been a successful manager of big stores for years and know things they don't. Everything they know came from books; what you know came from people. They need people who know people." She got the job. That made my day!

I did turn down one opportunity to meet a world-renowned figure. I'm still not sure I handled that one right. It was before a solo show at the beautiful historic Wheeler Opera House in Aspen. Headlining the best theater in town gave me a sense of great accomplishment. In the 1970s, NGDB was the hot act, and John Denver and Jimmy Buffett came to sit in with us there on the same night. But on this chilly Aspen night, with a packed house, Steve Coors (a fan from the beer family) came backstage to excitedly tell me, "Hey, I brought Robert McNamara to see your show!" I didn't hear anything else he babbled about after that.

The memory of visiting the Vietnam wall with my boys six years earlier vividly flashed back. In the late 1970s, McNamara had said, "I think I made a mistake" about sending the men now on the wall over there. My neighbor McEuen found his final resting place there thanks to McNamara, and the guy should be in jail. I spent the last half hour before the show pacing, not wanting to go on with him there. I wanted to go out and tell the audience, "The man who admitted to needlessly sending 58,000 Americans to their death is here tonight, and I can't play until he leaves." I declined meeting the former car salesman and secretary of defense.

In the end, I didn't have the cojones to do it and went on without mentioning the special guest. I even got an encore from the Aspen crowd. I was not proud; this was my job. I still don't know if it was right to chicken out on that, but the show must go on. I did wish Aspen Vietnam vet Duane had been there. It bothered me until I got busy again.

I was grateful that the Deadwood Jam bookings kept me on the phone so much the next week. It was tough booking eight national acts. I had to focus to negotiate with agents, and that kept me from dwelling on McNamara. I'd loved presenting concerts and festivals since Dylan in 1965. When I was in charge I could exercise my own taste, and my goal was to make a show where people could have fun. It reminded me of putting on backyard carnivals as a kid and the days at Disney. In the 1990s, I had also produced some corporate shows (Ironman Triathlon, JanSport, and others) and had become good at it. My last corporate show was my third for JanSport. I decided to find out just how good I was. After confirming with cofounder Skip Yowell that he approved my suggestions for that year, I booked Leon Russell, KoKo Taylor, and Jimmy Ibbotson, plus the sound, staging, lights, and catering, all in fifty-eight minutes, and called Skip back to say, "It's done."

Since nothing came out of any of these experiences or ideas that would excite the bandmates—like my often-suggested idea for an annual Colorado show, new merchandise, set changes, or new photos, or *anything*, I kept digging for other outlets. It was the audience and what NGDB did as a unit though that was important—only *we* could go out and do what we did. The good memories, feelings, and music we brought to the audience mattered more than my personal complaints or group differences. I knew I would never sing a hit record like Jeff or Ibby had, so I kept busy with some documentary film scores and solo gigs. But it was time for change. For me, the main point of all the offstage pursuits was to build my solo career with the diversity of creative things so I could draw more to a concert.

The next several years brought more of the same Dirt Band except that Ibby left the band around 2006 on a bad day for all of us that seemed to last years. It was bad that his voice and music and good energy would be gone, but his various drug demons had been showing up on stage and during travel. Simply put, it wasn't easy traveling and performing with someone who responded to "good morning" by silently scowling and flipping you off. Traveling was also very hard on Ibby, and he was saying, "I'm tired," a lot. Jim's departure didn't change the band's creative dynamic at all. Even with the supposed problem of him "holding us back" gone, nothing improved.

Then, at a post-Ibby band meeting with the manager, we were kicking around ideas about what we could do that would be new, since it had been four years since the last album. The new manager suggested, "Maybe we could make a DVD?"

I jumped in with, "Great idea! Lots of potential! I've produced two. One with Ibby won four awards, including 'Best of Show,' the other was with Paul Williams. . . . He said it's the best thing he has made. I understand the process of surround sound mixing, six-camera shoot, et cetera. With us? It could be great!"

Over a minute of deafening absolute silence followed my eager outburst, then the manager said, "Well, maybe a new CD?" It was embarrassing. I wanted out. I did tell the others that their excuse for not making a record—that it was too hard to deal with Ibby—was no longer understandable nor acceptable. He had been gone almost four years. The next year the *Speed of Life* album would finally come together.

My most important NGDB-related accomplishment of the decade happened because of Bob Carpenter, who wanted to cowrite a song with me. We wrote "Earthquake" for that album, and it was great fun. Equally gratifying was that Bob wanted me to fingerpick guitar on his "Something Dangerous" song. This was the first time any of them other than Ibby had been excited to work with me, and it meant a lot to me. Always clever Bob, a multitalented keyboards man and a singer with great pitch, reminded me of a nice version of a high school bully in many ways, often trying to convince you to eat or drink something you didn't want. Working with him on that was a pleasure. It felt like I was in a band. I just couldn't believe how it took so long to make the album, as if we had an unlimited budget. The problem was that we were funding it ourselves, and the slower we moved, the more money was spent. It took over six months, costing about $160,000 (*at least* a hundred thousand too much), and was met with a lot of silence. It was really time for a change.

L.A. was wearing thin for both me and Marilyn, and it seemed time for a change there, too. After much discussion with her about L.A. doldrums in the business and NGDB, and life for both of us, I, too, was done with L.A. Too many fish in the bowl. I sold my car, put about three quarters of our stuff in storage, and headed to New York City. Though a smaller bowl with more fish, its challenges were appealing. Raised in the Bronx, Marilyn would be going to home turf, and I'd be making a new home. That decision led to an exciting five years of life in New York for us. I needed to get about ten things done and see where they would take me. In a sense, I was going to New York in order to grow up.

24

Digging into the Apple

Unlike laidback L.A., Manhattan inspires you to do things—work, study, and learn, get out there and make it happen, mingle with the entire pastiche of the world's people. Everybody's busy! I had loved it since our 1967 Bitter End debut, when I turned the rental car right on a red light (almost a death penalty in NYC) and chipped a cab's taillight.

The cabbie jumped out and started yelling. "Hey, hippie! You blind? Can't see the big yellow car? What am I gonna tell my dispatcher? What're we gonna do about this?"

"What about twenty bucks?" I offered.

"Fine!" The cabbie snatched the twenty out of my hand and was gone before I got back in the car. From that moment, I knew I would love it there.

It's hard to stay depressed in the Apple. I could pick up my mood just by walking the streets. The years on York and 88th were great in many ways, although I was further away from the rest of my family than ever before. That made it difficult emotionally, but made it extra exciting when anyone visited. Marilyn always made it great when they came to see us.

I knew some things could happen in my life and career just by being conveniently based in The City. Right off, I got a call to sing and play with fifty goats, a cow, and twenty kids for a *Sesame Street* music video of "Oh, Susanna!" The shoot, on a Long Island farm, was incredibly cool. It was my first video where I had to lip-synch the singing, which was exciting. We recorded the song at about eight in the morning, shot that afternoon, and we were done! Next.

Soon after, I guested on *All Night with Joey Reynolds*, his famous late-night talk show on WOR-FM. That led to about twenty more times over the ensuing five years, bringing along Matt Cartsonis, David Amram, Martha Redbone, and Jon Mark Fletcher—all great musicians with whom I've worked regularly in the new century—and whomever else I could entice to go to lower Manhattan after midnight. I was exploring new music and people for hopeful use in the near future. It was like rehearsing on the radio. During one show I even interviewed the great Les Paul, who was a pioneer both musically and technologically. Immortalized by Gibson's iconic Les Paul guitar, I asked which invention was his favorite. He said, "They're like children. I love them all!" I had seen him play and shook his hand at the famed Iridium on Broadway two years earlier, when he was only ninety-two.

I met and interviewed fantastic singer Lou Christie one night, which was especially exciting since his "Lightning Strikes Again" was the first single I ever bought, at age seventeen. The multimillion record seller had three distinct sections, and he told me he did it all live in one take! No wonder I liked it. Joey often gave me a ride back uptown in his Mercedes around three in the morning, and his chats about old showbiz in the seemingly deserted city were great. That my visits and his open door invitation had nothing to do with the Dirt Band made me feel vibrant and valued. Reynolds said, "John, you're a real radio guy. Call anytime!"

Joey liked it when I came on with road reports, like when I told him about one of his favorites, Merle Haggard. At a West Virginia festival, backstage after our set, Merle's bus driver answered my timid knock on his bus door. "Hi, I'm John McEuen and I was wondering, if Mr. Haggard—"

I heard a loud voice from inside. "John McEuen! Come on in here and sit a spell." We talked about Bob Wills, other fiddlers, and the *Circle* album, and I got to tell him some Vassar Clements stories. We had one thing in common: we both were not as good as we wanted to be as fiddlers, yet had played with the greatest ones. It was a great visit I'd never imagined possible, to be treated as an equal by someone who basically defined his genre. I tried to share that story with the Dirt Band, but they weren't interested. But Joey was.

Late one rainy night during our second year in New York, I got the strangest call ever, from L.A.! A woman with a high voice was telling me that her husband was my biggest fan and had just passed away.

"Wayne always wanted to meet you," she said. "He played banjo, guitar, piano, and other instruments, and was your biggest fan. He has all your solo albums." I was excited that he liked my solo records the best, and marveled, as she spoke with grace, and in the present tense, of "how much Wayne will love this." I asked what Wayne did, and she explained, "Wayne Allwine was the voice of Mickey Mouse for thirty-five years, and the heart and soul of the mouse. Some said 'the mouse made the man.'" Russi—his wonderful widow's name—wanted me to do a few songs from the *Circle* album and play his banjo at his burial service. I gladly accepted this honor.

When I asked what she did, she answered with a laugh and higher voice, "I'm the voice of Minnie!" Now I figured I was being punked, but she filled me in. "Thirty years ago I auditioned for and got the job of Minnie. Wayne was the final approval. The next year, we married. Disney wouldn't allow us to make that public for years, afraid if we divorced, the papers would splash 'Mickey and Minnie get divorced!'" But Wayne knew Russi was right for him, and they had a magical thirty years together. People at the service said Wayne always knew what was right for Mickey, too, and would stand up for Mickey's character, refusing lines scriptwriters tried to put in Mickey's mouth that Wayne didn't think Mickey would say. Apparently, the studio always deferred to Wayne's judgment in those cases. For instance, Mickey would not say "dude." That was a good life lesson—stand up for what you believe in.

A happy group of about a hundred family members and Disney coworkers gathered on the peaceful grounds of Forest Lawn that sunny Sunday, laughing and sharing stories about a man who lived a full happy life, who saw the humor where others may not have, and who treated all people as friends. The life they honored was the kind of life I wanted to live. How strange my life is, to have this experience, I thought. Then it got bizarre.

After my twenty-minute set, the ever-smiling Russi handed me Wayne's long-necked banjo. "John, it's time to play the song." I started the Mickey song on Wayne's banjo. As notes of the Mickey Mouse Club theme rang across the grass, it was clear why we felt comfortable listening to what Mickey had to say: with no color, ethnic, political, or age boundaries, Wayne spoke to all of us, through Mickey. He was everyone's friend.

All gathered around the casket as I played, in the shadow Walt Disney's crypt. The second time through, everybody sang, and when I say "everybody," I mean the voices of Minnie, Goofy, Kermit, Gonzo, Fairy Godmother, and others. At the appropriate moment in the song, it wasn't just some nobody who wailed "Donald Duck," it was Donald f-ing Duck! It got stranger. As Wayne was lowered in to his resting place, people sang, "Now it's time to say goodbye." The words were very tough to hear. Then "M—I—C," and Russi said, "See you real soon." Then, "K—E—Y," and everybody answered, "Why? Because we love you." There wasn't a dry eye on the lawn, but the happy and sad tears honored both the man and what his life stood for. Twelve doves, released a pair at a time, circled the area and flew over Walt's crypt on their way home. Someone later said I put the fun back in funeral.

One crisp, spring, Upper East Side morning, Steve Martin called from his very Upper West Side place, asking if I could come over to listen to his banjo songs. We spent an hour or so going over his many tunes, which led to my producing his album of original music, *The Crow*. I was on top of the world producing that, recording in five cities including Dublin (with the great Mary Black). I loved Steve's music, and he gave me free rein producing it. Thank you, Steve. I also enlisted friends Vince Gill (whom I met when he was seventeen, playing rhythm guitar in Byron Berline's fiddle band) and Dolly Parton to sing, and Earl Scruggs to pick!

Steve turns off his comedy switch when working like this, as he takes his work very seriously. But his knack for finding humor in things is always present. I remember it coming out when he needed to count off one of the songs so everybody could start together.

"OK, here we go. One, two, three, four—" and he started playing. I had to stop him.

"Steve, for a studio count-off, the last number is silent so it doesn't ring around the room."

He said, "OK, I get it. Everybody ready? Here we go . . . one, two, four—" Everyone cracked up and laughed for a minute, then he did it right. Like my mother had said, he was always on. We won a Grammy for Best Bluegrass Album that year. Well, excuse me!

When Levon Helm's office called the next year to invite me to play his Midnight Ramble in Woodstock, New York, for his seventieth birthday, I felt like I had arrived. I'd open and sit in!

Levon had made an indelible mark on the world and had reached me the first time I saw him, at the Band's concert at Pasadena's Civic in the late 1960s. *Music from Big Pink* was the rage, inspiring many with its exciting new blend of acoustic instruments and drums. Our "Mr. Bojangles" recording approach was a direct descendent of the Band's album, which I'd listened to fervently during the *Paint Your Wagon* job. Even more influential than Levon's music was the kind of man he was. He loved life so much that he made you like yours more. His joy, his music, that contagious beat, his humility, and willingness to share were qualities you don't often find in someone of his cultural stature.

I'd asked the bandleader, Larry Campbell, at sound check if we needed to run over "Circle" with the piano guy. His answer was, "That's Donald Fagen [of Steely Dan]." We didn't run it. After sound check, Levon and I talked about when he was in a horrible Salt Lake City club fifteen years before with his blues band. It was in the mid-1990s, during a lull in his career, and I went to see him that night. I expected him to be down about a tiny dark room with bad sound and a crowd of only about ninety people, but as we chatted and waited for his stage time, you would have thought he was going on at Carnegie Hall.

After my set at the barn (Amram joined me), Marilyn and I stood about three feet from Levon in the packed barn as he laid down the beat for the dozen other players and about three hundred people. Marilyn, a great singer herself, grew up to different drums and was not aware of Levon's deep impact nor his music. I thought for sure she wouldn't want to hang there too long, so close to the drums. By the fourth song, she looked at me and said, "I get it now, he *is* magic. He doesn't play loud!" She wouldn't move a foot. Virgil Caine and his stories took us all away. Two hours later, Levon called me up to finish the night with a couple of NGDB songs, and we all played "Diggy Liggy Lo" and "Circle."

Everyone in the room loved him, and they knew he loved them for being there. We all did. And now I could say, "I played Woodstock!"

Other unexpected calls were ahead. The great David Amram asked me to play with him at a tiny jazz club, the Cornelia Street Café, in the Village. I called on him many times, too. I played solo shows, and concerts with Amram, Martha Redbone, Pete Seeger, Eric Anderson, Tom Chapin, Ed Helms (when he was a struggling nascent movie star), and others. I remember sitting in midtown on a "Why Hunger?" fund-raiser with Tom when he called up Pete to do a few songs. I whispered to Tom, "Should I leave now?" as it seemed the stage should be ceded to a legend like Seeger. Tom responded, "No. You belong here," and for once, I felt like I did. It was Pete's red *How to Play the Five-String Banjo* book that got Steve and me started. I sat in with my old friend Jose Feliciano at the Iridium, a club that was to be a very meaningful part of my future three years later.

Occasionally the Dirt Band played the Apple. It was funny to see them as tourists where I now considered myself a local. Being comfortable in New York gave me confidence, while they seemed worried about things visitors worry about in the big city. I grabbed a cab home from B. B. King's after work. Knowing they would not go to the Reynolds show at midnight, I didn't invite them. I would have if Ibby was in the band then. He would've done it great.

Playing music with others was always fun and they had respect for me, but inside the NGDB structure, I rarely heard anything other than "don't do that" or "we can't do that." Music became the thing we only did during the show. I just didn't get it. Jeff's guitar playing was better than ever, and the shows, though the same every night, were good, like NGDB nostalgia. Around this time, Jeff took away my stage vocal mic because he thought it "made the stage look better." He didn't want me talking. That same year I was honored with the Best in the West Solo Performer Award by Folk Alliance. I tried around year forty-seven to get the guys to play "Earl's Breakdown," our 2004 Grammy-winning song that I could rip on, but Fadden's comment of "I hate that fucking song" shut that idea down in a heartbeat. With NGDB I was living in the Land of No.

Walking through Washington Square one brisk, sunny, early spring 2012 day, I was telling Marilyn more blather about the importance of the Greenwich Village music scene, and how the folks who had gathered in the Square in the 1960s influenced my life. It was a happy day. Then my cell phone rang with a call from Steve Martin.

He simply told me, "Earl died last night. Didn't know if you had heard." Steve and I most likely would not have had a music career if it had not been for Mr. Scruggs. Steve said his worst swear word, "Darn. It's too darn bad. What a great thing we knew him." That changed the day, but Marilyn reminded me of how fortunate we were to have known him. That helped.

The next day Earl's oldest son, Gary, called. "John . . . would you play at dad's memorial? It'll be at the Ryman in a few days." Of course I said yes. I'd walked up those back steps under so many different circumstances, never predicting this one.

On the Opry's Ryman stage at the memorial, I faced those colored north windows that I had looked through that hot August summer night forty-seven years earlier, in those pre-NGDB years. The electric shock I'd felt when Earl and Lester brought Maybelle out seemed recent. I was now facing a full house, listening to music and talk honoring Scruggs, with everyone in the room touched one way or another by that man and his music.

Standing behind Earl's casket, I recounted my teenage dream to pick with Earl, one which all those pickers in the packed Ryman understood. When I started playing "Soldier's Joy," the duo we did on the *Circle* album, the emotions were instantly sad and happy. Sad he was gone, happy that I had known the man who was the catalyst to my musical life; the one who simply said, when I asked if he would record with NGDB, "I'd be proud to."

I told the audience how, a couple years earlier at a Q & A session at the Hall of Fame, Earl was fielding questions from the audience. Someone asked, "Earl, to what do you attribute your long marriage—over fifty years—to Louise? With the difficulties of this business, what made it work out? Do you have any advice in that regard?" Earl's reply brought the house down when he simply said, "Oh, be nice." He was—to everyone.

———————

In my last year in New York, Gregg Allman's camp asked me sit in with the Allman Brothers Band at the historic Beacon Theater. It turned out to be their 234th sold-out night, and it was a great show, with Gregg singing better than ever. We finished the night with "Circle." I ended up on their CD that came out later, and what a shock that was! They sent me an unexpected check for $200! I thought about when Phish had me on their Las Vegas DVD/CD, and their office called to have me sign off on the rights. I asked if there was any payment. That answer was no.

I sensed that multimedia was the future of stage shows, and dug in, learning more Final Cut Pro editing and getting long-range plans ready. I had presented the idea to the band of using some wonderful footage for our shows, but Fadden and Jeff told me, not surprisingly, that "it's distracting, boring. People don't want to see video. No." I tried another angle.

Stephen Kessler, a genius friend and fan, spent a lot of time cutting Dorthea Lange Depression-era photographs to the music of Fadden's song, "Workin' Man." To many people, the song honored what is often called "the greatest generation," showing that putting people to work can accomplish great things, like building a nation or winning a World War. I was excited to show it to Fadden, but he got up in the middle of playback and stormed out, loudly barking, "Who said you could put fucking pictures to my fucking song!" As he left, I said, "Hmm, does that mean you don't like the edit?" He was always like that. The two times I tested the video in concert (unknown to them) some of the audience cried; all clapped for the song more than ever. Then I dropped it.

As the world dives deeper and deeper into the digital age, new technologies open up new opportunities. If you maintain your curiosity and your spirit of adventure, there are plenty of new tricks for old dogs to learn. Internet genius Ruthie DiTucci called me in New York City in 2010, and I jumped in to help with the design of syndicatednews.net, a news/entertainment website. There were more things on the horizon than could be imagined, but Ruthie had imagined many correctly and wanted me to be a part of the company. I had never been a CEO, until now. The site has been growing steadily since its inception. I have interviewed dozens of people for it, written stories, and proudly featured NGDB many times for its entertainment sections. (I invite you to check it out: snn.bz)

25

Full Circle: I Didn't Know
I Would Get Here from There

It's all good, as they say in the twenty-first century, and that's from a twentieth-century guy who's made a living playing music, some of it from the nineteenth. In perhaps the sweetest of all accomplishments, I felt my life come full circle in 2012 by recording an album—*The McEuen Sessions*—with my sons Jonathan and Nathan. Always the one commanding attention even before a guitar came to his hands, Jonathan seemed to know very early whenever a camera was going to take a picture and he'd make sure he was in it. Thirty years earlier when young Jonathan played in the local high school production of *The King and I*, he was still in sixth grade. He killed. After months of rehearsal, it ran for four weeks, was extended for two more, and every performance was packed. On the play's closing night I found him alone in a broom closet, crying, and asked what was wrong.

"What am I going to do now?" he sobbed.

I said, "I think you are in show business. Practice." He would become Dave Mason's favorite guitar picker years down the road, and continues to work long hours toward success in his own music career.

Nothing brings it all back home like making music together with two great players who happen to be your sons. A most memorable moment of those sessions was when the youngest, Nathan (now thirty-six), balked at my suggestions on the recording of a song, saying, "Why do we have to do it that way? . . . How come? . . . Do I really have to?" He had opinions about everything, and frequently challenged me.

Finally, Jonathan stared across at him and asked, "Which one of you has platinum records on the wall? Maybe we should listen to the one who does." I was happy to see how both had grown over the years, and that the younger one was trying to stand up for his views. The time was coming that I would stand up for mine.

As a band, NGDB accomplished things no one will ever equal, not even ourselves: *Paint Your Wagon*, "Mr. Bojangles," recording with dozens of other great artists, opening for Jack Benny, touring Russia, three pop hits, twenty country hits, some great benefit concerts, and fifty years of touring. The *Circle* album has become the *Dark Side of the Moon* of country music.

We made an impact on many lives.

Around the time "Mr. Bojangles" was inducted into the Grammy Hall of Fame, we were honored with a star on the walk of fame in Nashville—presented by Garth Brooks and placed between Elvis and Hank Williams. Garth later put out an album and wrote in an album's liner notes, "I went to see Nitty Gritty Dirt Band in college . . . during a fiddle solo, John McEuen leaped over the monitors and past the edge of the stage and landed in between John Mathiason and me. McEuen never missed a lick of that solo. That moment is forever etched in my soul." But, like a jockey not acknowledging the horse, Jeff sternly refused to put that on NGDB's Facebook page. It was like the 1972 Shreveport review being thrown in my eggs again.

NGDB delivered a lot of shows and music that people loved. I could've just shut up and taken the ride, as our success was the dream of so many. But the set had been the same for ten years or more. Some fans were telling me about songs they missed hearing; some reviewers even made comments like "the Dirt Band was great . . . but [it's] disappointing there is nothing new." There was so much other music we could do, even more of our own.

I was never a good leader for this group, and I never really wanted to lead. I just wanted the team to occasionally believe in me enough to let me call a few plays. My comments and suggestions earlier in the career led to successful things, but since 2002 my best talents were being marginalized: fingerpicking and flat picking guitar, bluegrass and frailing banjo, dobro, fiddle, songwriting, arranging, production, song suggestions, show ideas, and set order. I really could not figure out why it was so much more difficult.

In the middle of our forty-ninth summer as a band, I requested a band meeting to talk about many things we could do. With an incredible brand to be proud of, NGDB needed to bring our best out to audiences for the fiftieth anniversary year. Jeff had sung hits we were no longer playing live. Fadden was great at so many things that could enhance the show (like the "Fish Song"), and Bob's piano and voice talents could be spotlighted better. We could play more bluegrass, add *Circle* songs, do a section of jug band music with film I'd edited from the past fifty years projecting behind us, use footage from Russia that I'd shot. CHANGE THE SET. Those were my thoughts. I was excited to start talking about new things the Dirt Band stage could have, drawing from what I had been doing on my own. I wanted to do it with them. We needed to draw on all of our strengths.

The night before, I sent each bandmate a resume of my work away from NGDB, an assessment of experience I had to draw from, hoping it didn't sound arrogant; not trying to impress, I was trying to land a job with the band in which I'd been playing for most of half a century and use some of that experience.

The meeting started in a forgotten road hotel room with the comment, "We don't care about anything you've done," and was over fairly soon after that. I made a new assessment of my NGDB future that clear summer night in a forgotten hotel parking lot, as they showed me yet once again how we weren't partners, nor brothers, and seldom friends on that Dirt Band road. It was the summer of my discontent.

I was no longer willing to sacrifice the things I can do—that I'd worked so hard to get good at—for a diminishing role in the NGDB. We—I—needed new things.

Just prior to our fiftieth anniversary shows, the manager wrote a press release saying that "plans are said to be extensive" for the coming touring year. Calling him, I jumped in with a bunch of suggestions, along the lines of what I'd proposed in the failed band meeting, with some additions. He blew smoke for a while. None were of real interest to him. To this day I can't figure out why, other than I just didn't get it. In responding to my comments he ended one e-mail with "You are a complete nut job. . . . Take a time capsule back to 1966 and start from scratch. Thanks for the laugh. –Steve." That was the nice part. (The whole letter is on my website.)

I was now seventy, and that was too far back to go. That shook me and I couldn't sleep for a week. NGDB had already made ten albums and been around the world three times before this manager had even been born. He'd never managed anyone before, but the guys thought he was great. (The extensive plans were hiring the "Fishin' in the Dark" writer to play bass and sing—which he did very well—firing Stan Martinez, our incredible road manager of thirty years, and getting a fog machine for the shows.)

My brother had been a great manager. Remembering that Steve the manager had never made anything helped me ignore him. Jeff just wasn't interested in anything new, and would say things such as, "Making CDs doesn't matter. No one buys them." I believe making things—a record, show, new music, film, book—is always important.

I brought up to Jeff in that last year, "You have only supported one song of mine in fifty years."

His answer was, "Well . . . there is one other . . . it was . . . uhhh," and then he mentioned some old song from 1976 that wasn't even one of mine. In my mind, you needed both the jockey and a horse to win a race. Sometimes I was the horse, running around with a fiddle, burning up a banjo or something. Sometimes I was the jockey along for the ride, playing along on a song, filling out the sound, or providing steady backup. Both were needed to win. I finally realized then it never really was a team.

In 2015, I learned I was actually *not* in Nitty Gritty Dirt Band, Inc., but merely an employee like a roadie. I had wrongly assumed the "brothers and friends" were again "partners" when I rejoined fifteen years earlier. I was stupid to not ask about it. Ironically, I had hired Bob in 1978. This explained why many years earlier his wife told people at a party, in front of Marilyn, that "John plays in Bobby's band." He knew back then. I told Marilyn to ignore her, especially when she later said to her "John's just a hired hand." The organization of which I was one of the founders, and had been corporation president of for twenty-one years, had decided in the autumn of its run that it was better to exclude me. It apparently was their plan since 2002. After asking several times for a year if I could again be a corporate member, Fadden sarcastically delivered the final news that winter at the Sarasota airport as we headed to work: "We think it's better this way." It was a devastating awakening. This camel just received one more straw. I now better understood the previous fifteen years of exclusion their ignoring my e-mails, and why it was more difficult. Another plan for my life had to be developed.

I got to work developing a new record. It would be my tenth recording project since 2004.

I know if NGDB had not been in my life a lot of great things might not have happened to me. Reflecting on the years since 9/11, most new accomplishments have been my own work. I tried to involve the band in many of them, but with their continual reluctance it no longer mattered to me. We all have our own points of view about what to do, and the others are apparently happy with being the stalwart Americana icon NGDB has become. NGDB earned it. It had been a lot of work, hard traveling, and we had done it well—and there were some laughs along the way. I wanted to do more. For the same reason that, as a teenager, I wanted to get in the paper by writing a check on a watermelon, I still felt there were things to do that would get in the paper, and get seen by people. I wanted people to know about what I was doing, not just what I had done.

As an employee in the band's golden anniversary year, that final summer I tried one last time to suggest two simple changes to songs: sixteen bars of one song (about forty seconds) to better spotlight Bob, and eight bars (about twenty seconds) of another. No one would even try it. Instead, they talked for five minutes about why they shouldn't. Another camel, like the one in 1965, just got another straw.

Thanks to Norman Chesky, I made my dream album in Brooklyn for Chesky Records. We'd met by chance at midnight at New York's famed Iridium when he helped me load out from a gig that came about from sitting in with Feliciano years earlier. He recognized me and said he had "a record company upstairs." At lunch the next day, the Chesky process intrigued me: all live around *one* microphone, no headphones, no overdubs, no mixing. An incredible selection of musicians contributed to the album, all friends from years on the road who I wanted to record with: David Bromberg and Jay Ungar (with their wives singing backup), Andy Goessling, Martha Redbone, John Carter Cash (his wife Ana Cristina sang, too), Matt, Amram, John Cowan, Skip Ward, Kevin Twigg. They all have great careers and are very well known in their respective fields, and we became a real band—and we listened to each other. Thankfully, Marilyn eagerly came and jumped in to sing during two twelve-hour days for first-take recording of songs I had chosen with the arrangements I wanted.

For Warren Zevon's "My Dirty Life and Times" (Matt's song suggestion) I enlisted Steve Martin to play banjo. At one point during the session, Steve asked, "What are you calling the album?" I hadn't really thought about it, but he had an idea. "Well, we're in Brooklyn. Why don't you call it *Made in Brooklyn*?" Which is exactly what I did. There we were, two banjo pickers who had started playing the same week in 1963 as Orange County teenagers, recording together fifty-three years later. Making *Brooklyn* was the most exciting time I'd had in the studio since the *Circle* album. Norm called me, twice, after the final sequencing of the album to tell me, "You've made a masterpiece! A masterpiece." Great news from the president of a label that had put out over four hundred records. *Brooklyn* received *Stereophile* magazine's Record of the

Month honor and great reviews. A few months later I put a bunch of us from the record—Matt, John Carter, and Martha—on the Grand Ole Opry and the music killed! It was Marilyn's and Matt's first Opry time, and she sang great. The way she looked would have melted an ice sculpture. I was hoping NGDB would let me sell *Brooklyn* on our concert's merchandise table, but as with my other albums, I was never allowed to sell anything at an NGDB show that I had made. Straws were piling up on this camel.

In July, after the *Brooklyn* sessions, John Carter Cash invited Marilyn and me to stay at Maybelle Carter's home in Hiltons, Virginia. We spent some wonderful time with one important member of the Carter Family fold: Rita Forrester, granddaughter of A. P. and Sara Carter. I don't know if Rita knew what it meant to me—a kid who had lived and learned in the grooves of Flatt and Scruggs' 1961 album *Songs of the Famous Carter Family* for the better part of my nineteenth year—to be talking to a direct descendant of A. P. Carter. Rita told us so many things about Carter history, knowledge I had hungered for as a teenager and relished hearing from the source in Maybelle's 1940's kitchen.

I could not have been more shocked when, a few weeks later, I opened a package from Rita containing a "token." She wrote that A.P. always wanted and bought "those heavy restaurant plates" for home, and that she thought I would appreciate one of those plates on which he had eaten his meals. I held it in wonderment with wet eyes. How could this be? That something I cherish more than a Grammy or other accolades came to me? I always wanted a Grammy—and I have two so far—but A. P.'s plate? I immediately tried it out with some eggs and toast while thinking about how to "Keep on the Sunnyside." That was not difficult.

Right after that, in September of NGDB's fiftieth year I was honored to be inducted in to the American Banjo Museum Hall of Fame. What an incredible honor for me! Glancing at incoming e-mail just before heading to the ceremony, the only one I opened was from Gary Scruggs. How ironic! An e-mail from a Scruggs. I thought he might be congratulating me. Instead, he asked, "Hey, have you seen this?" It was the Amazon link to an album to be available the next day. My life's work within NGDB was being represented without any knowledge or word about it to me. I had not heard a word about it in the months they spent putting it together. Even though their PR for *Anthology* says "supervised by Jeff Hanna and handpicked by the band," they'd intentionally kept it a secret from me. I had no idea.

For the very last show, the next month, my forty-five-year-old son, Aaron, flew to Fargo, North Dakota, October 22, 2017, to shoot some video of his dad's band that he grew up with, knowing it would be the final NGDB show for me. He wanted my grandkids (seven of them now) to be able to see what Granpabanjo had done, and to share with his siblings. Just before showtime the band sent the road manager to tell him to put the camera away—the band said "he doesn't have the right to do that! What is he going to do with it! He doesn't have any releases . . . We don't want people filming!" It didn't stop the usual fifty audience fans shooting videos. Only him. It was *very* disappointing, and I was astonished at their exclusion. Then I was hurt . . . then mad. But, not surprised.

Those reactions all took about two minutes, and I went on to play the show and did my best NGDB performance of the year. Afterward, I went to look for them, but for the first time ever they had all fled immediately for their hotel the second after walking off the stage. Aaron and I went to our airport hotel—well, McDonald's first, for a midnight snack. I told him, "That's life" and that I thought it was the perfect ending. They had just put the last nail in the camel's casket. It was time to go. So I did.

Though NGDB will always be a part of me, things are better than ever. Listening to rental car radios while touring (or now Pandora or Alexa), it is amazing to hear the impact of music from so many people with whom we grew up. Sometimes, even a NGDB record makes it to those classic airwaves along with those of many friends. Some are gone, some quit, some like me continue with their own pursuits, away from their original bands. Some do quite well, some do better than before. The shows I have been doing are going over fantastic. Using a lot of video, eight-millimeter film, classic stills from early days, and performing NGDB music that has not been on stage in years (and some that has), I also play a lot more *Circle* music and new songs that go over as well as the hits do. That is exciting! Les, John Cable, and Matt are inspiring to play with, and we play different shows every night. I also have a book coming out. Oh, wait—this is the book. It's hard to keep up! The touring dates are on www.johnmceuen.com along with photos, video, and some stories that did not make it in here.

I've lived the American dream of being in a band that touched so many; I still can't say exactly what went into that magical mix of factors that came together so well for so long. No one can. But I know that for a long time, much longer than *Billboard* magazine and some reviewers expected, it really worked. I have to thank Les, Ibby, Jeff, Fadden, and Bob, and especially my brother Bill, for creating a platform that I—*we*—could stand on and reach the world. WE made some history.

Now it is my turn to head out there and see what history I might create. I often say I'm the luckiest guy I know—doing what I want to do and getting away with it! There are so many *great* new players out there way beyond me, but I do feel like I am the best me I have been. I feel at the top of my performing and playing game and have show ideas audiences are loving to see and hear. It is difficult to put into words how exciting it is to develop something new, and then take it out to try it on the crowd. It's like practicing a magic trick for long hours, getting it down and ready in front of a mirror, and feeling it is time now to go do it. It's the people that make it worth the work and they in their way are your mirror . . . And Mom, the crowds are fine.

Time for me to get on stage now. I can't wait. It's the life I've picked, and I still feel excited—like the rope is getting ready to drop at the Disneyland entrance, and the show is about to start.

The road ahead . . . so much shorter than the one behind
It's been a long hard ride we shared, and often shined

Took so little time, but have to confide, there was fun while
it lasted
More than dreamed but last call came, so soon it seemed
And I answered

I was so much older then, I'm younger than that now . . .

Acknowledgments

F irst words of thanks go to my ever supportive mother, who in my teenage years made sure "if you're going to play the banjo professionally you need a good photo," and my father from whom I learned more than I realized at the time, and who gave me my first banjo. My brother Bill and his wife, Alice, for lifelong support, inspiration, and guidance; my kids Noel, Aaron, Andrew, Jonathan, Ryan, Nathan, and their mother, Kae; my wife Marilyn and her son, Richi; Ksenia McEuen and Allyson McEuen; my friends and supporters since high school Jim Arnold and Mike Van Horn; John Cable; Tim Cooney; Melody Dennis and Louie LaLonde; Rodney Dillard for your friendship and mentoring and Douglas Flint Dillard for your impickable playing; Scott Flanagan; Jon Mark Fletcher; Warren Floyd; Dr. Peter Hanson; Bill Hoyt; Dr. Khadivar; Kevin Nealon; Linda Rasmussen; Jim and Salli Ratts; Gary and Joanie Regester and family; Earl and Louise Scruggs; Gary Scruggs; Peter Starr; and Patty Williams.

And the other musicians, performers, actors, and engineers who have shown me so much: Gregg Allman, David Amram, Alan Arkin, Merel Bregante, David Burbank, Dom Camardella, Vassar Clements, Greg Crutcher, Bob Edwards, Ken Erlich, Jose Feliciano, Tom Honan, Billy Paul Jones, Tommy Lee Jones, Bill Keith, David Lindley, Steve Martin, Don Reno, Joey Reynolds, Linda Ronstadt, Dan Rowan, Leon Russell, Phil Salazar, Shelly Schultz, Nick Sevilla, Jon Sievert, Sissy

Spacek, David Starr, Mark Stouffer, Randy Tico, Merle Travis, Jerry Jeff Walker, Mason Williams, and of course Jeff Hanna, Jimmie Fadden, Les Thompson, Jim Ibbotson, and Bob Carpenter.

The business people and writers who gave me such great advice and inspiration: Josh Behrman, Mark Bliesner, Bob Cherry and Cybergrass, Phil CiganerJohn Copeland, Paul Corbin, Pete Gallagher, Richard Harrington, Ray Herbeck, Jack Hurst, Marty Klein, Jay Leno, Paul Lohr and Mary Matthews, Chuck Morris, Deborah Owen, Randy Poe, Lance Smith, Bob Stane, Mary Sue Twohy at Sirius/XM, Ron Wilson, Tommy Young, and Danny Zelisko.

Special thanks must go to my patient editor, David Sobel, from whom I learned more about writing than I had envisioned. David's guiding suggestions were essential as he looked from the outside and helped me better tell what I was trying to describe from the inside. I am thankful he stuck with me. David led me to my literary agent, Tom Miller at the Carol Mann Agency, who found the exact right person, senior editor Yuval Taylor at Chicago Review Press, to help guide me through a whole new process (for me)—publishing a book! And to all the staff at Chicago Review Press: Michelle Williams, Mary Kravenas, Olivia Aguilar, and my Word Hawk copyeditor Brooke Maddaford—my gratitude for your patience with a new writer.

Mom: thanks for having me.

Index

CPSIA information can be obtained
at www.ICGtesting.com
Printed in the USA
LVHW060353061118
596092LV00011B/28/P